Developing Mathematical Ideas

Number and Operations, Part 2

Making Meaning for Operations

In the Domains of Whole Numbers and Fractions

Facilitator's Guide

By
Deborah Schifter
Virginia Bastable
Susan Jo Russell

A new version of the Making Meaning for Operations Facilitator's Guide, *which highlights the Common Core content and mathematical practice standards, will be published by the National Council of Teachers of Mathematics.*

Go to http://mathleadership.org to find out about DMI facilitation institutes and online DMI seminars offered by Mathematic Leadership Programs at Mount Holyoke College.

Copyright© 2010 by Education Development Center, Inc.

This book was previously published by: Pearson Education, Inc.

Cover photo credit: Mike Flynn

Cuisenaire® is a registered trademark of the Cuisenaire Company of America, Inc.
Multilink™ is a trademark of NES Arnold, Ltd.
Unifix® is a registered trademark of Philograph Publications, Ltd.

Teaching to the Big Ideas

Developing Mathematical Ideas (DMI) was developed as a collaborative project by the staff and participants of Teaching to the Big Ideas, an NSF Teacher Enhancement Project.

PROJECT DIRECTORS   Deborah Schifter (EDC), Virginia Bastable (SummerMath for Teachers), Susan Jo Russell (TERC)

STAFF   Sophia Cohen (EDC), Jill Bodner Lester (SummerMath for Teachers), Lisa Yaffee (TERC), Linda Ruiz Davenport (EDC)

PARTICIPANTS   Allan Arnaboldi, Lisa Bailly, Audrey Barzey, Julie Berke, Nancy Buell, Yvonne Carpio, Rose Christiansen, Ann Connally, Nancy Dostal, Marcia Estelle, Becky Eston, Trish Farrington, Victoria Fink, Gail Gilmore, Nancy Horowitz, Debbie Jacques, Marcy Kitchener, Rick Last, Eileen Madison, Joyce McLaurin, Rena Moore, Amy Morse, Deborah O'Brien, Marti Ochs, Anne Marie O'Reilly, Hilory Paster, Jessica Redman, Priscilla Rhodes, Margie Riddle, Jan Rook, Doug Ruopp, Sherry Sajdak, Cynthia Schwartz, Karen Schweitzer, Lisa Seyferth, Susan Bush Smith, Diane Stafford, Liz Sweeney, Nora Toney, Polly Wagner, Carol Walker, and Steve Walkowicz, representing the public schools of Amherst, Belchertown, Boston, Brookline, Lincoln, Newton, Northampton, Pelham, South Hadley, Southampton, Springfield, Westfield, and Williamsburg, Massachusetts, and the Atrium School in Watertown, Massachusetts

VIDEO DEVELOPMENT   Susan Jo Russell, Judy Storeygard, David Smith, and Megan Murray (TERC)

CONSULTANTS, *MAKING MEANING FOR OPERATIONS*   Deborah Ball (University of Michigan), Jere Confrey (University of Texas at Austin), Megan Franke (UCLA), Erick Smith (University of Illinois at Chicago), John P. (Jack) Smith III (Michigan State University)

PROJECT EDITOR: Beverly Cory

This work was supported by the National Science Foundation under Grant Nos. ESI-9254393 (awarded to EDC), ESI-0095450 (awarded to TERC), and ESI-0242609 (awarded to EDC). Any opinions, findings, conclusions, or recommendations expressed here are those of the authors and do not necessarily reflect the views of the National Science Foundation.

Additional support was provided by the ExxonMobil Foundation.

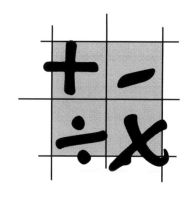

CONTENTS

Orientation to the Materials   1

Preparation for Seminar   9

First Homework   9

Maxine's Journal   *January 28,* Pre-seminar reflections   12

Session 1 • Making Meaning for Whole-Number Addition and Subtraction   15

Session Overview   15

Main Facilitator's Note   *Addition and Subtraction Problem Types*   17

Detailed Agenda   19

Maxine's Journal   *January 29*   34

Responding to the first homework   50

Session 2 • Making Meaning for Multiplication and Division   53

Session Overview   53

Main Facilitator's Note   *Situations Modeled by Multiplication and Division*   55

Detailed Agenda   57

Maxine's Journal   *February 12*   69

Responding to the second homework   83

Session 3 • When Dividing Doesn't Come Out Evenly   87

Session Overview   87

Main Facilitator's Note   *What is the Connection Between Division and Fractions? What Does It Mean for a Set of Numbers to be Closed Under an Operation?*   89

Detailed Agenda   90

Maxine's Journal   *February 26*   103

Responding to the third homework   114

Session 4 • Greater Than, Less Than, Equal To   117

Session Overview   117

Main Facilitator's Note   *What Is (and What Is Not) Addition of Fractions?*   119

Detailed Agenda   121

Maxine's Journal   *March 12*   134

Responding to the fourth homework   143

Session 5 • Combining Shares, or Adding Fractions   149

Session Overview   149

Main Facilitator's Note   *Representing the Same Story Situation with Two Different Expressions*   151

Detailed Agenda   153

Maxine's Journal   *March 26*   163

Responding to the fifth homework   177

Session 6 • Taking Portions of Portions, or Multiplying Fractions   181

Session Overview   181

Main Facilitator's Note   *Dividing Fractions*   183

Detailed Agenda   185

Maxine's Journal   *April 9*   193

Responding to the sixth homework   202

Session 7 • Expanding Ideas About Division in the Context of Fractions   207

Session Overview   207

Main Facilitator's Note   *How Can We interpret $\frac{3}{4} \times \frac{1}{2}$?*   209

Detailed Agenda   211

Maxine's Journal   *April 23*   219

Responding to the seventh homework   229

Session 8 • Wrapping Up   235

Session Overview   235

Main Facilitator's Note   *Contexts for Multiplication and Division*   237

Detailed Agenda   238

Maxine's Journal   *May 10*   245

Responding to the eighth homework   255

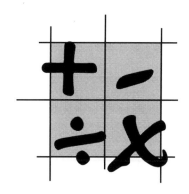

About DMI and Its Conception

The primary goal of Developing Mathematical Ideas (DMI) is to help teachers learn in a profound way the mathematics content they are responsible for teaching. To this end, DMI asks teachers to make sense of the content for themselves, recognize how the content of their grade is situated in the trajectory of learning from kindergarten through middle school, build connections among different concepts, and analyze student thinking from a mathematical perspective. Through this work, teachers learn how to orient their instruction to specific mathematical goals and develop a mathematics pedagogy in which student understanding takes center stage.

DMI is the product of decades of work in mathematics teachers' professional development on the part of the authors.

When I began teaching teachers of mathematics in the mid-1980s, a central goal for myself and my colleagues was to help teachers develop a pedagogy that supported students' mathematical understanding. In order to accomplish this, we designed professional development sessions that gave teachers the experience of learners in a mathematics class structured to promote sense making. These sessions were generally organized around mathematical tasks at a level challenging to the teachers, giving them opportunities to verbalize their own thinking and work together as a group to move their ideas forward.

The teachers were very engaged by these sessions in which they examined such topics as the structure of the place value number system, rules for comparing fractions, features of geometric shapes, and properties of the operations. However, through watching the teachers in this context, I came to see the need for them to learn more mathematics content, a perception that was reinforced when I visited their classrooms to support their teaching during the year. I was not alone in this assessment. Many of the teachers themselves—especially elementary and middle school teachers—said that they needed to learn more mathematics. They explained, however, that the traditional courses offered at the university would not help them. They did not need

1

lectures in which an instructor demonstrated procedures for solving particular problem types. Instead, they wanted to take courses taught in the same manner we were teaching them to teach, courses that would help them actively engage with mathematical concepts and delve deeply into the mathematics content they were responsible for teaching. Having had the experience of understanding through the lessons we had taught, they were thirsty for more.

I began offering such courses in 1989, and indeed, they were well received; the classes were always oversubscribed. However, after a time I became aware that, although the courses were satisfying teachers' thirst to understand mathematics content more deeply for themselves, their new knowledge did not necessarily carry over into their classrooms. In general, the teachers were not providing their students the same kind of opportunities to verbalize and develop mathematical ideas. I started to realize that there were additional skills, mathematical skills, that were part of the practice of teaching.

During that time, I was co-directing a project with Virginia Bastable and Susan Jo Russell, which involved thirty-six teachers recording events from their classrooms. Teachers wrote narrative pieces that captured their students' mathematical thinking. Through this writing, project staff and teachers together investigated how mathematical ideas developed across the grades.

Initially, I thought of these records of classroom discussion as raw data, to be used internally by project staff and participating teachers. But after I had collected several rounds of episodes and had begun to group them according to topic, I could see that they might profitably be used by other teachers as the basis of case discussions. Soon Virginia, Susan Jo, and I began to envision casebooks, each addressing a central mathematical theme, and organized into chapters, each focused on a subtopic. The resulting collection of cases would illustrate how related mathematical ideas arise in different classroom contexts and develop over the grades. In conjunction with lessons in which teachers dug directly into mathematics content, the cases could provide a mechanism for teachers to apply their new depth of mathematical understanding to aspects of classroom practice.

We selected cases to accomplish the following:

- to illustrate how the mathematics content teachers are working on arises in different classrooms at different grades

- to provide a model for teachers, helping them learn how to attend carefully to students' mathematical thinking, to follow their reasoning, to assess mathematical validity, and where the thinking is incorrect, to identify where the reasoning goes awry

- to highlight some of the major conceptual mathematical issues with which students struggle

- to present students' perspectives on the mathematics content, thus providing an opportunity for teachers to make new connections and understand the content even more deeply

Additional activities in each DMI seminar are similarly designed to help teachers bring their mathematics learning into the classroom. Teachers undertake homework assignments in which they capture and reflect on the mathematical thinking of their own students. They perform analyses of curriculum activities that highlight the mathematical goals of a lesson and the questions a teacher might ask in order to keep the focus on those goals.

The premise of the DMI materials is that the art of teaching involves helping students move from where they are into the content to be learned. It requires mathematical work on the part of teachers to determine what their students understand and how their understandings can be expanded. Teachers' chosen pedagogical strategies, then, should be based on both an understanding of the mathematics content to be learned and an assessment of students' mathematical understanding. DMI supports teachers in these efforts by offering activities that promote a deep understanding of mathematics content, along with cases that reveal how students develop ideas about that content.

Deborah Schifter
October 2008

The Developing Mathematical Ideas Professional Development Series

Developing Mathematical Ideas (DMI) is a professional development curriculum presented through a series of seminars. The work of each seminar includes, at its core, activities to investigate mathematics along with discussion of cases that illustrate students' thinking as described by their teachers. In addition, the curriculum offers teachers opportunities to share and discuss the work of their own students, to view and discuss videotapes of mathematics classrooms, to write about their own students' thinking (in essence, write their own "cases"), to analyze lessons taken from innovative elementary mathematics curricula, and to read overviews of related research.

DMI seminars bring together teachers from kindergarten through middle grades to

- learn mathematics content
- learn to recognize key mathematical ideas with which their students are grappling
- learn to support the power and complexity of student thinking
- learn how core mathematical ideas develop across the grades
- learn how to *continue* learning about children and mathematics

DMI consists of seven modules. Each module is focused on a coherent set of mathematical ideas, illustrating how those ideas develop across grades K–8. Each can be presented through eight 3-hour sessions of professional development.

- **Building a System of Tens (BST): Calculation with Whole Numbers and Decimals** Participants explore the base ten structure of the number system, consider how that structure is exploited in multidigit computational procedures, and examine how basic concepts of whole numbers reappear when working with decimals.

- **Making Meaning for Operations (MMO): In the Domains of Whole Numbers and Fractions** Participants examine the actions and situations modeled by the four basic operations. The seminar begins with an examination of the four basic operations on whole numbers and then moves to a study of the operations in the context of fractions.

- **Examining Features of Shape (EFS)** Participants examine aspects of 2D and 3D shapes, develop geometric vocabulary, and explore both definitions and properties of geometric objects. The seminar includes a study of angle, polygons, similarity, congruence, and the relationships between 3D objects and their 2D representations.

- **Measuring Space in One, Two, and Three Dimensions (MS123)** Participants examine different attributes of size, develop facility in composing and decomposing shapes, and apply these skills to make sense of formulas for area and volume. They also explore conceptual issues of length, area, and volume, as well as their complex interrelationships.

- **Working with Data (WWD)** Participants work with the collection, representation, description, and interpretation of data. They learn what various graphs and statistical measures show about features of the data, study how to summarize data when comparing groups, and consider whether the data provide insight into the questions that led to data collection.

- **Reasoning Algebraically about Operations (RAO): In the Domains of Whole Numbers and Integers** Participants examine generalizations at the heart of the study of operations in the elementary grades. They express these generalizations in common language and in algebraic notation, develop arguments based on representations of the operations, study what it means to prove a generalization, and extend their generalizations and arguments when the domain under consideration expands from whole numbers to integers.

- **Patterns, Functions, and Change (PFC)** Participants discover how the study of repeating patterns and number sequences can lead to ideas of functions, learn how to read tables and graphs to interpret phenomena of change, and use algebraic notation to write function rules. Participants also explore quadratic and exponential functions, with a particular emphasis on linear functions, and examine how various features of a function are seen in graphs, tables, or rules.

Components of a Developing Mathematical Ideas Module

The materials for each DMI module consist of a casebook, facilitator's guide, and DVD. To conduct a DMI seminar, each participant needs a casebook; facilitators need the casebook, the facilitator's guide, and the DVD.

Casebook The casebook includes an introduction and eight chapters. Participants prepare for each session by reading one chapter of the casebook. For the first session, participants should read both chapter 1 and the introduction to the casebook itself. The first seven chapters contain cases written by teachers of grades K–8, relating classroom discussion and describing the thinking of their own students. Chapter 8 is an essay that provides an overview of the mathematical ideas of the whole seminar.

Facilitator's Guide The facilitator's guide includes a session-by-session account for each of the eight sessions. Components of the facilitator's guide include

- a one-page overview of each session

- "Maxine's Journal," a narrative account of the session from the point of view of a facilitator, including examples of participants' writing and facilitator responses

- detailed agendas that describe the timing and activities of the session and list the goals for each discussion

- handouts such as math activity sheets, focus questions, and homework assignments to be duplicated for use in the seminar.

Session Overview This page summarizes the main goals of the session and provides a chart that indicates the order of the activities along with grouping suggestions and timing for each activity. The overview includes lists of what to do to prepare for the session.

Maxine's Journal This is a session-by-session narrative account of a seminar written from the point of view of a facilitator (Maxine). For each session, Maxine records small- and whole-group discussions, considers comments made by participants, and shares her own thoughts, questions, concerns, and decisions. Reading "Maxine's Journal" as preparation for a session allows facilitators to envision the main mathematical issues that are likely to emerge, provides examples of questions that facilitators can use to drive discussion, and presents images of ways facilitators and participants might interact. In addition, "Maxine's Journal" includes examples of participants' written work for the portfolio assignments, Maxine's responses, and her comments about what she was trying to accomplish with those responses.

Detailed Agendas These pages describe each activity of a session and the amount of time recommended for both small-group and whole-group work. Within an activity you will find suggested questions that can be used to shape each discussion. The agendas also contain boxed facilitator notes that provide mathematical background. The topics covered by facilitator notes in MMO are as follows:

Session 1
- Addition and Subtraction Problem Types (p. xx)
- Using a Number Line to Represent Subtraction (p. xx)

Session 2
- Situations Modeled by Multiplication and Division (p. xx)
- What Does the Remainder Mean in a Division Problem? (p. xx)
- Possible Answers to Story Problems Represented by 5/8 (p. xx)

Session 3
- What Is the Connection Between Division and Fractions? What Does It Mean for a Set of Numbers to Be Closed Under an Operation? (p. xx)
- Why Can't We Divide by Zero? (p. xx)
- In What Situations Do We Write 1/5? (p. xx)
- Strategies for Comparing Fractions: The Size of a Fraction Is Determined by Both the Size of the Pieces and the Number of Pieces (p. xx)
- Placing Fractions Relative to Each Other on a Number Line (p. xx)

Session 4
- What Is (and What Is Not) Addition of Fractions? (p. xx)

Session 5
- Representing the Same Story Situation with Two Different Expressions: How Is $6 \div (1/2)$ the Same as 6×2? How is $(5/6) \div (1/2)$ the same as $(5/6) \times 2$? (p. xx)

Session 6
- Dividing Fractions (p. xx)

Session 7
- How Can We Interpret $¾ \times ½$? (p. xx)
- How Are the Two Types of Division Seen in Problems with Fractions? (p. xx)

Session 8
- Contexts for Multiplication and Division (p. xx)

For sessions that include a DVD component, the agenda includes a summary of the video case or cases. These summaries are not full transcripts; rather they are brief narrative descriptions of the video content.

Handouts Pages to be duplicated for use in each seminar session include focus questions to guide the small- and whole-group discussions of the casebook chapters, math activities that participants work on to deepen their own mathematical understandings, and homework pages that describe the reading and writing assignments for each session. These handouts are located at the end of the agenda and are marked by a gray strip along the page edge.

DVD Cases While written cases allow users to examine student thinking at their own pace and to return as needed to ponder and analyze particular passages, the video clips offer real student voices in real time and provide rich images of classrooms organized around student thinking. The video cases show a wide variety of classroom settings, with children and teachers of different ethnic and language groups.

Preparing to Facilitate the MMO Seminar

Become familiar with MMO as a whole To become familiar with the flow of mathematical ideas in a seminar, we suggest that a facilitator read the introduction to the casebook, the introduction to the cases in each chapter, and the chapter 8 essay, "Highlights of Related Research." Then read all eight sessions of "Maxine's Journal" to get an image of the seminar as a whole from the point of view of a facilitator. As you read "Maxine's Journal," you may find it useful to examine some of the particular cases, focus questions, math activities, and homework assignments.

Prepare for recurring types of activities As you prepare for the eight seminar sessions, you will want to be familiar with all of the following.

Math activities Through activities designed for adult learners, the seminar participants develop, share, analyze, and refine their own mathematical thinking. MMO participants will deepen their understanding of the four operations, the relationships among the operations, and the meaning of fractions, and expand their means of representing and solving computational problems with fractions. Participants are often left with questions about the math; sometimes they analyze and discuss their own mathematical ideas and questions as homework. As a facilitator, you will respond to each participant's mathematical questions or pose additional questions to support each individual's mathematical thinking.

Case discussions In discussions of the casebook, participants examine the students' thinking, work on mathematical ideas for themselves, reflect on their own learning, and consider the types of classroom settings and teaching strategies that support the development of student understanding. The facilitator's guide lists goals for each case discussion, while "Maxine's Journal" allows you to see how the discussion might play out.

Viewing the DVD cases Through video, the teachers see episodes that capture both classroom atmosphere and student affect. Unlike the print cases, which allow for reading and rereading, these tapes give participants a view of children's mathematical thinking in process and offer practice in listening to students in real time. Some of the video clips are scenes of classroom work; some are based on interviews with a single student.

Sharing student-thinking assignments Several times over the course of the seminar, a session begins with pairs or groups of three participants meeting to share papers they have written, describing the thinking of their own students. As facilitator, you will read and respond to these writing assignments after participants have turned them in.

Discussing the chapter 8 essay This discussion at the last session of the seminar creates an integrated picture of the mathematical themes under consideration, connecting the events observed in the cases and in participants' own classrooms to the research literature. Some facilitators prefer to assign sections of chapter 8 throughout the seminar instead of assigning the entire chapter as first-time reading for Session 8. The homework portion of the detailed agendas indicates which sections of chapter 8 are appropriate to be assigned. In addition, the session overview page indicates which sections of chapter 8 will be useful for facilitators to read as background for that session.

Portfolio assignments Participants complete regular written assignments between sessions, sometimes reflecting on what they are learning in the seminar; other times taking a closer look into their own students' mathematical thinking. Responding to your participants' written reflections is an important part of the work of facilitating a DMI seminar. This facilitator-participant interaction helps teachers recognize how what they are learning in the seminar affects their classroom instruction and decision making. "Maxine's Journal" for each session includes examples of participant writing and a facilitators' response you can use for guidance in writing your own responses.

Identify connections between goals for the seminar and goals for each session Once you are familiar with the goals and components of the MMO curriculum as a whole, the next step is to prepare for individual sessions. For each session, you should read the cases first, then the related entry of "Maxine's Journal" and the suggested agenda. Finally, you should work through the activities in the session yourself; for example, do the math activity, view the DVD, and consider your own answers to the focus questions. As you do this work, think through the issues raised by that set of activities. What are the goals of the session as a whole? What ideas about mathematics, learning, and teaching should emerge as teachers participate in the investigations and discussions? How are these ideas illustrated in the cases? How might they arise in the other activities? What questions might you pose to call attention to these ideas?

Field-test facilitators offered suggestions about linking goals:

I realize now more than ever how important it is to be really prepared and to have thought through the issues, mathematical and otherwise, that might arise. Having a sense of the important points that you want people to be exploring and the direction in which you want them to be headed is crucial. However, it is important to realize that sometimes "the way there" might turn out to be different from the route you anticipate.

Have posters up front to keep the goals of each session to the forefront and continue to make connections to those goals during each experience of the session.

Make an overall outline of the whole course. Each time you plan a session, consider how that session fits into the overall outline of the course so you can sense how the ideas are building.

Plan ahead Besides planning for the ideas and issues that are likely to arise during discussions, you must think through the order of the activities and review the suggested timetable for each session, as detailed on the session overview page. Check the lists of items to duplicate and to obtain, and organize your materials so everything is ready ahead of time. Having the readings, handouts, DVDs, video equipment, and manipulatives at hand before a session saves time and allows you to concentrate on seminar participants during the session.

PREPARATION

MAKING MEANING FOR OPERATIONS

Pre-seminar Assignment

First Homework

This assignment is to be completed before the first session of the seminar. You will get more out of this work if you do the writing assignment BEFORE reading the casebook.

Writing assignment: Students' work samples

In the seminar *Making Meaning for Operations*, we will explore the way students engage with the topics of the elementary mathematics curriculum, with a focus on story problems representing the four operations with both whole numbers and fractions. Part of the first class session will be devoted to discussion of the mathematical goals we have for our students. In preparation for this discussion, please complete the following assignment:

Ask your students a question related to solving a word problem that involves whole numbers or fractions. Examine the set of student responses. Choose three students to write about: one whose work is strong, and two whose work is not so strong. Then write your analysis of these three students' work.

For each piece of student work, answer these three questions:

- What does the student understand?
- What is the student missing?
- What is your learning goal for each student?

Please bring two copies of the student work and two copies of your written analysis to the first session.

Reading assignment: Casebook chapter 1

In preparation for the first session, read the introduction to the casebook *Making Meaning for Operations*. Then read chapter 1, "Making Meaning for Whole-Number Addition and Subtraction," including both the introductory text and cases 1–7. Use the questions posed in the introduction to the chapter to guide your reading.

You may encounter ideas that are new to you as you read, particularly when you read cases written by teachers of grade levels you do not teach. Remember, the reading is in preparation for a seminar session in which you will have a chance to explore the mathematics involved in these cases in both small-group and whole-group settings.

Maxine's Journal

Introductory note

"Maxine's Journal" was created to convey a sense of what a DMI seminar might look like—the type of discussions that can take place, the type of lessons seminar participants can draw from the sessions—and how it might feel to facilitate one.

Maxine is a composite character and so, too, are the teachers in her seminar. Though Maxine is fiction, her journal entries describe events and individuals observed and recorded by the developers of these materials and by those who piloted the first DMI seminars. Through the specificity of Maxine's references, the reader can gain many insights of a more general nature.

Because "Maxine's Journal" is based on early pilots of DMI, the specifics of a given session as Maxine describes it don't always coincide with the activities suggested in the agendas in this facilitator's guide. For example, only in later pilots did facilitators show us the importance of giving teachers the chance to analyze lessons from innovative curricula and using exit cards to get feedback at every session. Since these weren't part of the experience of Maxine's composite group, such activities are not addressed in "Maxine's Journal." Similarly, some cases included in the casebooks and on the video were later additions. However, despite these adjustments, the major themes addressed in DMI have remained consistent.

Maxine used the DMI Number and Operations seminars over a full year, meeting with her group for three hours approximately every other week. She presented Part 1, *Building a System of Tens*, in the autumn semester and Part 2, *Making Meaning for Operations*, in the spring. The portion of her journal included here covers the second seminar. Her journal for the first seminar is in the facilitator's guide for *Building a System of Tens*.

Maxine's Journal

January 28

Pre-seminar reflections

This evening I'll be starting the seminar *Making Meaning for Operations* (MMO). Looking over the list of enrollees, I saw some who just completed *Building a System of Tens* with me, along with some newcomers.

As I think about what lies ahead, my goals for the seminar are clear. As with *Building a System of Tens*, I want teachers to come to see that mathematics is about *ideas*, that *they* have mathematical ideas, and so do the children they teach. I want them to learn how to analyze their students' thinking, to follow the students' reasoning, and to identify the conceptual issues the students are working through. And I want teachers to learn how to help students build on their own and, importantly, on their classmates' mathematical ideas.

Those members of the group who have already taken *Building a System of Tens* will expect to be challenged to think hard about the mathematics; they know the riches to be mined through examining student thinking. Will the newcomers follow their lead, or will they be intimidated by these "old-timers"?

On the other hand, the content of the goals specific to *Making Meaning for Operations* will be new to all. Instead of thinking about place value and how the base ten structure of the number system is exploited in calculation, we'll be taking a different slice through numbers and operations: What meanings can be given to the four basic operations? How are they related to one another? What kinds of situations do they model? And how do these meanings shift as we extend the domain from whole numbers to rational numbers? The teachers in the seminar will be working on the issues these questions raise for them, as well as for the students they teach.

When I planned the course last summer, I thought quite a bit about which should come first, *Building a System of Tens* or *Making Meaning for Operations*. I decided to offer *Building a System of Tens* first, even though it seems to switch the developmental order of things. We might assume that children need to understand, say, what addition is before they can devise procedures for adding, but what comes first for a child isn't necessarily what needs to come first for a teacher.

You see, almost all the teachers in my group entered the seminar with the notion that their responsibility as math teachers was to teach their students how to calculate—which meant, back then, to make sure their students learn to follow particular procedures. Many of them didn't think in terms of children's mathematical reasoning or how mathematics could be meaningful. In general, word problems provided dressing for calculation exercises; they were not used as opportunities to study what the operations do.

If I had begun with the ideas that come in the first part of *Making Meaning for Operations*, examining children's early understandings of addition, subtraction, multiplication, and division, the teachers would have been completely mystified—what does this have to do with their teaching? The topics in *Building a System of Tens*, place value and calculation, they could at least recognize, even though we were looking at them in ways that were completely new to them.

Having started in topic areas that, on the surface, seemed familiar, the teachers gradually began to see how understanding of the operations comes into play. For example, in case 13 of *Building a System of Tens*, they saw how Fiona sorted out her subtraction procedure by thinking about the context of the word problem (37 pigeons, 19 flew away). Also, as participants worked with their own representations—number lines, base ten models, arrays—they themselves had to return to questions about what the different operations do.

Now, with about three-fifths of the group new to DMI, I'll see how much of the content from *Building a System of Tens* is called upon.

SESSION 1

MAKING MEANING FOR OPERATIONS

Making Meaning for Whole-Number Addition and Subtraction

Mathematical Themes

- Young children can solve problems by counting before they learn to add and subtract; through solving such problems, they begin to develop meaning for the operations.

- The same situation can be represented by an addition and a subtraction sentence.

- Different kinds of situations can be represented by the same subtraction expressions.

Orientation	Whole group	5 minutes
Sharing students' work samples	Pairs	15 minutes
Chapter 1 case discussion (part 1)	Small groups Whole group	20 minutes 15 minutes
Math activity: Modeling story problems	Small groups Whole group	20 minutes 15 minutes
Break		15 minutes
DVD for Session 1	Whole group	15 minutes
Chapter 1 case discussion (part 2)	Small groups Whole group	30 minutes 25 minutes
Homework and exit cards	Whole group	5 minutes

Background Preparation

Read

- the casebook, chapter 1
- the detailed agenda for Session 1
- "Classification of Word Problems"
- "Maxine's Journal" for Session 1
- the casebook, chapter 8, sections 1 and 2

Work through

- the math activity: Modeling story problems
- the focus questions for Session 1

Preview

- the DVD, Session 1

Materials

Duplicate

- "Focus Questions: Chapter 1"
- "Math Activity: Modeling Story Problems"
- "Classification of Word Problems"
- "The Portfolio Process"
- "If You Have to Miss a Class"
- "Second Homework"

Obtain

- DVD player
- cubes
- index cards

Prepare

- a poster for the DVD discussion (see page 127)

Addition and Subtraction Problem Types

Each of these simple arithmetic expressions, 7 + 4 and 7 − 4, can apply to a variety of situations. Examining situations that each of these arithmetic expressions represents is a way to build mental images associated with the operations of addition and subtraction.

One way to make meaning for an operation is to consider the kind of story situations that are condensed into a particular arithmetic expression. For instance, 7 + 4 could determine the answer for either of these story contexts: "I have 7 apples and my sister gives me 4 apples. How many apples do I have now?" or "I have 7 blue marbles and 4 red marbles. How many marbles in all do I have?" Although one story describes a change (the number of apples I end up with) and the other a static situation (the number of marbles I have), they both involve the same relationship among quantities: 7 objects and 4 objects combined make a total of 11 objects.

Consider a similar approach to the operation of subtraction. The expression 7 − 4 could determine the answer to any of these story situations: "I have 7 apples and I eat 4 apples. How many apples are left?" or "I have 7 bananas and my sister has 4 bananas. How many more bananas do I have than my sister?" or "I have 4 pears. Yesterday I had 7 pears. How many pears have I eaten since yesterday?" The arithmetic expression isn't about any of the fruits, nor does it distinguish among the different structures of the three stories, but the relationship among the quantities is the same.

Picture each of these subtraction stories taking place in your mind. The mental images for each are different from one another: The first asks for the result of a change; the second, the difference between two quantities; the third asks for the change required to produce a given result. These differences are significant to children. Researchers studying how children react to such story contexts have identified and named these as being different problem types. In this session, we rely on the categories laid out by the research team of Thomas Carpenter, Elizabeth Fennema, and their colleagues.

The differences among the three problems can be seen more easily if we represent them with objects. For example, to represent the apple problem, we might put out 7 items and remove 4 of them. The answer is represented by the amount left. Such problems are commonly called *take-away*. Carpenter's team refers to them as *separating, result unknown*.

We could represent the problem about bananas by laying out 7 items in a row and then laying out 4 items alongside. The answer is found by seeing the number of items in the longer row that extend beyond the shorter row, or by finding the number of items needed to be added to the smaller quantity to make the two quantities the same. This is a *comparison* problem.

To act out the problem about pears, we would begin with 7 items. The question is, how many items would we need to remove in order to leave 4 items? This is referred to as a *separating problem with change unknown*.

Consider one other problem that could be solved by 7 − 4: "I have 4 plums, but I need 7 to make a plum cake. How many plums do I need?" To act out this problem, we would begin with 4 items and then figure out how many we must add on to get 7. This is referred to as a *joining problem, change unknown*.

Consistent with the action of this last problem, many children will write an addition sentence to represent the plum problem: 4 + __ = 7. This highlights the fact that a single situation can be represented by addition and subtraction. In fact, *any* subtraction problem can be seen as a missing addend problem. If $c - b = a$, then $a + b = c$.

In summary, there are two different ideas involved in examining problem types for addition and subtraction. One is that different kinds of story situations can be represented by the same arithmetic expression; the other is that the same story situation can be represented by either an addition or a subtraction equation.

SESSION 1

Detailed Agenda

Orientation   (5 minutes)

Whole group

Welcome the group by talking about the goals you have for their work in the seminar: exploring mathematics for themselves, examining print and video cases to learn how students develop these ideas, and also investigating and sharing their own students' work. Acknowledge that the name of the seminar, *Making Meaning for Operations*, may not carry much meaning for them at this point, but assure them that they will come to understand it though their work in the seminar.

Have participants introduce themselves, including the grade level they teach. Explain that sometimes they will be grouped across grade levels for small-group work, and other times they will meet in similar-grade-level groups.

Sharing students' work samples   (15 minutes)

Pairs

Have pairs share the examples of student work which they were asked to collect in preparation for the seminar. Tell them to read through each other's student work and written analysis before beginning any conversation. Ask them to discuss what they notice about the mathematical ideas the students are working on. They should discuss both what ideas are solid for the students and what ideas appear to be missing.

At the end of the discussion, describe your process for collecting and responding to their written assignments.

Case discussion, part 1: Solving problems by counting   (35 minutes)

Small groups (20 minutes)

Whole group (15 minutes)

The first three cases in *Making Meaning for Operations*, chapter 1, present examples of children who use counting strategies to solve problems that adults might solve by adding or subtracting. The students' methods often depend on acting out the situations described in the problems. The focus questions ask participants to look at word problems and student thinking in a way that is likely to be new for them. The emphasis is not on performing a computation but on understanding the nature of the operations. What is addition? What is subtraction?

Small-group case discussion   (20 minutes)

Organize the participants into small groups and distribute "Focus Questions: Chapter 1." Let the groups know they will have 20 minutes to discuss the first two questions. Assure them that there will be time to talk about the remaining cases later in the session.

Question 1, based on Denise's case, highlights confusions that arise in counting backward to solve a subtraction problem. Question 2, which is designed to help participants articulate their ideas about the nature of addition, restates a question raised in Dan's case: What is the difference between counting and adding?

The focus questions allow participants to explore the connections between the problem situations, the children's counting strategies, and the operations of addition and subtraction. As you work with the small groups, suggest they act out the stories in the problems with cubes to understand the point of view of the children.

Whole-group case discussion   (15 minutes)

As you call the group together for a whole-group discussion, let them know that while their work in small groups is the preparation for whole-group discussion, the whole-group discussion this time will be based on a new question. Suggest that they think about the conversations they have had and consider, "What are you noticing about the operations of addition and subtraction?" After giving participants 1 or 2 minutes to think, solicit comments.

The whole-group discussion should include these points:

- Addition and subtraction problems can be solved by counting strategies.

- Solving a subtraction problem by counting back requires paying attention to what you are counting, the spaces or the objects.

- The operation of addition is connected with the action of combining; subtraction is connected with actions of taking away and comparing.

- Children's counting strategies provide a way to get an answer to a particular problem as well as a way to begin to make sense of the nature of each operation; that is, the counting strategies highlight what actions are associated with addition and with subtraction.

Math activity: Modeling story problems (35 minutes)

Small groups (20 minutes)

Whole group (15 minutes)

In the math activity for this session, participants investigate the nature of subtraction and the variety of situations it encompasses. Participants may be surprised to realize that while the six problems can all be solved by writing 7 – 2 = 5, the situations they represent are, in fact, quite different. It is important that participants model the problems with cubes and represent them on number lines so that the actions associated with each problem, and how they are different, become visible.

For instance, while the first problem represents the familiar "take away" version of subtraction and would be modeled by laying out 7 cubes and removing 2 of them, the second problem presents a comparison situation that could be modeled by using 9 cubes in all, first laying out 7 cubes and then 2.

Small-group work (20 minutes)

Organize participants into small groups and distribute "Math Activity: Modeling Story Problems." Call attention to the directions about modeling each problem with cubes and a number line before writing any arithmetic expression. As you interact with groups, ask participants to show how their number sentences match the actions with the cubes or the way they modeled the problem on the number line.

As participants work on these problems they should encounter these two ideas:

- The single operation of subtraction models a variety of situations that are different from one another.

- The same situation can be modeled by both addition and subtraction.

As you work with the small groups, take note of the ways the participants model the problems with cubes and number lines to identify which of the six problems to bring to whole-group discussion. Look for a pair of problems that are modeled in different ways, such as 1b and 1c, or 1c and 1d. If you notice participants who have different approaches to the same problem, those would also be useful to bring to whole-group discussion.

Once participants have modeled all six problems, turn their attention to question 2: How these problems are similar and how they are not? After groups have had at least 5 minutes to discuss the nature of the problems on their own, distribute the chart "Classification of Word Problems." This chart represents a way to classify problems involving addition and subtraction by focusing on the actions involved in each story situation.

Using a Number Line to Represent Subtraction

Modeling subtraction problems on the number line provides a way to notice the distinctions between them. Consider problems 1a and 1c and a possible way to represent both the problem and the solution on a number line:

1a. Lydia has 7 candies. She eats 2 of them. How many does she have left?

1c. Lydia has 2 dollars. She wants to buy something that cost 7 dollars. How many more dollars does she need?

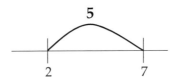

While the arithmetic sentence for both problems can be 7 − 2 = 5, their number-line representations differ. In the first problem, the answer is the value of a point on the number line; in the second, the answer is the length of a span between two points on the number line. The number-line model helps make visible the different structure of the problems.

Whole-group discussion (15 minutes)

Begin the whole-group discussion by asking for cube and number-line models for a pair of the word problems, such as 1b and 1c, that illustrate different representations for the same arithmetic expression. This provides a means to establish ways of representing story problems by paying attention to the action in the stories. Then ask the group what they noted about the operations of addition and subtraction by examining their models for these problems along with the chart, "Classification of Word Problems." You might want to share with the group that this classification scheme is based on research into the ways children react to word problems.

The discussion should highlight the following ideas:

- Focusing on the actions in a story problem highlights distinctions between problems that are represented by the same arithmetic expression.

- Given two problems that adults would call subtraction, children may react in different ways, counting back to solve one problem and adding up to solve the other.

See "Maxine's Journal," lines 241–281, for an example of this discussion.

Break   (15 minutes)

Viewing the DVD: Representing subtraction on the number line   (15 minutes)

Whole group

In general, the DVD clips in DMI offer participants the opportunity to see of students presenting their solutions, to hear students struggling to express their ideas, and to hear teachers posing questions to illuminate each approach. With the DVD, participants are able to listen to students in real time, to hear their tone of voice, and to see the children's writing. While the print cases allow for detailed analysis, the DVD clips add a visual image of the kind of classroom scenes described in the print cases.

The DVD clip for Session 1 provides images of seventh graders working on ideas that are similar to those in the math activity participants did in this session. Before showing the clip, post the chart with the two word problems the students are working on. Ask participants to read the problems and to visualize the way they would model the problems on a number line. Suggest that as they watch the video, they take note of both the students' solution methods and the teacher's questions as he sets up the task.

In a brief whole-group follow-up discussion, prompt participants to compare the students' approaches to their own. If there is time, solicit comments on the way the teacher set up the task.

Case discussion, part 2: Adding and subtracting   (55 minutes)

Small groups (30 minutes)

Whole group (25 minutes)

The last four cases in chapter 1 present these main questions:

- What are the connections between the action in the story problem and the way a student represents it?

- How is it possible that the same problem can be solved with both an addition and a subtraction sentence?

- What do the connections among a story situation, a number-line model, and an arithmetic expression illustrate about the relationship between addition and subtraction?

If you want to be sure participants have time to talk about the issues involved with negative numbers, suggest that they work with focus questions 4–7 first and then turn to question 3 if they have time.

On the other hand, if you are not planning to include negative numbers in the whole-group discussion, suggest that they begin with focus question 3. In that case, after 20 minutes, advise small groups to spend the last 10 minutes talking about questions 5 and 6 if they have not already done so.

Small-group case discussion (30 minutes)

Call the group's attention to part 2 of the focus question handout and let them know they will have 30 minutes to discuss these questions in small groups. Focus question 3, based on Jody's case 5, invites participants to examine how a single story situation can prompt some young children to add and some to subtract. Question 4, based on Machiko's case 6, presents the thinking of fourth graders finding "differences" by adding. Question 5, based on Kina's case 4, asks participants to discuss a child's reaction to the differences in two subtraction situations that adults might see as the same. Focus questions 6 and 7 are again based on Machiko's case 6. Question 6 looks into the different ways a class of fourth-grade students use number lines to represent finding the difference between two numbers, and question 7 focuses on a student method that uses negative numbers.

As you interact with the small groups, ask questions such as these:

- How is it possible that the same problem can be solved with either an addition or a subtraction sentence?

- Do you see similar examples in other cases in this chapter?

- How is the thinking of these students similar to or different from the thinking you did in the math activity?

If the use of number lines in this way is new to your participants, suggest that they spend a significant amount of time on question 6, articulating the connections between the ways the students are thinking about solving problems and the ways they model their solutions on number lines.

As you listen in on the small-group discussions of the number-line work in Machiko's case 6, choose the work of one or two students for the focus of the whole-group discussion. Look for examples where participant groups have differences of opinion about the student work, or where participants talk about learning something new from the way the students used the number line.

Whole-group case discussion (25 minutes)

Begin the whole-group discussion by asking, "What did you notice about addition and subtraction as you discussed these cases?" After a few comments, turn to question 5 and ask for comments about Zenobia's thinking. Use the last half of the discussion time to look at the number-line models from case 6.

The whole-group discussion should include these points:

- The same problem may be solved by some children with addition and by others with subtraction.

- The term *difference* is the name for the result of subtraction, but to find two numbers with a given difference, addition may be used.

- Two subtraction situations that may seem the same to adults can be seen as very different by children.

- Examining the ways in which a student uses a number line to model a problem can illuminate the way the student is thinking.

Homework and exit cards (5 minutes)

Whole group

Distribute the handout "The Portfolio Process" and answer any questions about maintaining a portfolio. For their portfolio, participants can use a binder, a folder, or any other means of keeping a collection of their written work and your responses. Explain how important reading and responding to papers is for you as the seminar facilitator; knowing their thinking helps you plan for the next session. They should also understand that the writing assignments are carefully designed to move their ideas forward and will often be used as a basis for class discussion. Establish a routine for collecting and returning assignments.

Also distribute the handout "If You Have to Miss a Session" or orally explain your expectations about attendance. Emphasize that the ideas of the seminar build from session to session. Missing any session will jeopardize their continued understanding and active participation in class activities.

Distribute the "Second Homework" handout and have participants read the writing assignment. Let them know that this kind of assignment, in which they write about their own experience with students, will occur three times during the seminar.

You might begin by commenting, "Sometimes people read the cases in the chapter and wonder if their own students think about math ideas in similar ways. This assignment is a chance to check that out." Point out that they are to include their analysis of their students' work as part of their written reflection. "Tell us what you make of what the students did. What did *you* learn about your students' thinking by closely examining their explanations or written work? What questions does their thinking raise for you?"

Explain that they will be discussing their papers with two other participants at the next session. Ask if there are any questions about the assignment.

Then announce that each session will end with a period of reflective writing on index cards that you call *exit cards*. Let the participants know that this is a time for them to think about the experience of being in the seminar and to share their feelings and learnings with you. Point out that, like the homework, their exit-card responses are invaluable to you as you plan sessions. The exit-card questions are usually of two types: one about the math content of the seminar, and one about the seminar experience. Since exit cards are a way for participants to communicate with you, they should sign their names.

As the first session ends, distribute index cards and pose these exit-card questions:

1. What mathematical ideas did this session highlight for you?

2. What was the session like for you as a learner?

Before the next session...

The pre-seminar assignment you collected from participants at this session has two purposes. The main purpose is to provide participants with material for an end-of-seminar reflection. That is, in Session 8, they will revisit what they wrote in this assignment and reflect on any changes in their thinking. The second purpose is to give you a glimpse into the participants' classrooms.

It is important to provide a response to participants' writing for every seminar session. However, in this case, it is not useful to respond individually to the written analyses that participants offer before they have begun to work on the ideas of the seminar. Instead, provide a written response to the whole group. Read over the samples of student work and make a list of the mathematical topics the students are grappling with. This will provide the group with a sense of the range of mathematics the participants are working with in their classes. For more information, see the section in "Maxine's Journal" on responding to the first homework.

Make copies of both the papers and your responses for your files before returning the work.

DVD Summary

Session 1: Representing Subtraction on the Number Line

Seventh-grade class with teacher Bruce Kamerer (5 minutes 30 seconds)

Students in this class work on two problems:

1. I have 375 candy bars. I sell 90 of them. How many candy bars do I have left?

2. I am taking a trip to visit my sister in Delaware. I drive 90 miles and then stop to rest. The total distance to my sister's house is 375 miles. How much farther do I have to go?

The teacher asks them to represent both problems using a number line, to write a number sentence for each, and to solve the problem.

After about 20 minutes, the teacher asks several pairs of students to share their work. One pair of girls explains their work.

For the first problem, they create a number line from 0 to 375. "Then you have to take away 90 candy bars from 375, and you get 285."

For the second problem they explain that they started at 0 on the number line and then jumped to 90. The teacher emphasizes that they started the trip at home, which is represented by 0 on the number line. They go on to explain that they had to find the distance from 90 to 375. It had to be 90 plus a number that equals 375. They show two number sentences they used to represent this problem: ___ + 90 = 375 and 375 − 90 = ___. They explain that they found the second number sentence because of inverse operations. The teacher asks them how they used inverse operations to determine the second number sentence.

Note: On the DVD, the students use the term *inverse operations* to mean that subtraction undoes the operation of addition. If $a + b = c$, then $c - b = a$.

Poster for DVD Discussion

Set up a poster to show the two story problems from the DVD clip. Display this poster during the whole-group discussion of the DVD.

---

1. I have 375 candy bars. I sell 90 of them. How many candy bars do I have left?

2. I am taking a trip to visit my sister in Delaware. I drive 90 miles and then stop to rest. The total distance to my sister's house is 375 miles. How much farther do I have to go?

SESSION 1

MAKING MEANING FOR OPERATIONS

Focus Questions: Chapter 1

Case discussion, part 1

1. In Denise's case 3, Susan works on a problem, getting an answer of 6 one day and 7 the next (lines 265 to 288). What is the logic behind each answer? What is the mathematical issue involved in this problem?

2. In case 1, Dan asks, "When do children move from merely counting to actually understanding addition?" What does Dan mean by this? Do you see children who understand addition in these cases? Explain your examples. Do you see children who "merely" count in these cases? Explain your examples.

Case discussion, part 2

3. In Jody's case, case 5, the children display a variety of ways of solving a single problem. Examine the methods of Latasha, Jessie, Maya, and Antoinette. What does each student's method show you about his or her mental image of the problem? What connections do you see between the action in the story problem and the ways each student represents it?

4. One of Machiko's students in case 6, Alex, says you can add or subtract to find numbers with a difference of 153. How can that be true if the term *difference* is meant to indicate the result of subtraction?

5. In case 4, Kina relates a story about the thinking of Zenobia. What similarities and differences do you see between the problem Zenobia is working on and the game that Kina refers to? What connections do you see between this case and the chart, "Classification of Word Problems"?

6. The students in Machiko's case 6 use number lines to express their solutions. Discuss the methods of Donny, Reesa, Brad, Katie, and Alex. How are they the same and how are they different?

7. In the fourth-grade class presented in case 6, the students encounter negative numbers as they work to find pairs of numbers with a difference of 153. What ideas about addition, subtraction, and negative numbers do they call upon as they make sense of this?

SESSION 1

MAKING MEANING FOR OPERATIONS

Math Activity: Modeling Story Problems

1. Model each of the following six problems with cubes or counters by acting out the situation. Then act out the problem on a number line. After you have modeled each problem, write an arithmetic sentence that captures the action.

    (a) Lydia has 7 candies. She eats 2 of them. How many does she have left?

    (b) Lydia has 7 candies and Juan has 2 candies. How many more candies does Lydia have?

    (c) Lydia has 2 dollars. She wants to buy something that costs 7 dollars. How many more dollars does she need?

    (d) Yesterday Lydia had 7 balloons. Some of them burst last evening. Today she has 2 balloons left. How many balloons burst?

    (e) Yesterday Lydia had some balloons. Today Juan gave her 2 more balloons. Now she has 7 all together. How many balloons did she have yesterday?

    (f) Lydia has 7 crayons. 2 are red and the rest are green. How many green crayons does she have?

2. How are these six problems alike? How are they different?

3. What connections do you see between the six problems and the information in the chart "Classification of Word Problems"?

SESSION 1

MAKING MEANING FOR OPERATIONS

Classification of Word Problems

Problem type: Join

Result unknown

1. Connie had 5 marbles. Jim gave her 8 more marbles. How many does Connie have altogether?

Change unknown

2. Connie has 5 marbles. How many more marbles does she need to have 13 altogether?

Start unknown

3. Connie had some marbles. Jim gave her 5 more marbles. Now she has 13 marbles. How many marbles did Connie have to start with?

Problem type: Separate

Result unknown

4. Connie had 13 marbles. She gave 5 marbles to Jim. How many marbles does she have left?

Change unknown

5. Connie had 13 marbles. She gave some to Jim. Now she has 5 marbles left. How many marbles did Connie give to Jim?

Start unknown

6. Connie had some marbles. She gave 5 to Jim. Now she has 8 marbles left. How many marbles did Connie have to start with?

Problem type: Part-part-whole

7. Connie has 5 red marbles and 8 blue marbles. How many marbles does she have?

8. Connie has 13 marbles. Five are red and the rest are blue. How many blue marbles does Connie have?

Problem type: Compare

9. Connie has 13 marbles. Jim has 5 marbles. How many more marbles does Connie have than Jim?

10. Jim has 5 marbles. Connie has 8 more than Jim. How many marbles does Connie have?

11. Connie has 13 marbles. She has 5 more marbles than Jim. How many marbles does Jim have?

Adapted from "Using Children's Mathematical Knowledge in Instruction," by E. Fennema, M. L. Franke, T. P. Carpenter, and D. A. Carey, 1993, *American Educational Research Journal, 30 (3)*, p. 558. Used by permission of the authors.

SESSION 1

MAKING MEANING FOR OPERATIONS

The Portfolio Process

As a participant in the DMI seminar *Making Meaning for Operations*, you will complete writing, reading, and sometimes mathematics assignments for each session. In fact, you already did the first of these in the pre-seminar homework, as you wrote about the work of three of your students and read the cases in the first chapter of the casebook.

You will write a reflective paper for each class session. Some of these writings will be read and considered in small-group discussion; all are opportunities to communicate with the facilitator of the seminar. The facilitator will collect your paper at the end of each session. At the following session, your paper will be returned to you with a written response from the facilitator. Please save both your writing and these responses in a folder that will serve as your seminar portfolio.

There will be a total of nine papers, one to be turned in at each session and one—the final portfolio review—to be completed at the end of the seminar. In all cases, the purpose of the assignments and written responses is to stimulate your thinking. The portfolio will be a record of your work and will also serve as a tool for reflection. Particularly toward the end of the seminar, you will be able to look back over your work and think about how your ideas changed.

SESSION 1

MAKING MEANING FOR OPERATIONS

If You Have to Miss a Class

DMI seminars are highly interactive, providing many opportunities for you to express your own ideas and to listen to the ideas of your colleagues. Much of what you learn in the seminar is developed through small-group and whole-group discussions. You will get the most from the seminar, and will be able to contribute positively to the learning of everyone in the group, if you make every effort to prepare for each session and attend the entire time.

Frequently, ideas that are introduced in one session are expanded upon and developed more fully in later sessions. Thus, every session is important. If you find that you are unable to attend a particular session, or might miss a part of a seminar (by coming late or leaving early), please contact the facilitator as soon as possible. Make arrangements to turn in assignments and to obtain copies of the assignments that you will miss.

When you are absent, you are also responsible for turning in a reflective paper describing your responses to the focus questions on the cases discussed at the session you missed. This is in addition to the regularly assigned work. You also need to turn in your work on the math activity that the group did while you were absent. If at all possible, meet with a classmate to discuss the session you were not able to attend.

These requirements are designed to minimize any loss of learning in the event that you must miss a session.

SESSION 1

MAKING MEANING FOR OPERATIONS

Second Homework

Reading assignment: Casebook chapter 2

In the casebook, read chapter 2, "Making Meaning for Multiplication and Division," including the introductory text and cases 8–12. Consider the questions posed in the introduction to this chapter as you read the cases.

Writing assignment: Examples of student thinking

It is likely that reading the cases and working on the mathematics in this seminar have made you curious about how your own students think about the mathematics they do. This assignment asks you to examine the thinking of your students as they work on the two types of problems shown in the DVD clip. Choose numbers that are appropriate for the grade level you teach.

1. I have 375 (or 55, or 15) candy bars. I sell 90 (or 30, or 8) of them. How many candy bars do I have left?

2. I am taking a trip to visit my sister. I drive 90 (or 30, or 8) miles and then stop to rest. The total distance to my sister's house is 375 (or 55, or 15) miles. How much farther do I have to go?

Ask your students to

- make a number line model for each problem.
- write a number sentence for each problem.
- solve the number sentences.
- explain how the two problems are similar and how they are different.

Consider your students' work. What did you expect? Were you surprised? What did you learn from examining their approaches? Write up your questions, how your students responded, and what you make of their responses (your expectations, your surprises, and what you learned). Include specific examples of student work or dialogue. Examining the work of just a few students in depth is very helpful.

At our next session, you will share this writing with colleagues in the seminar. Please bring three copies of your writing to share and to turn in.

Note: You will be asked to prepare similar assignments that involve investigating students' thinking in preparation for Session 4 and Session 6. Check your classroom schedules and lesson plans to make time to complete these assignments.

Session 1
Making meaning for whole-number addition and subtraction

Maxine's Journal

January 29

We met last night for the first session of *Making Meaning for Operations*. There are 20 teachers representing 11 school systems: urban, rural, and college town. They span grades from kindergarten to middle school.

Nine participants took *Building a System of Tens* with me last fall; the rest are new to DMI. It seemed that, at times, the "DMI veterans" were demonstrating how to participate in the seminar, but I don't think they dominated all the conversations. I was pleased with participation on the whole.

This first session focused on the meaning of addition and subtraction—the relationship between these operations, the different kinds of situations that are modeled by them, and how students build an understanding of them. It was interesting to see how relevant these issues are to all the grades represented in the seminar.

Orientation

I didn't spend a lot of time on introductions at this point. Participants gave their name, what grade they teach, and where they teach.

Then I made a few of my own introductory comments. "Our group spans a wide range of grade levels. This might be unusual for you, and you might be wondering why a kindergarten teacher would be in the same professional development seminar as a middle school teacher. I ask that you keep an open mind about it for now, because I'm quite sure that, by the end of the seminar, you'll find that those who teach a different grade will contribute to the richness of your experience. Some participants in the room have just finished a seminar with me, and they can vouch for the value of working with a group that spans the grades.

"In this seminar, we'll be exploring the four basic operations: addition, subtraction, multiplication, and division, and the kinds of situations that they model. We'll begin by looking at the meaning of the operations in the realm of whole numbers. Later, we'll consider how those meanings are refined when we extend the domain to include fractions.

"Those who teach at higher grades are often stymied by what their students find confusing. That is, middle school teachers often expect their students to understand all the content that was to have been covered in elementary school, and they carry on as if that were true. But elementary school covered a lot of terrain, much of which is very difficult. By examining cases from lower grades, you middle school teachers will have the opportunity to identify some of the ideas your students still need to sort out. Also, by understanding how younger students put ideas together, you will be better prepared to build on those ideas, to link them to the new content you are responsible for teaching. One question you might consider is this: If your students are having difficulty how the operations work with fractions, do they have a strong enough understanding of how the operations work with whole numbers?

"Those of you who teach lower grades will have the opportunity to learn how the ideas you work on are extended and refined in later grades. You lay an important foundation. With a deeper understanding of what is in store for your students as they go through school, you will know what to emphasize. You will be able to take advantage of opportunities to point your students toward ideas that, when solidly understood, will put them in good standing for their later work.

"Almost everyone who takes this seminar learns to think about the operations in new ways. You will all have an opportunity to learn some mathematics and examine your own process of learning. Periodically in the seminar, I'll ask you to reflect on that experience and consider implications for your teaching."

Sharing students' work samples

I continued to address the group: "You were given a few tasks to prepare for this session. One of these was to bring in samples of student work. I asked you to pose a question that involved solving word problems to your students. So to start, I'd like you to meet in pairs to share the samples you brought. Explain to your partner why you selected these samples and what you see as next steps for these students."

As participants got to work, I went from pair to pair to listen in. I didn't intervene at this point. Mainly, I was trying to get a sense of who these individuals are and how they interact. I have collected what they brought, and I'll get a chance to look it over to see what some of their ideas are at the beginning of the seminar. At the end of the seminar, participants will have an opportunity to review what they brought to this first session and to think about whether and how their ideas have changed.

When the time was up, I described to participants the seminar portfolio they will be keeping. I explained that they would keep in their portfolio a copy of the samples they brought in to this session, together with all of their work for subsequent meetings, as well as my written responses to their assignments. I suggested that they also keep in their portfolios whatever notes they might take in class.

Case discussion, part 1: Solving problems by counting

The rest of the session was dedicated to an examination of the operations of addition and subtraction of whole numbers, considering issues that arise from kindergarten through middle school. To start, we examined cases about young children who are just encountering the operations of addition and subtraction through word problems, which they solve by counting. We would look at the remaining cases from chapter 1 in a second case discussion in the final hour.

I asked the teachers to turn to their groups to discuss Denise's and Dan's cases with the following question in mind: What connections do you see between counting and the operations of addition and subtraction? I was impressed that in this first session, participants stayed close to the cases to think about what the students were able to do and where their errors lay.

I began the whole-group discussion by suggesting we first look at Mike's strategy in Dan's case at line 41. Andrea skirted my suggestion to look specifically at Mike and instead commented on the idea of counting on: "I have kindergartners, and this is first grade. I was looking at how, if they were given 5 spiders and they had 8 more to count, they were able to start counting on from 6. My children aren't at that level yet. I've tried to get them to do it on their own, but they don't. I even try to do it with them, but they still don't do it."

As Andrea was talking, I had the sense that this wasn't a complaint; she didn't seem to be reporting a problem. Rather, this was something she had noticed about the way people learn.

Carol commented, in support of Andrea, "I think the issue is developmental. I have third graders who still start from 1."

Even though, on the face of it, Carol's comment is valid and a worthwhile contribution to the discussion, I get a little nervous when I start hearing teachers say, "That's developmental." Too often, I've seen people use that label to get themselves off the hook. If "it" is developmental, there isn't anything the teacher can do. The child just has to grow into "it." The word *developmental* can mark the end of discussion and the end of thought. But at the same time, I think there *is* something developmental about the issue Andrea and Carol were talking about.

I chose to steer the conversation toward the mathematics of counting on: "Whether this is developmental or not, what is 'it'? Can you put into words what the math is we're talking about? What ideas are in here, what mathematics has Andrea been working on with her kindergartners?"

No one took on my question directly, but after a pause, Nadra spoke. "It's quicker to do it that way; it's just quicker. I find you have to show kids how to do it; they don't come up with it on their own. It needs to be taught."

Beatrice responded to her, "But what Andrea is saying is, it doesn't work to teach it."

Nadra replied, "Well, it doesn't work for Andrea because she teaches kindergarten. I teach first grade. But I agree with Andrea that the children don't come in knowing this. They just can't do it on their own. They need to practice and practice, and they have to know to say the number after, so they don't have an extra 1 in there. We practice that and practice that."

Nadra spoke with vehemence. I was aware she was defending a perspective different from the approach Beatrice's point reflected, and I wondered if she was feeling some tension. Then Camisha, who teaches second grade, added, "And when I get them from you, they continue to count that extra 1." Because she said it with a bit of humor, everyone laughed.

What was striking to me was that individuals in the group were articulating different, conflicting points of view. Nadra was saying that if you show kids how to count on and get them to practice it enough, they'll learn it. Andrea, Beatrice, and Camisha were arguing that it's not merely a matter of having the teacher demonstrate and the children practice. Nor is it merely a matter of the children getting older, as Carol seemed to imply. There's something more that has to happen—though the teachers weren't saying what that is. I wonder if they are thinking about the agency of the child, that there's something a child needs to figure out for herself or himself.

Anyway, Camisha continued to explain how counting on is still not there for many of her second graders as they work on double-digit addition and subtraction with base ten blocks. When they count up a representation that consists of rods and cubes, they touch each unit on the rods, starting at 1 and counting by ones.

I pointed out that, for some children, sticking with their method—starting at 1 and counting by ones—might be good for them because it helps them stay connected to the quantity being considered. I also suggested that in adding, say, $3 + 5$, a child needs to keep track of three quantities—a group of 3, a group of 5, and a group of 8. Counting each group starting at 1 might help the child. I had decided to offer this because I was worried that people were too ready to judge counting on as better than starting at 1, without thinking about the mathematics that is involved in all of this. I wanted to push on the mathematical issues.

After a pause, Elspeth remarked, "It never ceases to amaze me what we ask of children. When we teach them to count, we say, this is 1, this is 2, this is 3 . . . ." As she said each number, she pointed to a cube. "For each number, we point to a single cube, but we know we mean all of them, the whole set. But what does the child see?"

Several of the teachers picked up on this, talking about the difference between counting as making certain sounds, like singing a song in a language you don't understand, and counting as connected to quantity.

Carol said, "You know, I was thinking about Dan's question. What *is* the difference between adding and just counting? I don't think it's about knowing addition facts. Kids can know their facts without having an idea of what adding is really about. But maybe that's it, whether they have ideas about quantity. They might count to solve an adding problem, but I'd say they understand if they get the idea that you put two quantities together."

This was an idea worth highlighting, and so I asked if anyone could paraphrase what Carol had said. Gaye spoke up, "I agree with Carol. If the child is thinking about joining two quantities to come up with a total, that's adding. It doesn't matter if the child is counting from 1, counting on, or using addition facts."

Then Marina brought us back to the case: "You know at one point, Mike was counting on his fingers—1, 2, 3, 4, 5—and later he was using those same fingers to be 14, 15, 16, 17, 18. What does Mike think of 'fiveness'?"

These comments pleased me. In the case, it's clear that Mike can solve the problem correctly; he adds 13 + 5 by using his fingers and counting on. But Carol's, Gaye's, and Marina's points brought everyone's attention to the fact that there is more to it: What does Mike know that enables him to do this?

Iris turned the question around: "What is missing for a child who starts at 1? I have a child who does that, and when I try to show counting on, he just echoes what I said and can't do it himself." Iris posed the flip side of Marina's question; instead of asking what the child who counts on understands, she asked what is missing for the child who can't. But then she brought us back to the frustration of the teacher trying to teach counting on to a child who doesn't get it. Could we get back to the first part of her remarks to dig into the idea?

Unfortunately, the responses skipped over the child's thinking and went right to teaching behavior:

ODETTE: OK, suppose I have a student who always goes back to 1 and doesn't use counting on. What do I, as a teacher, do?

AMBER: Make them practice.

AN-CHI: Use bigger numbers so they won't want to go back and count them all.

BEATRICE: Give them a lot of experience doing things, and then they might start doing it. But they should be doing other kinds of things, not just focus on this counting on.

I decided to remind the group that there is more than one student for each teacher in a classroom and suggested there might be something important in how the children interact among themselves as they attend to one another's strategies. This comment was followed by a long pause. Did my comment mean anything to the teachers? Why was there no response?

It seemed a dead issue, so I invited the group to turn to Denise's case. But instead of getting into its content, Maalika talked about the level of analysis Denise engaged in. She pointed out that Denise has a set of goals for all the children, but she also looks very carefully at what each child does. "She explains what she knows about what children understand in general and then uses that to study what her kids are doing. I really admire her." Is Maalika saying that this is a goal she holds for herself?

Maalika's comment was followed by several stories that initially seemed unconnected. Camisha said she was recently at a family gathering where her 4-year-old nephew talked about his age and that of his 1-year-old sister: "Now we're 1 and 4. When I am 5, she'll be 2; and when I am 6, she'll be 3." Camisha said she was really surprised he understood all of this and wanted to know how. "But there were several other adults there and nobody else seemed to think much of it. I'm going to see him next week, and I'm going to ask him."

Amber referred to a child in her school who couldn't answer the question, "What number is before 5?" The other teachers at Amber's school thought this indicated the girl didn't know her numbers, but Amber said that when she asked her a few more questions, it turned out she's an ELL student, struggling to learn English. Upon hearing the word *before*, she thought "B4," and so didn't understand the question.

As all of this was going on, I was trying to figure out why these comments were coming out now—what they had to do with one another and what they had to do with the cases. But as I think back this evening, I wonder if the teachers (particularly those for whom this is a second DMI course) weren't evidencing how they are learning to see mathematics through the eyes of their students. They are becoming curious about how children put ideas together and are beginning to look at student errors for the sense that may lie behind them.

Iris now brought us back to Denise's case: "I always find it confusing to count on the calendar, and now I can see why—it's hard to keep track of when you're counting the numbers and when you're counting the spaces between them." Several teachers concurred.

Joseph returned to our earlier conversation. "In my group, we talked about how there isn't really a true difference between a counter and an adder. There's a continuum. There's a comfort zone when you add, but if you feel unsure, then you count. You even see adults in the supermarket counting on their fingers."

I then asked the group, "And what would we say addition is? What characterizes the operation?" I got two responses at the same time.

DOFI: Combining numbers.

CATHLEEN: Combining quantities.

I said, "Before I ask the same question about subtraction, I want you to look at some story problems."

Math activity: Modeling story problems

The purpose of the math activity was to work on different types of situations modeled by subtraction. I handed out a page with the following problems:

(a) Lydia has 7 candies. She eats 2 of them. How many does she have left?

(b) Lydia has 7 candies and Juan has 2 candies. How many more candies does Lydia have?

(c) Lydia has 2 dollars. She wants to buy something that costs 7 dollars. How many more dollars does she need?

(d) Yesterday Lydia had 7 balloons. Some of them burst last evening. Today she has 2 balloons left. How many balloons burst?

(e) Yesterday Lydia had some balloons. Today Juan gave her 2 more balloons. Now she has 7 all together. How many balloons did she have yesterday?

(f) Lydia has 7 crayons. 2 are red and the rest are green. How many green crayons does she have?

Before they got to work in small groups, I made some comments about the activity. "You can see that these problems all involve 7 and 2, and in fact, I can tell you that the answer to each problem is 5. Obviously, solving these problems isn't the point of the activity. There's something else, more subtle, that I want you to pay attention to. As you'll see, there are ideas here that are relevant for all of your students, even if they are working with much larger or different kinds of numbers. I want you to represent each of the problems in two ways: with cubes and with a number line. And by looking at these representations, I want you to think about what is the same and what is different among all of these problems."

I acknowledged that some participants might not be used to representing problems with cubes, and others might not be used to representing problems with number lines. I suggested that they help each other, but if they were having any problems, they should call me over.

As the group got down to work, it was quiet for only a few minutes before Odette exclaimed, "Oh, my gosh, I need all nine cubes!" I went to her and asked what was bothering her. "Look," she said, pointing to problem b. "Whenever I ask my kids to do something like 23 – 18, some will make a pile of 23 cubes and another pile of 18. When they do that, I push the 18 cubes away and tell them they're doing it wrong. But, look at this. I have one pile for Lydia's 7 candies and a second pile for Juan's 2. There are times when it's right to show both numbers."

Spencer then helped Odette represent the same problem on a number line. He commented, "When we look at the number line, we're finding the distance between 7 and 2. It isn't as obvious that the problem involved 9 cubes all together."

Maalika said she'd like to see two number lines, one for each child.

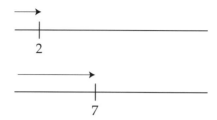

Odette commented, "That looks more like my cubes. It seems more like there are 9 altogether."

When we came together for discussion, the first comment was from Celeste: "Why are we being directed to use the number lines? I don't think this is necessarily the most efficient way to represent this. Sometimes I think it's more difficult to represent it."

I explained that at this point, we're not looking for efficiency. We're looking to see what we can learn about subtraction, the contexts modeled by the operation of subtraction, and what the different representations offer. I asked, "What new insights arose from your work on the problems?"

Joseph responded: "It seems to me that the fourth and fifth problems are much more complex than the first and sixth." I asked him why, and he said he didn't really know; they just seemed harder. I asked what other people thought, and they agreed with Joseph. So I turned the question to the group, "Why do problems (d) and (e) seem more complex than the others?"

Elspeth said she wasn't sure she could explain, but she wanted to give it a try. "Look, here in the first problem I've got these 7 candies," she said, holding up 7 cubes. "And I eat 2. It tells me exactly what to do. I remove the 2 cubes and see what I have left." She took away 2 cubes and counted up the remaining 5. "Now look at the fourth problem. I start again with 7. This is how many I had yesterday. Then it says today I have 2. It tells me what I have in the end. It doesn't tell me what happened in between; it doesn't tell me what I'm supposed to do. It was different when it said, 'Eat two candies.' This time I have to figure out what to do so that I end up with 2 balloons."

In the meantime, Maalika brought in another point: "'Lydia has 2 dollars and needs 7.' That seems like addition; it's a missing addend problem." She acted it out, first showing 2 dollars and then adding on to get 7.

Karran said, "Sure. You could think of it as 2 + *something* = 7, but couldn't you do that for *all* of them?"

Gaye appeared to agree. "Yes, it works for all of them, but for some it works better than others." When I asked Gaye what she meant, she shrugged, so Elspeth stepped in once more. "It has to do with acting it out again. If you say you had 7 candies and ate 2, how can you act that out as addition? You ate 2 and now they're gone. To think of it as addition, you have to start with this image of 2 candies in your stomach, but that's kind of weird. It's hard to start out with 2 and think of the action of the problem as adding on to make 7."

Amber had been listening to the conversation, but now burst out with agitation, "How can you add to solve a subtraction problem? I teach my students to look for key words to tell what operation to use. If the key word tells you to subtract, how can you add? This will completely confuse them!"

Spencer said gently, "It might be confusing to us even before it's confusing to them."

Beatrice added, "Maybe key words isn't the best way to solve word problems."

Marina, who had been in my DMI seminar in the fall, said, "These classes make me rethink a lot of what I do. So now I need to think more about key words."

I chose to reframe Amber's comments before moving on: "We might begin to think about word problems in new ways—what purpose they serve in learning, how students learn to solve them. Amber has brought up an important point: Key words may not be a reliable strategy for solving word problems. That's something to think about as the seminar continues."

At this point, I handed out the chart "Classification of Word Problems," which comes from a paper written by the Cognitively Guided Instruction Group at the University of Wisconsin ("Using Children's Mathematical Knowledge in Instruction," by E. Fennema, M. L. Franke, T. P. Carpenter, and D. A. Carey, 1993, *American Educational Research Journal, 30*, pp. 555–583). This concise chart summarizes the results of an extensive research program on children's thinking about addition and subtraction contexts. We'll read more about this work in chapter 8, "Highlights of Related Research," which we'll be discussing in Session 8, but for now I wanted the group to see an organized way of thinking about 11 different categories of addition and subtraction word problems.

The teachers took time to look over the chart, and Karran asked the first question. "Is there a typographical error, or is it right that one row has two problems and the rest have three?"

I said that was a good question; it's not a typographical error, but if we try to figure out why one row has just two problems, that might help us understand the chart. "Let's look at the second row to see what's going on there. Do any of the problems seem like the ones we were working on?"

Elspeth was the first to speak again. "This is like what I was saying about the candy and the balloon problems. Problem 4 on the chart is like our problem (a), and problem 5 on the chart is like our problem (d). And their problem 6 is like our problem (e)."

An-Chi said, "Problem 9 is like our problem (b)."

Dofi added, "Problem 2 is like (c)."

Marina said, "And problem 8 is like (f)."

Karran had been quiet, so I turned back to her and asked where she was with her question.

"I see it," she said. "At least, I see some of it. In the first two rows, all the problems are about some action. You start with a certain amount, you add some more or take some away, and then you end up with a certain amount. So there are three different amounts, like they say in the columns—the amount you start with, the amount you change, and the result, and any of those amounts might be unknown. But in the third row, just like problem (f), you just start with these two amounts and put them together. Either you don't know how much there is altogether, or you don't know what one of the parts is. But having a missing part doesn't give you two different types of problems. That's the answer to my question before, but I still need to figure out what's going on in the fourth row."

Labeeba said, "Wow. Who'd have thought that 7 minus 2 could be so complicated? It's amazing there are so many ways to think about it."

It seems to me that our math activity and the classification chart gave participants a lot to digest in a short amount of time. Elspeth, Gaye, and Karran had a handle on a good amount of it. For the others, I'm satisfied if they start to recognize that these different ways of thinking about addition and subtraction exist.

Viewing the DVD: Representing subtraction on the number line

In the first activity after our break, we viewed a DVD of seventh graders working on these two subtraction problems:

1. I have 375 candy bars. I sell 90 of them. How many candy bars do I have left?

2. I am taking a trip to visit my sister in Delaware. I drive 90 miles and then stop to rest. The total distance to my sister's house is 375 miles. How much farther do I have to go?

The eighth graders created the following number lines to solve the problems.

Problem 1

Problem 2

The relationship between addition and subtraction had arisen in the previous discussion, but I chose to use the video to highlight that relationship again. After viewing the video, I began by asking about the different actions in the problems.

Spencer referred to the "Classification of Word Problems" chart and said, "The first one is separating with result unknown."

I looked around to see if everyone agreed and saw heads nodding. Then Carol said, "The second one is 90 plus something is 375."

I asked if there are any other comments about the second problem. Spencer again went back to the chart and said, "It's joining with change unknown."

An-Chi said, "You can see on the number line. It's finding the distance between 90 and 375."

Celeste added, "You can also call it *difference*. You're finding the difference between 375 and 90."

I commented, "Carol gave us an addition sentence, and Spencer called it a joining problem. But An-Chi and Celeste used the words *distance* and *difference*, which imply subtraction. Is it both addition and subtraction?"

Iris said, "I like to use the word *change*."

I acknowledged that we could use the word *change* as well. "But what's going on here? Is it an addition problem or a subtraction problem?"

Cathleen said, "Well, actually, there's no such thing as subtraction or division."

Cathleen was speaking from her background as a secondary teacher. Within a formal system, one might think of subtraction as adding an inverse and of division as multiplying by a reciprocal, and in that sense there are two basic operations. But in the context of elementary and middle school mathematics, there are definitely four basic operations. The important point is how they are related.

Many teachers looked at Cathleen strangely after she made that comment. I wanted to acknowledge what she said, but also indicate that this is not what we're talking about here. So I said, "Cathleen is speaking from the perspective of a formal system that students may study later. If you take the DMI seminar *Reasoning Algebraically About Operations*, we'll discuss that notion then. But from the perspective of the students in the cases and the video, there *is* such a thing as subtraction. I think everyone would agree that the first problem about selling candy bars is a subtraction problem. Can you tell me about the driving-to-Delaware problem?"

Gaye suggested, "I think you can use either addition or subtraction for that problem."

Celeste said, "You can think of it as addition: You've gone 90 miles, and you have to add the miles you're still going to drive to make the whole trip of 375 miles. Or you can think of it as subtraction: The whole trip is 375 miles, and there are two parts—the amount you've driven and the amount you still have to drive. You subtract the part you've driven to get the amount you still have to drive."

Spencer took us back to the first problem. "You know, you can change the way you think about the candy bars, too. There are 375 candy bars separated into two groups—the bars you've sold and the bars you haven't sold. You can add those two groups to get 375."

I nodded and looked around the room. "Celeste says the trip-to-Delaware problem can be seen as either addition or subtraction, and Spencer says the candy-bar problem can be seen as either addition or subtraction. Do you think that can always happen? Can any subtraction problem be seen as addition, and vice versa?"

Beatrice said, "I think any subtraction problem can be seen as a missing addend problem, and any missing addend problem can be seen as a subtraction problem. I'm not sure if I'm ready to say that *any* addition problem can be seen as subtraction."

I suggested we let that question settle as we moved on to the next set of print cases.

Case discussion, part 2: Adding and subtracting

I asked participants to move into their small groups to begin discussion of the last four cases in chapter 1. They were good about getting right down to work.

Dofi, Karran, and Elspeth were discussing Kina's case 4. Elspeth said, "When I read this case for homework, I couldn't tell what was going on with Zenobia. The two problems seemed to be the same to me. Now, looking at the 'Classification of Word Problems' chart, I can see that there's a difference. In the word problem, Max had 3 blocks, found some more, and now he has 7. It's a joining problem with a missing change. In the hiding game, there isn't a change. Max can see 3 blocks, and he knows there are some more hidden, for a total of 7 blocks. That would be a part-part-whole problem."

Karran added, "The difference between those problems seems so subtle to me. But to Zenobia, it makes a big difference; she can understand one, but not the other."

Dofi reflected on implications for her students. "This is something I'll need to pay attention to. I think I'll give these two problems to my class and see what they do with them."

Joseph, Andrea, and Odette were looking at Jody's case 5. Joseph offered, "Jessie said she could solve the sticker problem both ways: $14 - 6 = 8$ and $6 + \_\_ = 14$."

Andrea said, "You know, when we look at that problem, we would call it subtraction. There were 14 stickers between the two girls; Yvonne had 6; how many did Sabrina have? We would all say 14 − 6. But almost all the kids in the class added! Jessie said it was subtraction, too. But look at all the other solutions. Liza wrote 6 + 8 = 14. Cecile added. Joe added. Annette said, 'I took 6 cubes. Then I said, how many more cubes should I get to get to 14?' Doesn't that sound like adding?"

Gaye told her group she was reminded of their earlier discussion about "Insects and Spiders" (case 1). Mike was able to count on his fingers, 1, 2, 3, 4, 5, and later those same fingers stood for 14, 15, 16, 17, 18. Gaye was interested in Damien's use of the number strip (in Jody's case 5), where he called the number after 6 *one* and counted up from 1 to 8, landing on 14. "I can see now that it must be really hard for little kids to keep those two meanings in their heads."

Celeste was interested in Cecile's and Joe's methods, both of which relied on doubles. She commented, "Cecile said, because she knew 7 + 7 = 14, she could move 1 from one of the 7s to the other to make 6 + 8. Joe started with 6 + 6 = 12, knowing he needed to add on 2 more to get 14."

I asked, "Does 7 + 7 = 14 appropriately represent the problem?" Beatrice said that as long as the child could explain how 7 + 7 connects to the numbers in the problem, it's a good answer. Other teachers agreed that they'd be pleased if some of their students thought about the problem this way.

I decided to spend most of the whole-group discussion on Machiko's case 6, but first I wanted to check in about Kina's case to make sure the group understood the distinction between the two problems she had given to Zenobia. Once we clarified those issues, I said, "In Machiko's case, once again we see students adding for a problem about difference. What's going on there?"

Spencer said, "When you're trying to find the difference between two numbers, you subtract them. But in this case, the teacher told the class what the difference is. They needed to find two numbers that have that difference."

Celeste said, "Here's a problem where it really does make sense to look at a number line. At least, it makes it clear to me."

I asked Celeste to come to the board to show us what she meant. She said, "Let's say you want to find two numbers whose difference is 20. That means you want to find two numbers on the number line that are 20 apart. So let's just pick any number on the number line."

―――――――――――|―――――――――――

Celeste drew a number line and marked a spot for any number. Then she continued, "I want to find another number that is 20 away from that. So I take my number and add 20; that gives me the second number. If I subtract those, the answer is 20."

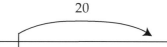

Karran added, "Actually, there are two numbers, one on the right and one on the left. The one on the right is 20 more, and the one on the left is 20 less." Karran came to the board and added to Celeste's number line.

Iris said, "Now that you're explaining it that way, I can see it. You add 20 to get the number to the right, and you subtract 20 to get the number on the left."

I then suggested we turn to the student work Machiko gave as an assessment at the end of the case. "In what ways is the work similar, and how is it different?"

Karran said, "I like what Brad did; it just looks so neat."

Celeste commented, "Yeah. His diagram looks like what you just did on the board."

I was hoping the discussion wouldn't be only about student work participants liked, but what it demonstrates about student thinking.

Gaye took us into that territory. She said, "Actually, there are three students whose work looks like Karran's. They all picked a number and found a larger number that gave a difference of 134 and a smaller number that gave a difference of 134."

Joseph said, "Brad did it in just one jump. Donny and Katie showed smaller jumps. Katie made jumps of 100, 30, and 4; Donny made jumps of 130 and 4."

Odette said, "Donny made one of his numbers 134, and that made it easy for him. He already knows that 134 and 0 have a difference of 134. Then he added 134 to 134 to get the other number."

Spencer said, "I wonder if Katie picked 200 to start with, just to make sure she wouldn't run into negative numbers."

Karran said, "Brad didn't worry about that. He knew that $100 - 134 = -34$."

Beatrice brought our attention the work of the other two students. "I'm intrigued by what Reesa and Alex did. They didn't find just two pairs of numbers. They showed how you could find infinitely many pairs of numbers. In fact, Reesa wrote, 'I know that $n + 58$ gets your answer.' She means that if n is one of your numbers, then $n + 58$ is the other."

Spencer asked, "Is this kid already doing algebra?"

I let that question go, as An-Chi pointed out the rule Alex stated: "He first showed a bunch of pairs of numbers whose difference is 134, and then

Maxine's Journal, Session 1

he said, 'When you add one to one number, you have to add one to the other to keep the same difference.' I never thought of that before. But he's right!"

Elspeth said, "I'm curious about Reesa's number line. She wrote 'n + 58' but her number line shows 53 + 1. I'm just wondering if she realized that."

I used Elspeth's question to emphasize a point I wanted to make. "Elspeth has posed a very interesting question, one that we might get in the habit of asking. When we read the cases, we do have some evidence of what students did, but we don't have the opportunity to ask students further questions. We might make conjectures about what students would say or do. When we study the cases, we learn how to pay careful attention to student thinking and consider what we might ask them if they were in front of us. But you also have your own students, and when they are in front of you, you can ask them questions. In fact, you'll have just such an opportunity as you do your homework for the next session."

Homework and exit cards

I distributed the homework assignment and gave participants a chance to read it. Then I explained, "For each of our sessions, you will have a reading assignment. Most of the time, it will be the cases in one chapter. Pay careful attention to the chapter introduction. It gives you a sense of the ideas addressed in the cases and poses some questions for you to think about as you read."

Then I explained the writing assignment. "For some of the sessions, you will write about the thinking of your own students. The assignment suggests some problems you give to your students, and you will write a description of what they do. In your write-up, be sure to include your questions, your students' responses, and what you learned from their responses."

I distributed the handouts about keeping a portfolio and missing class sessions. Then I asked that participants respond to the exit-card questions:

1. What mathematical ideas did this session highlight for you?

2. What was the session like for you as a learner?

Throughout the session I had felt that all the participants were engaged, and the exit cards confirmed that sense. As I wrote in the introduction, teachers at different grade levels found the content relevant. For example, I got these responses from middle school teachers:

> CELESTE: I enjoyed looking at the work of younger students, seeing how the foundation is built and also trying to put myself in the place of a child who's 5 or 6 or 7. How would I approach the problem?

KARRAN: I always enjoy reading the cases to see how students think. Sometimes when I am working with students myself, the time goes by so fast I feel that I maybe missed a good look at their process. Reading the cases gives me ideas of what to look at in the limited time I have.

From primary-grade teachers:

DOFI: I could think more about the concepts because the focus was on smaller numbers and simple equations. That was helpful because with the more confusing equations, I can't focus on concepts.

ELSPETH: The idea I found interesting is that a lot of subtraction problems can be solved with addition—that in fact, based on the context of the problems, at times using addition makes a lot more sense. I used to think that adding to find the answer to a subtraction problem should be saved as a strategy for algebra class.

And from upper elementary:

ODETTE: I really liked the chart on classification of word problems. It is helpful and informative to see the different problem types.

JOSEPH: This session highlighted the importance of students' understanding the *action* in the problem, because this will guide them toward addition or subtraction instead of searching for a key word. This also shows that one may decide to add or subtract to get the right answer.

I was a bit worried about Amber, who seemed agitated at times during the seminar. She wrote, "The session was fine. I liked how it was broken up into different parts."

Andrea, who had been with me in the *Building a System of Tens* seminar last fall, wrote, "I talked aloud today more than I did in the entire last seminar. This group of people seems to make me feel more comfortable." I suspect that it's not entirely the group of people, but rather that Andrea is developing more confidence in herself.

Responding to the first homework
February 1

For homework, participants had been asked to make a written assignment to their class related to word problems for whole numbers or fractions, and then choose a sample of three students' work. For each sample, they wrote about what the student understands, what is missing for the student, and what their learning goal for that student is.

I was pleased to see that many participants did not consider simply whether students got correct answers or not. They looked at the work to find evidence of understanding. Overall, this assignment gave me some good clues about the participants in the group.

I was also pleased to see that most participants selected work that pertained to the content of the seminar, although a few selected work that was more relevant to *Building a Systems of Tens*. In these cases, students solved calculation problems that didn't involve interpreting a story context.

Because participants had done this assignment prior to the first session, before we began working on these issues together, I knew it wouldn't be very productive to respond to individual participants. Instead, I wrote a message to the group as a whole. In it, I chose to identify ideas I noticed in their students' work, whether or not participants had mentioned these ideas. I thought that if I began to name them, the teachers would start to notice them.

Dear MMO seminar group,

It was very interesting to read your responses to the first writing assignment. Your classes are working on many of the big ideas that lie at the heart of the seminar. Even though all this work is related to *Making Meaning for Operations*, as you can see from the following list, the students in your classrooms are thinking about quite a range of mathematics. Some of the ideas may seem unique to a certain age group, but there are important ways in which many classes are working on related ideas.

Here are some of the mathematical ideas I found in your work. Take a look and consider which of these are related to the work of your students.

- Counting accurately to solve problems
- Representing quantities
- Moving from counting all to counting on
- Understanding different types of subtraction problems

- Understanding missing addend problems
- Understanding part-part-whole situations
- Understanding the action in a word problem
- Representing problems with equations
- Representing problems with number lines
- Representing problems with pictures

Some of the ideas in your students' work also reflect the content of *Building a System of Tens*, the seminar some of you took last fall.

- Decomposing numbers by place to solve problems efficiently
- Keeping track of decomposed numbers

And of course, there are important aspects to students' work, regardless of the mathematics content, which some of you emphasized:

- Developing perseverance
- Recording thinking clearly

I look forward to our continued work together.

Maxine

SESSION 2

MAKING MEANING FOR OPERATIONS

Making Meaning for Multiplication and Division

Mathematical Themes

- When working with multiplicative situations, students frequently find it challenging to coordinate the different units: the number of items in a group and the number of groups.

- The variety of students' methods for solving story problems involving multiplication and division illustrates relationships among operations.

- Different kinds of situations can be represented by the same division expression.

Sharing student thinking	Pairs	20 minutes
Discussion: Norms for learning	Whole group	20 minutes
DVD for Session 2	Whole group	10 minutes
Chapter 2 case discussion	Small groups Whole group	30 minutes 25 minutes
Break		15 minutes
Math activity: Story problems for division	Small groups Whole group Small groups	25 minutes 25 minutes 5 minutes
Homework and exit cards	Whole group	5 minutes

Background Preparation

Read

- the casebook, chapter 2
- the detailed agenda for Session 2
- "Maxine's Journal" for Session 2
- the casebook, chapter 8, sections 3 and 4

Work through

- the focus questions for Session 2
- the math activity: Story problems for division

Preview

- DVD, Session 2

Materials

Duplicate

- "Focus Questions: Chapter 2"
- "Math Activity: Story Problems for Division"
- "Third Homework"

Obtain

- interlocking cubes
- DVD player
- index cards

Prepare

- six posters for the math activity (see p. 65)

Situations Modeled by Multiplication and Division

Just as there are different situations that get condensed into addition or subtraction expressions, there are different situations that can be represented by multiplication as well. Consider these two situations:

a. There are 5 elephants. Each elephant has 4 legs. How many legs are there on all the elephants?

b. I have 4 packs of gum. Each pack has 5 sticks of gum. How many sticks of gum are there?

The elephant situation represents 5 groups with 4 objects in each group. The packs of gum situation represents 4 groups with 5 objects in each group. In our work, we consider both of these situations to be modeled by 5 × 4 or 4 × 5.

In some communities, people establish conventions about which factor in the multiplication sentence refers to the number of groups and which refers to the number in the group. For example, in Japan, the elephant problem would be represented as 4 × 5, the gum problem as 5 × 4. On the other hand, in most textbooks in the United States (though not all), the convention is reversed: the elephant problem is modeled as 5 × 4, the gum problem as 4 × 5. For our purposes, what's important is the notion that each of the factors represents something different, regardless of which occurs first or second in the expression. After all, the result of the multiplication is the same, no matter what the order of factors is.

These story situations for multiplication also point out a very significant difference between the operations of multiplication and addition. While the arithmetic expressions for 5 + 4 and 5 + 4 appear very similar when written out, applying each to a situation illustrates that in an addition problem, the two addends and the sum all stand for the same kinds of quantities (5 apples + 4 apples = 9 apples). This is not true for a multiplication expression. In a multiplication situation such as the legs on the elephants or the packs of gum, one number indicates the number of groups, the other indicates the number of items in each group.

Division expressions are also mapped to different story situations. For instance, 12 ÷ 3 provides the answer to both of these situations:

a. There are 12 apples to share among 3 people. How many apples will each person get?

b. There are 12 pears. I am placing them into bags that hold 3 pears. How many bags will I fill?

In the apple situation, the number of groups is known and the number in a group is to be determined. In the pear situation, the number in each group is known and the number of groups is to be determined. Drawing a model for each of these situations illustrates these distinctions. Even though the answer to both is 4, in one case the 4 represents each person's share, and in the other, the 4 represents the number of bags.

	Apple Problem	Pear Problem
Begin with 12 items	X X X X X X X X X X X X	X X X X X X X X X X X X
	XXXX XXXX XXXX	XXX XXX XXX XXX
	Make three groups	Make groups of three

The apple problem is technically labeled as *partitive* or, more informally, as *dealing*—this term is suggestive of dealing out the objects. Similarly, the pear situation is labeled as *quotitive* or *measurement*—a reference to the idea that examining the question *How many 3s in 12?* is a way to measure 12 in units of size 3.

These examples illustrate interpretations of multiplication and division of whole numbers. Later sessions will introduce multiplication and division of fractions, which will require extending the interpretation of the operations.

SESSION 2

Detailed Agenda

Sharing student thinking (20 minutes)

Pairs

Organize participants into pairs to discuss the written homework assignment in which they examined the thinking of their own students. While it is important that each participant have his or her own paper read and discussed, each pair can also be looking for common themes and ideas that arise in the student thinking in both classrooms.

Announce that pairs should read each other's papers before beginning any discussion. Their conversation should reflect ideas from both papers. They might begin by sharing what surprised them or what they discovered about their own students' thinking. The discussion can also include what was the same and what was different in the ideas of the two sets of students.

At the end of the activity, let the group know that you will be reading and responding to all of the papers. Remind them of the procedure you established for collecting papers.

Discussion: Norms for learning (20 minutes)

Whole group

Now that participants have had a chance to work together for a session, this is a good time to collect ideas from the group about how to keep the focus on learning as they work together. Suggest that participants think about these two questions:

- What do you do to make this a good learning experience for yourself?

- What do you do to make this a good learning experience for others?

After a few minutes of "think time," ask the group to offer statements describing the way the seminar should operate to make it a good learning experience for all. Examples:

Allow time in small-group work for individuals to think before talking.

Be prepared for sessions—everyone should have something to contribute.

Listen carefully to take in another person's ideas.

Find ways to disagree without being disagreeable.

Start and end each session on time.

Be open to a new idea or perspective.

Allow just 20 minutes for this discussion. The list does not need to be comprehensive or complete. The activity is designed to help participants know that reflecting on their own learning process and considering the dynamics of the group are part of the seminar. Some facilitators post the list in the meeting room and encourage participants to add to it as the seminar continues..

Viewing the DVD: Early multiplication and division (10 minutes)

Whole group

The DVD for Session 2 provides images of students using counting strategies to solve multiplication problems. The first two segments (a first-grade class and a group of fourth graders) illustrate connections between repeated addition, skip counting, and multiplication.

In the third DVD segment, two third graders are explaining how they solved the problem, *How many legs do three elephants have?* The segment concludes with comments from their teacher. Embedded in their conversations are issues of equal-sized groups, the connections between counting strategies and multiplication, and the need to keep track of both the number of groups and the number of things in a group.

After viewing the DVD, let the group know there be no whole-group discussion of the video. However, participants should look for the issues raised by the DVD as they come up in different contexts in the print cases.

Case discussion: Early multiplication and division (55 minutes)

Small groups (30 minutes)

Whole group (25 minutes)

The cases in chapter 2 present students working on multiplication and division. The chapter brings up the following main themes:

- In making sense of multiplication problems, children need to keep track of both the number in the group and the number of groups, and this is neither easy nor obvious.

- Children solve problems that adults might consider to be division by using addition, subtraction, or multiplication.

Distribute the handout "Focus Questions: Chapter 2." Let the group know that it is OK if they do not get to all of the focus questions. Remind them that the goal of the small-group time is to clarify their ideas, and that they need not rush through the questions just to finish. Assure them that you will mention any specific questions you would like them to address before the whole-group discussion.

Small-group discussion (30 minutes)

Focus question 1, based on Bella's case 8, invites participants to analyze five different kindergarten students' representations of a multiplication problem. Question 2, based on the same case, asks participants to examine the thinking of a student who is trying to work through a multiplication situation.

Focus question 3, based on Janine's case 10, and question 4, based on Melinda's case 12, ask participants to consider older students who are sorting out the same issue as Bella's kindergarten student in question 2: that in multiplication, you need to keep track of both the number in the group and the number of groups. Focus question 5, based on Nisha's case 9, asks about the thinking of students as they match arithmetic expressions to a visual display of tiles. Focus question 6 focuses on the thinking of students in Georgia's case 11 as they use a variety of operations to solve "division" problems.

As you work with the small groups, help them stay focused on the specifics of the cases by asking for line-number references to support their ideas. After 15 minutes, suggest they move on to questions 5 and 6 if they have not already done so.

Whole-group discussion (25 minutes)

The main points to come up in the whole-group discussion should include these:

- In order to make sense of multiplication, students need to grapple with the idea of number in a group and number of groups; this is a multiyear process.

- Explicitly connecting representations to arithmetic sentences can help students note the relationship between repeated addition and multiplication.

- Examining the operations that students use to solve problems provides a window into the ways they are thinking about the both the situations and the operations.

Remind participants that the small-group work is designed to help them use the thinking of the students in the cases to expand their own thinking about the operations. Indicate that many of the small groups had similar conversations (if this is true), and that you are not going to repeat those conversations in the whole group. Then pose these questions:

- What are you noticing about the operations of multiplication and division as you discuss the thinking the children in the cases?

- What is involved for students as they work to make sense of these operations?

See "Maxine's Journal," lines 145–402, for an example of this discussion.

Break (15 minutes)

Math activity: Story problems for division (55 minutes)

Small groups (25 minutes)

Whole group (25 minutes)

Small groups (5 minutes)

This activity illustrates the importance of the problem context in making sense of division. While all the problems to be written will be represented by $32 \div 5$, the numerical answers will vary with the situations. In the same way that the math activity for Session 1 was designed to expand the participants' conceptions of subtraction, this activity helps them reconsider division.

What Does the Remainder Mean in a Division Problem?

Consider the division problem $32 \div 5$. Looking simply at the numbers, the mathematical answer is either $6\frac{2}{5}$ or 6.4, because $5 \times 6\frac{2}{5}$ and $5 \times 6.4 = 32$. Frequently, elementary textbooks suggest that the answer to $32 \div 5$ is 6 remainder 2. A more mathematically precise way to note this is to say $(5 \times 6) + 2 = 32$; that is, there are 6 groups of 5 in 32, with 2 items not in any of the 6 groups.

However, when this division expression is derived from a situation, the reality of the situation determines how to account for those 2 items that don't belong in any group. For instance, consider these three situations:

- There are 32 children to place in my classroom. I have 5 tables in my room. I want to place the children at tables as evenly as possible. How many children will sit at each table?

- There are 32 children to take on a field trip. A school van holds 5 children and 1 driver. How many vans will I need to transport the children?

- I have 32 yards of material. It takes 5 yards of material to make a costume. How many costumes can I make?

> In the classroom-seating problem, since all of the children must be seated and since children cannot be divided into parts, some tables will have 6 children and some tables will have 7. The 2 "left over" children are distributed among the 5 tables. The answer in this case is "6 or 7"; that is, 6 at some tables and 7 at others.
>
> In the field-trip problem, since all of the children need to be transported, 7 vans will be needed. Six vans will be fully occupied and the 2 children "left over" will need a seventh van.
>
> In the costume-sewing problem, I can make 6 costumes; $\frac{2}{5}$ of a costume or 0.4 of a costume is not sensible, since a costume cannot be broken into parts.
>
> In each of the above situations, the objects (children and costumes) must remain whole. If the context allows for objects that can be divided up, different responses are possible. For instance consider these two situations:
>
> - I plan to run for 32 miles over the next 5 days. How many miles will I run if I run the same distance every day?
>
> - I have $32 to share with my 4 brothers. How much money will we each get?
>
> Both of these situations illustrate cases in which the objects to be divided (miles and dollars) can be broken apart. The answer to the first of these is $6\frac{2}{5}$ miles or 6.4 miles. The answer to the second is $6.40. The difference between working with miles and dollars is not apparent in this example. If the problem were 32 ÷ 3, there would be a significant difference. Distance measured in miles is a continuous quantity; therefore there could be a reasonable answer ($10\frac{2}{3}$ miles per day). However it isn't possible, in our system of dollars and cents, to express $10\frac{2}{3}$ dollars.)

Small-group work   (25 minutes)

Place the teachers in small groups and ask each group to write a story problem for 32 ÷ 5.

Collect two or three examples, asking after each one, "Does anyone have a problem situation that is different from those that have already been offered?" Distribute the math activity handout and display the six posters for collecting different types of story problems. Point out that as participants come up with new problems for the different solutions, they should write them on the appropriate posters.

If the teachers are having trouble varying their word problems, you might refer them to the problems in Georgia's case 11. As you circulate among the small groups, keep an eye on the collection of answers. If you see one or two posters with limited or no responses, call attention to this and ask groups to concentrate on those answers for the remaining time. By collecting responses in this way, participants will be able to see a variety of problem situations for each possible answer.

Note: Participants should understand that although answers to particular story problems involving 32 ÷ 5 may vary, it is incorrect to write 32 ÷ 5 = 6 or 32 ÷ 5 = 7. This notation is used to express the numerical answer 32 ÷ 5 = 6.4. The variation among the answers in this activity is related to how we interpret the numerical answer differently, depending on the specific story situation.

Whole-group discussion (25 minutes)

Begin the whole-group discussion by asking if anyone has questions about any particular problem situations that have been posted. Once any difficulties have been resolved, focus the whole-group discussion on these questions:

- What is it about the story context that determines whole-number answers such as 6, 7, and "6 or 7"?

- What is it about the story context that discriminates among the three whole-number answers?

- What is it about the story context that provides the possibility of answers expressed with decimals or fractions, such as $6\frac{2}{5}$ or 6.4?

- What do you notice about the answer 6 remainder 2?

This discussion should bring up the following factors:

- In some contexts, the objects or the groups can be broken apart, and in others they cannot.

- Some contexts require that the entire amount be accounted for, and some allow for leftovers.

- Some contexts are more likely to produce fractions as answers and some decimals, even though $\frac{2}{5}$ and 0.4 are equivalent.

Small-group discussion: Story contexts for 5 ÷ 8 (5 minutes)

Once these points have been clarified, ask participants to move back into their small groups to think about question 2. Suggest that they examine their responses to 32 ÷ 5 and think explicitly about the story contexts from this discussion as they work with the 5 ÷ 8 problems. "How can you adapt those earlier problems so they would result in the given answers for this new task?"

When there are 5 minutes left, let the group know there will not be a whole-group discussion on this third question, but that they will continue to think about it for homework.

> **Possible Answers to Story Problems Represented by 5 ÷ 8**
>
> *Answer:* 0
> It takes 8 yards of material to make a wedding dress. I have 5 yards of material. How many of these dresses can I make?
>
> *Answer:* 1
> I have 5 children to transport and a van holds 8 children. How many vans do I need?
>
> *Answer:* 0 or 1
> I have 5 children to place in my room. I have 8 tables. I want to place the children at the tables as evenly as possible. How many children will be at each table?
>
> *Answer:* 0 *remainder* 5
> I have $5. Tickets for a ride cost $8. How many rides can I buy? (I can purchase 0 rides and have $5 left.)
>
> *Answer:* $\frac{5}{8}$ or 0.625
> I want to run 5 miles over the next 8 days. I plan to run the same amount every day. How many miles should I run each day? Or: I have 5 gallons of liquid to put into 8 containers evenly. How much liquid will be in each container?

Homework and exit cards (5 minutes)

Whole group

Distribute the "Third Homework" sheet. Point out that the writing assignment is based on problem 2 from the math activity.

If you are planning to assign the reading of chapter 8, "Highlights of Related Research," in sections throughout the seminar rather than all at once at the end of Session 7, it is appropriate to assign sections 1 and 2 at this point. Let participants know they won't be discussing this reading at the next meeting, but that these sections are pertinent to the work of the past two sessions and thus make useful reading at this point in the seminar.

Distribute index cards and pose these exit-card questions:

1. What was important or significant to you in the mathematics discussed at this session?

2. What do you want to tell the facilitators about how the seminar is working for you?

Before the next session...

In preparation for the next session, read what participants wrote in their student-thinking assignment and write a response to each participant. For more information, see the section in "Maxine's Journal" on responding to the second homework. Make copies of the papers and your response for your files before returning the work.

DVD Summary

Session 2: Early Multiplication and Division

The DVD for this session includes clips from three different classes.

Ways to Make 16: First-grade class with teacher Malia Scott (3 minutes)

The first sequence on the DVD shows a first-grade class examining ways to make 16. Jason breaks 16 into 2 + 2 + 2 + 2 + 2 + 2 + 2 + 2. The teacher records this chain on the board, and Jason counts eight 2s. Serena confirms that he has enough 2s, going to the board and counting by 2s as she points to them: 2, 4, 6, 8, 10, 12, 14, 16.

Jason, who wrote the problem, explains that he thought about it this way:

$$\underbrace{2+2}_{4} + \underbrace{2+2}_{4} + \underbrace{2+2}_{4} + \underbrace{2+2}_{4}$$
$$\underbrace{}_{8} \quad \underbrace{}_{8}$$

And he knew 8 + 8 is 16.

Counting by 25s: Fourth-grade class with teacher Angela Philactos (1 minute 20 seconds)

In the next sequence, we see a group of fourth-grade students counting to 400 by 25s. It is still important to keep in mind the quantities represented by the numbers in the "counting-by" chant. They use cubes connected in 5 × 5 flats to model the situation as they count 25, 50, 75, 100, 125, … up to 400. The teacher asks them, "Is there any way you can organize those [flats of cubes] so I can tell at a glance how many?" The students then group their cube-flats in stacks of four, or 100 cubes each.

How Many Legs on Three Elephants?: Third-grade class with teacher Nancy Horowitz (4 minutes 20 seconds)

In the third sequence, two third-grade students share their approaches to the problem, "How many legs do three elephants have?" One student, Ebony, draws three circles with four slashes in each one.

4 legs × 3 circles (elephants, each with 4 legs) = 12 legs

David uses the arithmetic statements, " 4 + 4 = 8, so that's two elephants, and if we add another elephant, it's 12 legs, 8 + 4 legs = 12 legs."

The video concludes with comments from the teacher, Nancy Horowitz. She talks about the difficulty, for children who are starting to multiply, of keeping track of the number of groups versus the number of items in the group, and knowing what the answer stands for—in this example, is it elephants or legs?

Posters for the Math Activity

Prepare six sheets of easel paper, each labeled at the top with one of the possible answers to story problems solved by 32 ÷ 5. Post these to collect the story problems that articipants write while working on the math activity in small groups.

$6\frac{2}{5}$	6.4	6 or 7	6	7	6 remainder 2

Session 2 Detailed Agenda

SESSION 2

MAKING MEANING FOR OPERATIONS

Focus Questions: Chapter 2

1. In Bella's case 8 <old case 6>, children are working to answer questions that we would consider multiplication. Consider the representations offered by Jason, Rashad, Carlita, Kenya, and Flora. How does each illustrate multiplication? How are they the same and how are they different?

2. Also in Bella's case, consider the thinking of Junior in lines 513–526. What ideas about multiplication is he is grappling with? What does his confusion illuminate about the nature of multiplication?

3. In Janine's case 10, we see children working on a multiplication problem, making mistakes and sorting out their confusions. Where did these children get confused? How did they sort it out? How are the ideas in this fourth-grade class similar to Junior's confusion in Bella's kindergarten case?

4. Consider Melinda's case. Explain the thinking of Su-Yin, and also that of Derrick and William. What ideas about multiplication and division are highlighted by the thinking of these children?

5. In Nisha's case 9, we see second graders writing arithmetic expressions to represent the ways they determined the total number of tiles in an arrangement of 15 tiles. What ideas about multiplication are they developing? What connections are there between this work in second grade and future work on multiplication?

6. In Georgia's case 11, we see students using addition, subtraction, and multiplication to solve problems that most of us would consider division problems.

    (a) In particular, consider Vanessa's work on the first two problems (lines 112–130). Vanessa subtracts to solve one problem and adds to solve the other. Why do you think she uses different operations for these two problems?

    (b) Consider the work of Cory (lines 134–149) and Matthew (lines 160–180). What does each student's approach indicate about his thinking about division?

SESSION 2

MAKING MEANING FOR OPERATIONS

Math Activity: Story Problems for Division

1. Write story problems for 32 ÷ 5 so that the question you pose would be answered by each of the following.

    (a) $6\frac{2}{5}$

    (b) 6.4

    (c) 6 or 7

    (d) 6

    (e) 7

    (f) 6 remainder 2

2. Write story problems for 5 ÷ 8 so that the question you pose would be answered by each of the following. Consider how to modify your responses from problem 1 so they fit the 5 ÷ 8 situations.

    (a) $\frac{5}{8}$ (b) 0.625   (c) 0 or 1   (d) 0   (e) 1

Session 2 Detailed Agenda

Session 2

MAKING MEANING FOR OPERATIONS

Third Homework

Reading assignment: Casebook chapter 3

In the casebook, read chapter 3, "When Dividing Doesn't Come Out Evenly," including the introductory text and cases 13 to 16. Consider the questions posed in the chapter introduction as you read.

Writing assignment: Story problems for 5 ÷ 8

You may have worked on this problem briefly in the seminar. This assignment provides the opportunity for you to revisit your thinking by writing your own answers. Your writing can also include questions you have about any parts of the problem that are still confusing or unclear. Seminar facilitators will read what you have written and respond to your ideas and questions.

1. Write story problems for 5 ÷ 8 so that the question you pose would be answered by each of the following.

   (a) $\frac{5}{8}$ (b) 0.625   (c) 0 or 1   (d) 0   (e) 1

   One way to approach this task is to examine the stories your group wrote for 32 ÷ 5 and determine how to modify them to match 5 ÷ 8.

2. For each problem, explain what it is in the story context that makes the answer appropriate for the situation.

Session 2
Making meaning for multiplication and division

Maxine's Journal

February 12

As participants entered the room, they seemed to be excited to share their student-thinking assignments. Even before I brought the group together, Odette spoke up to tell the following story.

She said that she had set up her class to work on the subtraction problems from the MMO homework assignment. When it was time to go to lunch, one boy who wasn't done asked if he could stay in the classroom to finish his work. He then remarked to his teacher, "This is so much better than when we did math!" Odette was shocked. What did he think math was? Doing pages of problems, apparently; definitely *not* talking about his own ideas. "What do the other children think math is?" she wondered.

Elspeth reported that a parent and child had recently visited her class because they were going to be moving into the school district. Initially, the child was nervous, but soon became comfortable enough to sit at a table with other children while his mother sat at the back of the room. While the children were working on a problem individually, Elspeth said she overheard the visiting child ask one of her students what subject he was doing. When he replied he was doing math, the visitor wrinkled up his face and asked, "That's math?" The student responded, "What's math like in your class?" When the visitor said they do things like 3 + 5 = 8 and 2 + 3 = 5, Elspeth's student exclaimed, "That's *all* you do in math? We do much more than that!"

Elspeth's story is like Odette's; both are about children's sense of what math is. However, Elspeth's youngster recognizes that mathematics is much more than rehearsing math facts. Odette's students still need to revise a view of mathematics identified with years of doing worksheets. I'm pleased the teachers are hearing and noting their students' ideas about what mathematics is, and I'm glad they are reporting this to the seminar.

Once Odette and Elspeth told their stories, I oriented participants to this session's work. I said, "Last time we met, we considered the meanings of addition and subtraction. First we looked at the work of young children who were counting to solve problems, and then we examined the work of older students, up through seventh grade. We thought about the variety of contexts that are represented by addition and subtraction, the relationship between those two operations, and how they can be represented with discrete objects like cubes and with a number line."

"Today we'll be doing similar work with multiplication and division. We'll view students' work through print and video cases, and we'll do some mathematics for ourselves. You have noticed that the cases in this chapter are from kindergarten to fourth-grade classrooms, but the ideas in them have important implications for later grades."

"Before we get to the cases, we'll take a few minutes for you to discuss your student-thinking assignments with another participant, and we'll also take a few moments to talk about how we function as a seminar group."

To the last point, Nadra asked, "Did we do something wrong?"

Gaye assured her, "Don't think about it that way. We did the same thing in *Building a System of Tens*. It's really helpful to talk about how to work together."

Sharing student thinking

For homework, participants had given their students the two problems from the DVD clip from Session 1: "I have 375 candy bars. I ate 90 of them. How many do I have left?" and "I am taking a trip to my sister's house. I drive 90 miles and then stop to rest. The total distance is 375 miles. How much farther do I have to go?" Teachers working at the lower grades modified the numbers to be appropriate for their class. I organized participants so each was paired with someone who taught at a different grade level.

Student responses were often quite similar, but some pairs were intrigued by the differences. For example, most of Beatrice's students wrote 375 – 90 for the first problem and 90 + __ = 375 for the second. On the other hand, Karran's students saw both problems as subtraction and initially said there was nothing different about them. Eventually, one student said, "They are both subtraction, but different kinds of subtraction. One is taking something away, and the other is finding how many more you need to get to the other number."

Discussion: Norms for learning

Near the beginning of the seminar, it is important to take a few minutes to consider group norms—how we can interact together to support both our own and one another's learning. The trick here, as Nadra's comment at the opening of the session points out, is to avoid making people feel chided. Discussion of behavior often occurs in classrooms only when something is amiss, but in this case, participants in the seminar have been doing fine. Even so, it's useful to articulate some of the behaviors and attitudes that make the seminar function well.

I started out by reading some of last session's exit cards. "Many people are writing about things that are working well for them," I said. "For example, someone wrote, 'This way of working in small groups helps me to practice and understand better.' Someone else said, 'For me, the cooperative learning process is a very positive way to learn.'"

I went on to say that the way we are engaging in the seminar often requires negotiation. "It's useful for us to talk together about how to work so that everyone can learn. What kinds of things should we be thinking about?"

Participants seemed reluctant to speak until Camisha got us started. "I'm not thinking about rules for us," Camisha said. "It's more like, we need to pay attention to each other's thoughts. That's different from other courses I've taken. I've never been in a class before DMI where we needed to listen to each other so carefully."

Nadra said, "You know, we really come in at all these different levels. I teach young children; I don't teach middle school. I had to remind myself that it's OK to be the slowest person in a group."

Marina (who had been to a DMI seminar before) said, "I come here to ask questions that I never could ask before. Some of my questions I never even knew I had. Some things I just accepted and hadn't ever realized you could ask about them."

Odette said, "I'd like to mention the tug between thinking things out for yourself and moving on with the group. In the last class, I wasn't ready to move on when the group was."

"But Odette," Celeste objected, "the questions you kept asking about number lines turned out to be important for us all to be thinking about."

That felt to me to be an extremely useful insight, but before I could underscore it for the group, Elspeth spoke up. "Sometimes it's not. Sometimes, you just have to feel like you're in a muddle, but you don't know whether or not it's useful to the group to stick with an idea."

I said, "I do understand what you're saying. This is what I mean by some things needing negotiation. There are times when you might take a step back and ask the group if it's useful."

I let this idea sink in until I judged the pause had gone on long enough. Then I asked about reading the cases. "This is a different kind of reading. What kinds of things do you do as you read to prepare for class?"

This time, Marina responded first. "Usually I find one case that piques my interest. I generally have to stop reading and do the math the kids are talking about."

Gaye offered, "I have to read the cases more than once. First I just read the whole chapter to get a general sense. Then I reread the introduction carefully, and read the cases slowly again with those questions in mind. When I read slowly, I start to realize that some of the things happening in the cases are like my own class. Or sometimes, after I read the cases, later in the week I notice the same thing with my students."

Elspeth agreed. "Something like that happens to me, too. After I read the cases, when I'm in my own classroom, questions pop into focus as I'm listening to my students."

"It's like all of a sudden you're alert to things," Beatrice observed, "and so now you start to hear them. Maybe the kids were always saying this stuff, but I never noticed it before."

Gaye, Elspeth, and Marina are among those participants who took *Building a System of Tens* before this seminar, and so they have more experience reading cases. I was glad that the new participants had a chance to hear their perspective. But I wanted to make sure others knew they could speak up, too. I asked if anyone new to reading cases had something to add.

Spencer said that he enjoyed reading the cases, but he hadn't been in an elementary classroom since he graduated from fifth grade, and so it's hard for him to picture what it looks like.

Nadra laughed and said, "Last time, that's how I felt reading the middle school case. But seeing the video helped."

Gaye said, "I teach elementary school, but I felt the same way when I read the first cases for *Building a System of Tens*. It really helped me to see the video. It changed the way I read cases."

I said that in this session, we would get a chance to see elementary classrooms on video, so maybe that would help Spencer read the K–5 cases.

DVD and case discussion: Early multiplication and division

I next turned on the video, which shows children in three classrooms (first, fourth, and third grades) working on preliminary ideas for multiplication and division. Then I said, "We're not going to have a whole-group discussion about the DVD now. As we just said, it's helpful to have images of students in classrooms. As you discuss the print cases, you might refer back to the video, since some of the same issues arise."

Small-group case discussion

As participants settled into their small groups, Maalika didn't hesitate to start talking. "I've been thinking about what it means to count by something. Kids learn a chant, 2, 4, 6, 8, or 5, 10, 15, 20. But we can ask them questions to help them think about what it means."

"Yes," Carol said, "I was thinking about that, too. It's not just about little kids, either. We saw fourth graders showing what it means to count by 25s, and then by 100s."

Joseph, Andrea, and Labeeba were discussing Bella's case 8 about the kindergartners who were asked, "If you have three rabbits, how many legs are there?" Joseph noticed that Kevin represented the problem using 15 keys: 3 stood for rabbit bodies and 12 stood for legs. He found it surprising that Kevin could keep track of which keys to count and even got the right answer. Andrea suggested that it was probably important that it was Kevin's own representation.

Labeeba said, "In our last session, we asked the question about whether the children in the cases about counting were adding, or was it just counting.

Well, it seems to me that Bella's students are doing multiplication. They're counting groups of things, and isn't that what multiplication is?"

I sat down with An-Chi, Camisha, and Iris as they turned to Janine's case 10, "Candy Canes in Packages." An-Chi started explaining that what the teacher was talking about at the end of the video was the same issue that Letitia was struggling with in the case. Later, when I stopped by Karran's group, they were discussing Melinda's case 12, and Karran was saying, "Su-Yin is confused about what are seeds and what are kids, like the teacher on the video was saying. And wasn't that Junior's problem in Bella's case?" I was pleased that many participants were noticing this important point.

Whole-group case discussion

There were several points I wanted to highlight in this discussion, first among them, various representations of multiplication. I said, "In the print and video cases, we see a number of ways to represent multiplication. I think it would be a good idea for us to consider these together. What do we see?"

As participants began flipping through the cases, Andrea said, "We can start with the kindergartners in Bella's case. Jason drew a picture of bunnies and showed four legs on each bunny."

Iris suggested, "We can look at Rashad's and Carlita's arrangements of keys. Rashad used a key for each bunny and also used keys for legs. It's almost like he created a model of a bunny out of keys. But Carlita arranged her keys into three rows of four. It actually looks like an array."

I stopped to clarify the meaning of the term *array*: an arrangement of items with equal rows and equal columns. Spencer added that you can think of the items as arranged in a rectangle.

Karran brought our attention to Kenya's picture, which depicted cubes arranged into an array. I drew an array on the board, a little more carefully than Kenya could manage.

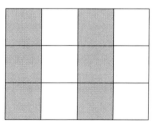

I said, "This is an important image to represent multiplication. You can think of it as 3 rows with 4 cubes in each row; or as 4 columns with 3 cubes in each column; or you can think of it as a rectangle with one side of 4 units and the other with 3 units. You can see all of that in one representation."

Carol said, "Some of the kids in Nisha's case saw multiplication in an array, too. Look at line 55, where Patrick said, 'I see this 3-by-4 rectangle.'"

Celeste mentioned that Flora (in Bella's case 8) arranged her rocks into a row. "She might have counted out three groups of four, but her representation doesn't show the groups, so it isn't very illuminating."

I acknowledged that, although this representation might have helped Flora solve the problem, once the rocks are arranged in a row, it's hard to see what was multiplied.

Gaye said, "What we saw on the video was a little more abstract. The girl there drew three circles with 4 lines in each. Each circle stood for an elephant, and each line was a leg."

Maalika added, "The fourth graders on the video showed multiplication with groups of cubes. They first had 25s arranged in arrays, and then they grouped four of those to show groups of 100."

I said, "At our last meeting, we spent quite a lot of time looking at addition and subtraction on a number line. Can you show multiplication on a number line?"

Cathleen said, "Sure, this shows 3 × 4," and came up to show us.

Now I was ready to move to a second topic. "Three children in this chapter were struggling with something that I'd like to talk about: Junior in Bella's case 8, Su-Yin in Melinda's case 12, and Letitia in Janine's case 10. I heard several people talking about this in small groups, but I want to make sure it's something we all recognize."

Dofi said, "What was happening with Letitia was like what the teacher said on the video. It says in the case, 'she kept confusing 10 and 10 groups of 6.' It was hard for her to keep straight when she needed to count candy canes and when she needed to count packages."

Nadra said, "And it was the same thing with Su-Yin. She was getting confused between what's a kid and what's a seed."

I asked, "What about Junior?"

Celeste responded, "In our small group, we couldn't get what was happening with Junior. We thought he was just out to lunch or wasn't paying attention. But maybe it was just overload for him to think about baskets and eggs at the same time."

Spencer said, "I'm looking at these three kids and how old they are. Junior is in kindergarten, and, like Celeste said, maybe it's just overload for him. He can't think about it at all. In second grade, Su-Yin can think about seeds and kids at the same time, but loses track and doesn't seem to be able to get back on track. Letitia is a fourth grader. She also loses track, but when the teacher asks her a question, she gets back on track."

Gaye pointed out, "But there are other children in the cases who can figure this out."

Spencer responded, "Yes, I know. But maybe these kids illustrate something that is developmental. It's not that they stand for every student.

But maybe for kids who have trouble with this, as they get older they have the ability to sort it out."

Spencer was making an interesting point. In contrast to the discussion in Session 1, when I was concerned that the phrase "it's developmental" would put an end to thought, here Spencer was looking closely at what distinguishes the kindergartner from the second grader and the fourth grader.

Then I raised the next issue. "Let's take a moment to contrast this aspect of multiplication with addition. What happens in addition?"

Beatrice said, "In addition, everything is the same."

Cathleen added, to clarify, "The units are the same for both addends. In multiplication, the units are different for the two factors."

I nodded, "That's true of all the multiplication problems in the cases. And that's exactly what those three children are struggling with."

Then I said, "Let's turn to division. Georgia's students were working on division, weren't they? What did you see in Georgia's case 11?"

It turned out my question was too general. The teachers could see that although Georgia had given her students division problems, they had used every operation except division to solve them. Even though they found the case engaging when they met in small groups, now as they talked, there was a ho-hum feeling. "So the children use different operations. That's good. I don't see why Georgia thinks there's a problem."

Well, I do want teachers to appreciate children's different solution strategies, but I think there is still something else to think about. So I asked, "Do you think there's anything important for children to understand about division as a distinctive operation? What makes division different from addition, subtraction, or multiplication?" And that got more people thinking.

Beatrice said that she asks her students to solve problems in more than one way so that they can see linkages between operations. If they solved the same problem with addition and multiplication, then they could see what was the same and what was different about adding and multiplying. I was pleased to hear this remark. She wasn't just talking about a pedagogical strategy that she had been told to use; she was talking about what students learn when she employs that strategy.

Marina remarked that Vanessa used addition for one problem and subtraction for another. Why did she subtract to solve $24 \div 8$ and add to solve $36 \div 6$?

Odette reiterated the conjecture Georgia had offered, that it depended on the size of the number. If it's easier to visualize the number 24 in her head, then Vanessa is more likely to subtract. If 36 is harder to visualize, then she'll build up to it.

I know that's what Georgia said she was thinking, but because I didn't find that conjecture plausible, I asked the group if there might be something in the wording of the problem, the actual situation described, that makes one of them seem more like addition and the other seem more like subtraction.

There was a buzz in the room, so I suggested that the teachers spend a few minutes talking to a partner. When we came back together, Dofi explained how she saw it: "For the first problem, you have 24 shirts in front of you and you need to put them in the drawers. So first you pick up 8 and put them away; that leaves 16. Then you pick up the next 8 and put them away; that leaves 8. And then you put the last group of 8 in a drawer. That makes 3 drawers. Each time you took away 8, and that feels like subtraction. In the second problem, you need 36 cans; that's what you're trying to get to. So, first you put one 6-pack in your shopping cart and then you put another 6-pack in the cart. That makes 12 cans. You keep adding 6-packs to your cart until you have enough for everyone—36. That feels like addition."

After Dofi spoke, there was a long pause. It was almost as though the teachers were savoring the clarity of Dofi's explanation. Then Spencer continued: "You know, as an adult, I would never have paid attention to those things. I would just know they are both division problems. Now I see that if children are actually looking at the problem and are engaged in acting out the problem—in their heads or with pictures or manipulatives—they would think these problems are totally different. It's amazing to me that children would think that these are different kinds of problems, and I never noticed that."

After another pregnant pause I said, "We don't see in the case whether or not Georgia's students used manipulatives or drew diagrams. But let's think about this for a moment. How can we represent division?"

Dofi spoke first. "We don't see a picture of it, but Vanessa might have acted it out with cubes, just like what I said. She gets 24 cubes for 24 shirts and then starts putting away groups of 8. Or she can start collecting groups of 6 until she has 36 cans." As Dofi spoke, she held up collections of cubes for us to see.

Iris stared at Dofi's cubes and exclaimed, "Oh, my gosh! I can see why division never made any sense to me!"

When I asked Iris to explain, she said, "We say '8 into 24,' but the 24 is what you have. You have 24 shirts. The 8 is an idea, an imaginary thing. It isn't real. And neither is the 3. So neither is the answer, nor what you are operating with. Neither the 8 nor the 3 are real objects, the way you have 3 apples and 8 apples."

After Iris finished, a number of teachers started speaking at once, so I gave them a few minutes to talk to their neighbors. I'm not sure everyone understood what Iris was saying—I'm not sure I did—but everyone seemed aware that she was saying something powerful.

After a few minutes, I brought the group together again and asked if anyone could paraphrase what Iris had said. Beatrice gave it a try. "When you see 24 ÷ 8, you might expect to see 24 things and 8 things. But it's not like that. You have groups of 8 and see that you have 3 groups."

Karran added, "It's the same thing we talked about in multiplication. When you do 3 × 4, the 3 and the 4 aren't the same thing. When you do 3 + 4, you can talk about 3 apples and 4 apples. But if you do 3 × 4, you have 3 elephants and 4 legs for each elephant—they're not the same thing."

Karran's right. Iris was addressing exactly the same thing we discussed earlier. Junior, Su-Yin, and Letitia were all struggling with coordinating multiple units. Similarly, division involves multiple units. Apparently, Iris had sorted out this idea with multiplication, but had never realized this is what division was about.

Before we moved on, there was one more point I wanted to make. I said, "Here are two problems, and I want you to draw a diagram for each."

1. Janice has 12 tulips to distribute equally among 3 vases. How many flowers go in each vase?

2. Michael needs 12 pencils. Pencils come in packages of 3. How many packages does he need?

I asked participants to work alone to sketch their diagrams and then turned around to write out the problems on the board. When I turned back, Spencer was chuckling, and several participants were leaning over to talk about what they had drawn. Coming together, we agreed that both problems could be solved with 12 ÷ 3, but were represented by different diagrams:

1. ☐☐☐☐ ☐☐☐☐ ☐☐☐☐   2. ☐☐☐ ☐☐☐ ☐☐☐ ☐☐☐

An-Chi declared, "I always thought that 12 ÷ 3 meant 'How many 3s are in 12?' That's like the second problem. But now I see that the first problem is also 12 ÷ 3."

Nadra said, "I always thought that, in division, you were told how many groups you had and you had to figure out how many in each group."

I then related a story a fifth-grade teacher once told on herself. She said she had been working with a special needs teacher in her classroom, and they asked the class to come up with a diagram for a division problem. When the two teachers met after class, they were both dismayed that half the class drew an incorrect diagram. But as they began talking, they discovered that they each thought a different half got it wrong. The two teachers had different pictures of what division was. They had a long discussion until they concluded there were different ways to think about division and all of the students had drawn correct diagrams.

At this point, several of the teachers commented about how much more time in their elementary curriculum is spent on addition and subtraction than multiplication and division. "All of kindergarten, first, and second grade is about addition and subtraction, and then all of a sudden in third grade, you do multiplication." I wasn't sure just what they meant, but I didn't think it was simply the amount of time spent on different operations, so I asked them to explain.

Odette said, "When they want kids to learn about addition, they have the children putting out 5 things and putting out 3 things and then seeing how much there is all together. There's also lots of work on what subtraction is. But with multiplication, they just do that quickly—3 × 4 is 3 groups of 4—and the rest of the year is learning to say multiplication facts. Very little time on what multiplication *is*."

They were making an important point. I said, "One thing the primary-grade teachers might think about is, How can you start introducing ideas about multiplication into your teaching? And higher-grade teachers, you might think about how to help your students get at that meaning." But I still wanted to push a little on the *teachers'* ideas about what multiplication is, so I shifted the topic. I pointed out that they saw multiplication as groups of things, like 3 groups of 4. "What would you make of the following problem? Jacob has 3 pairs of shorts and 4 T-shirts. How many outfits can he make with those items of clothing?"

I gave them a few minutes to work on this problem, and everyone came up with 12. Odette said, "I can see that you get the right answer by multiplying, but I don't know why it's a multiplication problem."

In response, Marina explained, "Look, you can think of one pair of shorts with each of the 4 shirts—that's 4 outfits; then the next pair of shorts with 4 shirts—8 outfits; and the third pair of shorts with 4 shirts—12 outfits."

Marina was showing how you could think of the outfits problem as 4 + 4 + 4, but it did give the teachers a sense that when you write 3 × 4, it could have more than one meaning.

Then Amber said, almost plaintively, "Why didn't anyone ever teach us this before? Why didn't I ever get a chance to think about this?"

The conversation got emotional as folks testified to their own experiences as math students. They had always felt this pressure to do things fast, they said; students were made to feel stupid, and if they couldn't do multiplication they got labeled as remedial.

"You know," Camisha confessed, "I've done that to kids, too. I've taught that way. I didn't know there was another way to do it."

"Yeah," Elspeth agreed. "But I've been trying to make it emotionally safer. The children need to know their facts, but it doesn't have to be done with flash cards and timed tests."

After a pause, I pointed out that they *are* getting a chance to think about this stuff now. Then I said that after break, I would have some division problems for them.

Math activity: Story problems for division

I began the math activity by asking every teacher to come up with a word problem for 32 ÷ 5, and then compare their problem with a neighbor's. When they had done that, I asked Iris to share hers.

In the past, when I've assigned a similar task, the first suggestion usually involved something like 32 cookies to be shared among 5 people. Each person got 6 cookies, there were 2 left over, and maybe someone would think of dividing up the remainder.

Iris's problem was different: "There are 32 children in the class and 5 tables in the classroom. If the children are arranged as evenly as possible, how many will be seated at each table?" When I asked the group what the answer was, none responded. They talked about the situation, but no one actually said, "6 or 7."

I decided to let that go and handed out the math activity sheet, pointing out that they already had a start on problem 1. I also mentioned that if, when we came back together, they hadn't finished all the work, we would concentrate on solutions for problem 1, discussing problem 2 only if there was time.

Everybody could get started, but it was interesting to see that different groups got stuck on different solutions. For example, some groups could find a problem whose answer was 6, but not 7; others found problems whose answer was 7, but not 6. Neither could see how the other answer was possible.

Other groups found it easiest simply to write a bunch of problems without aiming for a particular answer and then see what answers they gave. They came up with problems for most of the items that way.

But most groups had trouble inventing a problem whose answer was "6 or 7," until part way through the session, they looked up at the board and realized that Iris had already given it to them.

Some of the groups also had difficulty writing a problem for 6.4. They said that it was hard to think about contexts where you use decimals, except for money, and in that case the answer would be $6.40, not 6.4. "Decimals are for money and fractions are for food," according to Marina. "Isn't that weird?"

When the teachers were working in small groups, I noticed that a few had written math sentences reading $32 \div 5 = 6$ and $32 \div 5 = 7$. I took the time to point out that, even though the answer to the word problem was 6 or 7, the mathematical notation means something else. You can say that $32 \div 5 = 6.4$ or $6\frac{2}{5}$, but it's not correct to say $32 \div 5 = 6$.

Then I put posters on the wall, each headed with one of the six answers:

$6\frac{2}{5}$ 6.4   6 or 7   6   7   6 r 2

I asked participants to write their group's problems on the appropriate posters.

It was important for participants to see that some of the items they thought were easy, others found difficult, and vice versa. This counters the notion that in mathematics there is an absolute standard of this is harder than that. "Hardness" is not necessarily a characteristic of the problem. When they're having more difficulty solving one problem than another, it's not just that the problem is harder. There's something else going on.

When Marina compared the story problems on the posters for 6.4 and $6\frac{2}{5}$, she saw that some of them were the same and asked, "How can that be?"

Spencer explained that 6.4 and $6\frac{2}{5}$ are simply two different ways to write the same amount. He said, "If I run 6.4 miles and you run $6\frac{2}{5}$ miles, we've run exactly the same distance. It doesn't matter!"

Spencer was right. In fact, 6.4 = $6\frac{2}{5}$, and so, technically, any story problem whose answer is 6.4 also has an answer of $6\frac{2}{5}$. But Marina had a point, too. In some contexts, decimals are used more frequently, and in others, fractions.

Celeste said, "There are other answers that can use the same problem, too. For example, say you have $32 dollars to share among 5 people, and the question is, how much money does each person get? If you actually have 32 dollar bills and don't have any way to get change, then each person gets $6 and you don't distribute the other $2. Or you can say three people get $6 and two get $7. Or, if you can get change, then each person gets $6.40."

Celeste's point was different from Spencer's since, or course, $6.40 ≠ $6. Celeste has taken the same basic problem with slight variations to produce different answers.

The discussion of 6 remainder 2 was interesting. Beatrice declared, "There isn't a problem whose answer is 6 remainder 2! If you have such a problem, you have to ask two questions. Like you might say, *I need 5 yards of material for drapes and I have 32 yards. How many drapes can I make?* The answer is just 6. But what if I ask, *How many drapes can I make and how much material do I have left over?* There are two answers: 6 drapes answers the first question; 2 yards answers the second."

Beatrice's remarks created a stir, and I was pleased. I'm not so concerned about whether or not participants think you can have a problem whose answer is 6 r2, but rather that they see the complexity of that answer. I think that was what surprised the group, since students are often told that 6 r2 is the correct answer, especially if they haven't yet worked with fractions.

Toward the end of our math time, I asked people to consider problem 2 on the math activity sheet, which asks them to think of word problems for 5 ÷ 8. At first Iris blurted out, "What? You can't divide a smaller number by a larger number."

Karran said, "Sure you can." Iris turned red.

"Iris," I said, "You've been having all kinds of new discoveries about division today, and it might be that you have enough to think about already. Still, I'd like us all to think about why it might *seem* that you can't have 5 ÷ 8."

"Let's go back to the problems we made up for 32 ÷ 5," Spencer offered. "Like you had 32 cookies for 5 kids. Now let's say you have 5 cookies for 8 kids."

"It's just like the other problems," Carol declared. "You can have different answers."

"What do you mean?" I asked.

"It depends on whether you can cut up your cookies. If you have 5 cookies for 8 kids, you might just say forget it. The answer is 0—there's not enough to share. But if you cut them up, each kid gets $\frac{5}{8}$ of a cookie."

Participants had a few minutes to get into the problem in small groups, and then the time was up. I explained, "This is the question you'll work on for homework. Just as we did for 32 ÷ 5, I'd like you to write out different story problems for 5 ÷ 8. As you work on this, think about Spencer's suggestion, that you use the problems you created for 32 ÷ 5. Before you leave, make sure you have written down at least one story problem for each of the answers on the posters. For homework, you are asked to substitute the numbers 5 and 8 into those problems, and then make up an additional problem for each answer. You'll see that this assignment is relevant for the cases you'll be reading."

Homework and exit cards

I distributed the "Third Homework" sheet and gave participants a chance to read it. Then I posted the exit-card questions.

1. What was important or significant to you in the mathematics discussed at this session?

2. What do you want to tell the facilitators about how the seminar is working for you?

The exit cards give me a sense of what participants are taking away from the session. Some of the cards express key issues related to teachers' practice.

> ODETTE: What was significant for me today was realizing that the context in which a problem is presented can help kids think about more complicated math ideas.

> JOSEPH: I am impressed at the level of thinking we ask of students on a daily basis. Having to create problems to fit the answer helps me understand the complexity involved.

> MAALIKA: The problems about 32 ÷ 5 were challenging. It really re-emphasized how important context is. Sharing these examples with parents would help them understand that math is not all about quick recall of memorized facts. Children need to understand the problem.

Some of the middle school teachers wrote about what they get from examining cases from elementary classrooms.

> SPENCER: Seeing how multiple processes can be used to solve relatively simple math problems makes me realize that multiple processes can and should be used to solve more complicated, multi-step algebraic problems. That is, what I see in the cases with younger students

applies to my middle school students working on more complex content—they shouldn't simply be memorizing set procedures for solving particular problem types.

CELESTE: When I examine the thought processes of younger students, I see that sometimes I overlook or take for granted the skills my students have. I need to check this out.

I do appreciate it when participants let me know that they are intimidated by the mathematics. For example:

NADRA: The fractions in word problems make me nervous. I was never strong with them to begin with.

I'll need to help Nadra face her fear of fractions.

Responding to the second homework

February 15

For this homework assignment, participants had given students two story problems to solve, problems which many adults would identify as subtraction. Most of the participants wrote about how different students had different ways of thinking about the two story problems. The teachers, who after Session 1 already were surprised as they began to see the complexity of subtraction, now could see that complexity revealed in their students' thinking. For example, Dofi discovered that the second problem was much more challenging to her first graders than the first.

Dofi

I gave three of my students the following problems.

Problem 1: Max had 15 candy bars. He sold 8 of them. How many candy bars did he have left?

Problem 2: Mom was taking a trip to the store. She drove for 8 miles and then had to stop to rest. The total distance to the store is 15 miles. How much farther does Mom have to go?

All three students used the same equation for Problem 1: $15 - 8 = 7$. I had expected that this would happen because we have solved and talked about problems similar to this in class before. Two of the students used symbols to solve the problem (they both drew 15 X's and crossed out 8 of them), while the other used cubes. Again, this is what I expected. When asked why they subtracted, Student 1 said, "He is giving away stuff," while Student 2 said, "He didn't have as many candy bars as he started with." After examining their work, I learned that all three students understand that after you "take away" part of a group, you will have less than what you started with.

The surprises came with Problem 2. I was not sure what to expect from the students with this problem. All three of them used a different method to solve it, and all three needed more time than with Problem 1.

Student 1 used the equation $8 + 15 = 23$, and decided that Mom had 23 more miles to go. He solved the equation by first taking out 8 cubes and then 15 and counting up all the cubes. When I asked him about why he chose to add 8 and 15, he said that 8 and 15 were the numbers in the problem, and he added them together because "Mom was going to the store and that's not going back." I reiterated to him a couple of times that the total distance to the store was 15, but this did not change his thinking in any way. I believe this is because in the majority, if not all, of the problems he has solved in the past, he has had to use both numbers in the equation to find a sum or difference rather than a missing addend.

Student 2 used the equation 8 + 7 = 15. I asked him why he used addition, and he said he added because "She had to go more miles… She had to take a rest at 8 miles and she had 7 more miles to go." He also explained, "I knew 7 + 7 = 14 and 8 + 8 = 16, so I added 1 to 14 and took away 1 from 16, and that equaled 15."

Student 3 used the equation 15 – 8 = 7. To solve this equation, she drew 15 circles on her paper, crossed off 8 of them, and then counted the circles that were left. I asked her why she subtracted, and she said, "It is 15 miles to the store and she already drove the 8." I was surprised at the accuracy and level of her thinking because we have not solved problems like this in the past. It was interesting that she was the only one out of three to view this as a subtraction problem.

I was pleased that Dofi has begun to explore the complexity of subtraction with her first graders and isn't backing away from it. Rather, her writing about her students conveys the richness of their thinking. In my response, I wanted to give her more ideas to consider—approaches that might help Student 1 interpret the problem, particular hurdles many students in her class may need to overcome, and other questions that might be posed to further the thinking of all students.

Dear Dofi,

What an interesting description of the work three of your students did. Particularly fascinating is that they all solved the first problem essentially the same way, but did very different things with the second.

It sounds like you worked with each of the three children individually. I wonder what would have happened if they'd had a chance to discuss the second problem together. Would Student 1 have been able to make sense of either of his classmates' reasoning? Would Students 2 and 3 have been able to recognize that both their ways fit the problem and result in the same answer?

There is more to think about with Student 1. He isn't thinking about the problem in a way that actually matches the context. I wonder whether this context is too abstract for him to work on a new idea, and if there is another context that would make the ideas more accessible. What if he had 8¢, but needed 15¢ for something he wanted to buy? Or maybe he had 8 objects, but needed 15 for something he wanted to do? You said that he was the one student who used cubes to solve Problem 1 rather than drawing symbols on a page. Perhaps he still needs to be thinking about something more concrete than units of distance.

You might want to check out whether Student 1 (as well as other students in the class) believe the equal sign means "here comes the answer," so whatever he does has to result in a number that goes after the equal sign. Perhaps, once he decided the problem involves addition, adding the two numbers is the only possibility; he didn't consider that the appropriate equation could be 8 + __ = 15.

I also wonder whether any of the three children noticed that the two problems involved the same numbers—especially Student 3, who wrote the same number sentence (15 − 8 = 7) to solve both problems. Could they talk about what is the same about the two problems and what is different?

There is so much to pay attention to in making sense of subtraction. Have fun working on these ideas with your class.

Maxine

S E S S I O N

3

MAKING MEANING FOR OPERATIONS

When Dividing Doesn't Come Out Evenly

Mathematical Themes

- As students extend their concept of number to include fractions and zero, their ideas about the behavior of the operations must be reconsidered.

- The same quantity can be represented by different fraction names depending on what is taken as 1, the unit or the whole.

- The value of a fraction is determined by the relationship between the numerator and the denominator.

Chapter 3 case discussion	Small groups	30 minutes
	Whole group	30 minutes
Math activity: Comparing fractions	Small group	40 minutes
Break		15 minutes
Math activity (cont.)	Whole group	30 minutes
Planning for the student-thinking assignment	Groups of 2 or 3	30 minutes
Homework and exit cards	Whole group	5 minutes

Background Preparation

Read

- the casebook, chapter 3
- the detailed agenda for Session 3
- "Maxine's Journal" for Session 3
- the casebook, chapter 8, sections 5 and 6

Work through

- the math activity: Comparing fractions
- the focus questions for Session 3

Materials

Duplicate

- "Focus Questions: Chapter 3"
- "Math Activity: Comparing Fractions"
- "Planning the Student-Thinking Assignment"
- "Fourth Homework"

Obtain

- cubes
- graph paper
- index cards

What Is the Connection Between Division and Fractions?
What Does it Mean for a Set of Numbers to be Closed Under an Operation?

The example problems in the first three cases in this chapter, 5 ÷ 39 and 7 ÷ 4, illustrate a significant point about division. Division of whole numbers does not always result in a whole number as an answer.

This is different from what happens with the operation of addition. If you add any two whole numbers, you get a whole number as a result. In formal mathematical language, the set of whole numbers is closed under addition. However, consider what happens with the operation of subtraction: 3 − 8 = −5, and −5 is not a whole number. Some pairs of whole numbers, when subtracted, yield a whole-number answer, and some do not. The set of whole numbers is *not* closed under. In order to be able to produce an answer to every subtraction of whole numbers, a new kind of number must be considered—numbers that are less than zero, or negative numbers. In the DMI seminar *Reasoning Algebraically About Operations*, the set of numbers known as the integers (whole numbers, zero, and the opposites of the whole numbers) is studied.

The operation of multiplication is similar to that of addition: multiply any pair of whole numbers, and the product is another whole number. The set of whole numbers is closed under multiplication. Now consider division, where the situation is like subtraction. For 30 ÷ 5, the answer is 6, a whole number. However, 5 ÷ 30 does not have a whole-number answer. In order to produce an answer for all pairs of whole numbers, a new kind of number must be considered; numbers of the form $\frac{a}{b}$, where a and b are whole numbers and b is not zero.

A consequence of this definition is that $a \div b$ has as its answer $\frac{a}{b}$. For example, while we might consider the answer to 3 ÷ 4 by thinking 4 times what is 3; we could also say that 3 ÷ 4 is $\frac{3}{4}$. This relationship between division and fractions involves even more complexity. While the division problem is about two whole numbers, 3 and 4, the answer is a number that expresses a relationship between the original whole numbers. Thus, $\frac{3}{4}$ is simultaneously an expression of a relationship between the two whole numbers 3 and 4, and a single value with a specific place on the number line.

Session 3

Detailed Agenda

Case discussion: When dividing gives an answer less than 1 (60 minutes)

Small groups (30 minutes)

Whole group (30 minutes)

The cases in chapter 2, discussed in the previous session, began an examination of whole-number division. The cases in chapter 3 extend that work by presenting situations in which the divisor is less than the dividend. The chapter includes the following main questions:

- What happens when a smaller number is divided by a greater number?

- How does changing the context for a division problem affect the nature of the answer?

- How do the meanings of multiplication and division need to expand to address multiplying with 0 and dividing with 0?

The first two cases describe students struggling to make sense of the problem, $5 \div 39$. As the participants work to make sense of the students' quandaries, they may realize that they share some of the same confusions. Acknowledge that fractions embody complex mathematical ideas, and indicate that the remaining sessions of the seminar will be devoted to this topic. Suggest that they can use the thinking of the students to deepen their own mathematical ideas. The last case presents middle school students working to expand their ideas about multiplication and division as they try to determine what it means to use zero as a factor, divisor, or dividend.

The third case in this chapter is not considered in the initial case discussion, but it will be discussed as the context for a student-thinking assignment the group will be doing for homework.

Before beginning the small-group work, remind participants about the work they did in the previous session and as homework, creating word problems for $32 \div 5$ and $5 \div 8$. Suggest that the thinking they did with those problems will be useful as they work to understand the thinking of the students in these cases.

The cases of this chapter can support different kinds of discussions. If you want to concentrate on student thinking and classroom discourse, have participants discuss focus questions 1–4. Focus question 5 provides an opportunity for participants to work on their own mathematical ideas involving fractions. It foreshadows the work of the next three sessions of the seminar. Participants new to this kind of thinking will benefit from focusing on the other ideas in this session and deferring extensive work on this issue until after they have worked through Sessions 4–6. Question 6 examines what it might mean to multiply by zero; this can lead into a discussion of why it is not possible to divide by zero.

If you want to be sure your participants have time to talk about the issues raised in case 16 involving operations with zero, suggest they work with focus questions 3, 4, and 6 first, and then turn to the other questions if they have time. On the other hand, if you do not intend to include Jayson's case 16 in the whole-group discussion, suggest that small groups begin with focus question 1. Then, after 20 minutes, ask the group to spend the last 10 minutes discussing questions 3 and 4 if they have not already done so.

Why Can't We Divide by Zero?

In Jayson's case 16, Renee presents one explanation for why division by zero is not possible: if $6 \div 0 = n$, then this would mean $n \times 0 = 6$. To complete her argument, note that since any number multiplied by 0 is 0, there is no such number, n. It is not possible to determine a number that would satisfy the equation. This argument relies on the relationship between multiplication and division and our interest in having the mathematical structure of the number system be consistent.

Another approach is to consider the actions involved in a division story situation. One type of division story is modeled by the question "How many groups of 3 are in 12?" The action suggests gathering groups of 3 out of the 12 until the 12 has been used up, and then counting the number of times the action of taking 3 out of the 12 occurred. How many times can you reach into a pool of 12 objects and take out 3 of them? If this scenario is played out with taking zero objects, there is no end to the process. No matter how many times you reach into the pool of 12 and remove zero, the 12 objects will never be used up.

In the previous examples, the divisor was a non-zero number. The question arises, what would $\frac{0}{0}$ mean? Consider what happens if Renee's argument is applied. The multiplication sentence implied by $0 \div 0 = n$, $n \times 0 = 0$, does not result in a contradiction. However, a new kind of difficulty arises: n can be replaced by any number and the sentence remains true. This implies that $0 \div 0$ has infinitely many answers. For this reason, mathematicians have called $0 \div 0$ indeterminate.

For additional information on this topic, consult "Maxine's Journal," lines 507–550.

Small-group discussion
(30 minutes)

Distribute "Focus Questions: Chapter 3." Let participants know that this discussion is based on cases 13, 14, and 16, and that there will be an activity later in the session based on case 15.

Focus question 1 invites participants to examine the thinking of the children as they begin to notice the need to revise and expand their ideas about the operation of division. Question 2 focuses on what the word *number* means and how that meaning must shift or expand as new kinds of numbers are needed. Focus question 3 examines how the contexts students assign to a division problem affect the answers that seem possible.

Question 4 focuses participants on a particular section of case 14 as they analyze the classroom discourse to identify what idea each student contributes to the discussion. Question 5 invites participants to engage in mathematical analysis by asking them to link the diagram at the end of case 14 with various arithmetic expressions. Focus question 6 supports an examination of student and participant thinking about multiplying and dividing with zero.

Let your group know which of the focus questions they should concentrate on, and tell them the main ideas they will be discussing as a whole group.

Now that you have worked with these participants for a few sessions, it is likely you know something about the way individuals prefer to participate in case discussions. You might want to group participants with similar pacing together. Also, if you think some, but not all, of your participants will benefit from a discussion based on focus question 6, group them together and encourage them to include case 16 in their small-group discussion, even though it won't be addressed in whole group.

Whole-group case discussion (30 minutes)

Note: This summary includes comments about all of the focus questions. If you have varied the assignment of questions, refer just to the ideas below that are applicable to your group.

In discussing the focus questions 1–4, ask, "What ideas about division have been highlighted for you as you discuss these cases?"

Points that should arise in this discussion include these:

- One context for making sense of division when the divisor is greater than the dividend is to consider objects that can be broken into parts.

- Numbers between 0 and 1 are the result of dividing a number by a greater number.

In discussing focus question 5, invite participants to explain how they make sense of the various ways to name the fractional part in the diagram. Two main ideas will come up in the explanations:

- The name of the fractional part is dependent on what is interpreted as a whole, as well as how many parts the whole is divided into.

- It is possible to name a fractional part by identifying it as a sum or product of fractions.

In discussing focus question 6, participants should consider Renee's argument for why division by 0 is impossible, as well as Cameron's rebuttal. The discussion should establish the following:

- There is a difference between an answer that is the number 0 and a situation in which there is no answer.

- Zero divided by a non-zero number is 0.

- A non-zero number divided by 0 cannot be defined.

Some participants may wish to discuss the $0 \div 0$ situation as well.

This case discussion has introduced the idea of fractions in the context $5 \div 39$. The remaining sessions of the *Making Meaning for Operations* seminar will be devoted to exploring the topics of fractions in more detail.

In What Situations Do We Write $\frac{1}{5}$?

The number $\frac{1}{5}$ is sometimes written to represent each of these situations:

a. In a basketball game, for every 5 attempts Hank made to shoot a basket, he scored once. What fraction of all his tries did Hank make?

b. There are 5 people and 1 sandwich. If the sandwich is shared evenly, how much does each person get?

c. A model is constructed so that a length of 1 foot on the model represents 5 feet on the actual object. What is the scale?

d. There are 5 donuts left in a box. Someone eats one donut. What fraction of the donuts did that person eat?

e. In each hour of exercise throughout the week, Jamilla spent 12 minutes running and 48 minutes walking. What fraction represents the amount of time in each hour that Jamilla ran?

f. It takes a snail 5 seconds to move 1 foot. How fast is it going?

The differences among these situations are significant, even though the answer in each case can be represented as $\frac{1}{5}$. In situations (a) and (e), $\frac{1}{5}$ is really a shorthand way to say 1 out of 5. For every 5 attempts, Hank made 1 shot; for every hour of exercise, Jamilla spent 12 minutes running. These are expressions of a ratio relationship.

Situation (c) is a scaling situation; on the model, each linear dimension of the actual object is shrunk to $\frac{1}{5}$ of its length.

Situations (b) and (d) represent fractional relationships; the sandwich is cut into 5 equal parts, the total amount of donuts is divided into 5 equal parts.

Situation (f) involves a rate; the pace of the snail is $\frac{1}{5}$ feet per second.

Math activity: Comparing fractions (40 minutes)

Small groups

Distribute "Math Activity: Comparing Fractions" to the small groups. Ask participants to read the directions and let them know that the constraint of not using common denominators or converting to decimals is to help them develop rules about comparing fractions that are based on other attributes of the fractions. Draw a diagram such as the following to represent $\frac{2}{3}$, and suggest that this is the kind of representation they should use.

Strategies for Comparing Fractions
The Size of a Fraction is Determined by Both the Size of the Pieces and the Number of Pieces

Most people are familiar with the common denominator procedure for comparing a pair of fractions: Convert both numbers to fractions with the same denominator; the one with the greater numerator is the greater fraction. For instance, to compare $\frac{2}{3}$ and $\frac{5}{6}$, change them to fractions with denominator of 6 and compare $\frac{4}{6}$ and $\frac{5}{6}$. Which is more, 4 pieces the size of $\frac{1}{6}$ or 5 pieces the size of $\frac{1}{6}$? Why does this work, in general? By changing to the same denominator, we can fall back to ways we compare whole numbers: 5 is greater than 4. The common denominator is a way to assure that we are comparing 4 objects to 5 of the same objects. Eight cents is less than 10 cents. Eight dollars is less than 10 dollars. However, 8 dollars is not less than 10 cents. The common denominator procedure provides a guarantee that we are comparing two whole numbers of the same thing. Once we know the size of the pieces is the same, the fraction that represents more pieces is greater.

By attending to both the size of the pieces and the number of pieces, we can find other approaches for comparing pairs of fractions. For example, $\frac{4}{5}$ and $\frac{4}{7}$ can be described as a common numerator situation. Both fractions represent the same number of pieces, but the pieces are of different sizes. Since dividing something into more equal parts means each part is smaller, $\frac{1}{5}$ will be greater than $\frac{1}{7}$, so in this case, $\frac{4}{5}$ is greater than $\frac{4}{7}$ because 4 of the greater pieces is more than 4 of the smaller pieces. In general, this idea might be stated as: If you have the same number of pieces, the fraction whose denominator is less—that is, it has the larger-size pieces—will be the greater.

Consider $\frac{5}{6}$ and $\frac{7}{8}$. Each fraction represents a situation with one piece missing from the whole. The size of the missing piece (the denominator) determines which is the greater fraction. The smaller the amount missing, the greater the fraction. This can be generalized to situations in which the two fractions represent situations with two pieces missing, three pieces missing or, in general, the same number of pieces missing from the whole.

Comparing $\frac{3}{8}$ and $\frac{2}{9}$ provides a situation in which one fraction represents more pieces that are a greater size ($\frac{3}{8}$), so it is the greater fraction.

As you work with the small groups, encourage them to express their strategies with language that is descriptive of the situation, such as *the size of the piece* and *the number of pieces* rather than terms such as *numerator* and *denominator*.

Note: When groups reach problem 3, they are asked to consider a common denominator approach to resolving which is greater, $\frac{2}{5}$ or $\frac{1}{2}$. They are also asked to consider other ways to determine which of these two is greater.

Placing Fractions Relative to Each Other on a Number Line

Comparing fraction pairs by examining the size of the piece and the number of pieces seems to focus on the numbers that are in the numerator and the denominator. However, the purpose of the task is to determine the value of a third number, the fraction itself. For example, the fraction $\frac{4}{7}$, while expressed by writing a 4 and a 7, represents a specific value—a number or a point on the number line. The value of $\frac{4}{7}$ is determined by the ratio of 4 to 7. Placing fractions on the number line in relationship to each other focuses on the value of the fraction.

In order to place $\frac{4}{7}$ on the number line, first locate 0 and 1, giving you the size of a unit. Divide the unit into 7 equal parts. Beginning at 0, move to the right across four of these 7 equal parts. That point is $\frac{4}{7}$.

One way to determine where to locate $\frac{4}{5}$ is to consider its relationship to $\frac{4}{7}$ and use this strategy: If the number of pieces is the same, the fraction that represents the larger-size pieces (lesser denominator) is greater fraction.

To place $\frac{5}{6}$ and $\frac{7}{8}$, consider that the three fractions $\frac{4}{5}$, $\frac{5}{6}$, and $\frac{7}{8}$ are all examples of this situation: If both fractions have one piece missing from a whole, then the smaller piece (greater denominator) is the greater fraction.

With similar reasoning, the remaining fractions from the activity sheet can be placed to show this relative placement.

Note: These placements along the number line show correctly which numbers fall to the right or left of each other, but not necessarily their relative size.

Break   (15 minutes)

Math activity (cont.): Comparing fractions   (30 minutes)

Whole group

Use the whole-group discussion to establish useful strategies for comparing fractions:

- Comparing fractions with common numerators

- Comparing fractions with the same number of pieces missing from the whole

Begin the whole-group discussion by asking for a strategy that was generated by the fraction pair $\frac{4}{5}$ and $\frac{4}{7}$. Once this situation has been clarified, turn to $\frac{5}{6}$ and $\frac{7}{8}$. One explanation for this pair might be: If two fractions represent one part missing from a whole, the fraction with the smaller pieces (the one with the greater denominator) is the greater fraction because the missing part is smaller. After some discussion, ask if this strategy can be generalized. Does it need to be one part missing from a whole? Ask for a more general statement. You might want to ask the group to offer some examples for fraction pairs such as $\frac{7}{10}$ and $\frac{4}{7}$, or $\frac{3}{8}$ and $\frac{2}{7}$, to clarify this strategy.

These explanations focus on the meaning of the numerator and denominator in a fraction. In order to move the discussion into the idea that a fraction is a single value, represented by a point on the number line, pose this question: "What did you notice about fractions when you worked to place them relative to each other on a number line?" See "Maxine's Journal," lines 245–302, for an example of this discussion.

Planning for the student-thinking assignment (30 minutes)

Groups of 2 or 3, representing two consecutive grade levels

Let the group know that before the next session, they will take a problem involving fractions to their own students. In a written assignment, participants will share what they learned from examining their students' thinking. Distribute the handout "Planning the Student-Thinking Assignment."

Tell the groups to discuss Lori's case 15 first, focusing on the first two questions on the handout. They should then consider the problem they will be giving their students and develop responses to questions 3(a) to 3(d) as a group. Let them know that in the next session, they will return to these same small groups to share their own students' responses.

The assignment includes a variation that middle-grade teachers might use if they feel that "4 children and 7 brownies" is too easy to stimulate their students' thinking. On the other hand, if your seminar includes teachers of kindergarten or grade 1, you might suggest they offer a simpler situation to their students: 4 children and 5 brownies, or 4 children sharing 6 brownies.

Homework and exit cards (5 minutes)

Whole group

As the session ends, distribute the "Fourth Homework" sheet. Also distribute index cards and pose these exit-card questions:

1. What mathematics are you still wondering about from this session?

2. What was this session like for you as a learner?

Before the next session…

In preparation for the next session, read what participants wrote in their homework on creating story problems for $5 \div 8$ and write a response to each participant. For more information, see the section in "Maxine's Journal " on responding to the third homework. Make copies of both the papers and your response for your files before returning the work.

SESSION 3

MAKING MEANING FOR OPERATIONS

Focus Questions: Chapter 3

1. In MaryAnn's case 13, T.C. declares, "You can't divide a number that's lower by one that's higher." Why does this statement seem true? In what ways is it not true? Why does MaryAnn think the idea of "fair shares" would help T.C. and his classmates look at division differently?

2. In case 14, Darrell says, "I think 39 can't go into 5. I mean, it can go into it, but it's going to be a fraction, it's got to be a fraction. A larger number into a smaller number—5 can go into 39, but there's a remainder. No, it's not a remainder; it's not a number." What might Darrell be thinking? What do you think he means by "number"?

3. The students in MaryAnn's two cases realize that, in order to think through why $5 \div 39$ and $39 \div 5$ are not the same problem, they could use story contexts that are modeled by the arithmetic expressions. Modify their stories or make up some story contexts of your own that help you think about this.

4. Trace the development of the discussion in case 14 from Mitchell's conversation at line 185 to the end of the case. Explain what math ideas the following students add to the conversation: Leo, Cynthia, Tori, Maribel, Laila, Anthony, and Alejandro.

5. Explain the diagram offered by Cynthia and Leo near the end of case 14 (line 239) and consider the questions posed by the class at the end of the case (lines 244–259).

6. In Jayson's case 16, his friend Charlene's middle school students, who are exploring what it means to divide into 0 and to divide by 0, surface both important relationships and misunderstandings about the operations of multiplication and division and the nature of 0. Examine the following passages to discuss this: Cameron beginning at line 157 (including his drawings), Cameron beginning at line 212, Ashley beginning at line 233, and Renee at line 237.

SESSION 3

MAKING MEANING FOR OPERATIONS

Math Activity: Comparing Fractions

You may know how to compare fractions by converting them into decimals or by making common denominators. *Do not do that here.* Explore these problems by drawing diagrams to determine which one of the pair is greater. You will get more from this activity by following these directions.

1. Using diagrams, determine which fraction in each pair is greater:

   (a) $\frac{4}{5}$ or $\frac{4}{7}$ (b) $\frac{5}{6}$ or $\frac{7}{8}$ (c) $\frac{3}{8}$ or $\frac{2}{9}$

   What general statements about the relative sizes of fractions can you make based on these examples? Be as precise as you can as you write the statements. You might need to try some more examples to check your statements.

2. Use your reasoning from problem 1 to place the six fractions ($\frac{4}{5}$, $\frac{4}{7}$, $\frac{5}{6}$, $\frac{7}{8}$, $\frac{3}{8}$, and $\frac{2}{9}$) on this line, showing their positions relative to each other.

   Take note of your reasoning as you decide where to place each fraction.

3. Consider this fraction pair: $\frac{2}{5}$ and $\frac{1}{2}$. Explain which fraction is greater. Place these fractions on the line with the other six. What new issues come up for you? Why might you want to use common denominators for this work? Can you find another way?

4. Make up some fractions of your own and see if you can determine where they should be placed. Are some easy to determine? If so, which ones and why? Are some harder to determine? If so, which ones and why?

SESSION 3

MAKING MEANING FOR OPERATIONS

Planning the Student-Thinking Assignment

1. In case 15, we see first-grade students working to determine how to share 7 brownies among 4 children. Discuss the approach of each of these children: Matthew (lines 35–60), Diane (lines 65–73), and James (lines 74–90). What ideas about fractions do these children have? What ideas are missing?

2. Revisit the case to examine the questions that Lori asks. How would you characterize her questions? What do you imagine Lori's purpose to be in posing these questions?

3. For the next session, you will collect and analyze the work of your own students as they work on the problem of 4 children sharing 7 brownies. If you feel this problem is too easy for the grade level you teach, pose both this question and the variation.

> *Problem:* There are 7 brownies to share among 4 friends. How many brownies would each friend get? Solve this problem with a diagram and with an arithmetic sentence. Describe the connections you see between the diagram and the arithmetic.
>
> *Variation:* There are 4 brownies to share among 7 friends. How many brownies would each friend get? Solve this problem with a diagram and with an arithmetic sentence. Describe the connections you see between the diagram and the arithmetic.
>
> One student offered this solution to the variation:
>
>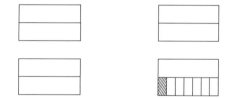
>
> Each person gets $\frac{1}{2}$ plus the shaded amount.
>
> Is this correct? If so, explain why, and tell how it matches the answer you have. If not, explain why it is incorrect.

   (a) Write out ways you would expect your students to work on this problem.

   (b) What mathematics might they draw on to do this work?

   (c) What might be conceptual hurdles for them?

   (d) What kinds of questions might you ask to be sure you understand what your students are thinking?

SESSION 3

MAKING MEANING FOR OPERATIONS

Fourth Homework

Reading assignment: Casebook chapter 4

In the casebook, read chapter 4, "Greater Than, Less Than, Equal To," including the introductory text and cases 17 to 21. Use the questions posed in the introduction as a guide for your reading of the cases.

Writing assignment: Sharing brownies

Ask your students to work on the brownie problem, 4 children sharing 7 brownies. For middle school classes, you might also pose the variation given on the planning sheet. For kindergarten and grade 1 classes, you can modify the original problem to 4 children sharing 5 brownies, or 4 children sharing 6 brownies.

Take notes on what your students did and the questions you asked to uncover their thinking. Select the work of four or five students to share at our next seminar meeting.

Write about what happened and what you learned by working with students on this task. Your writing should include the examples of student work and why each one is of interest to you.

Please bring three copies of this writing to the next session to share with your colleagues.

Session 3
When dividing doesn't come out evenly

Maxine's Journal

February 26

Now we are into our extended exploration of operations with fractions, which we'll be doing from now to the end of the seminar.

Many teachers in this group don't teach fractions, so this feels like foreign material to them. "You know, what you are drawing on here is what I learned when I was in junior high school, and I haven't used them since." That's what Iris had to say about fractions. In fact, I'm hoping some of the primary-grade teachers, Iris among them (as well as Nadra, who wrote about her fear of fractions on her exit card after Session 2) will discover that it *is* appropriate to begin to explore some fraction-related ideas with their young students.

None of the upper-grade teachers spoke up in response to Iris's comment, but I suspect they'll be finding themselves in foreign territory, as well. In fact, most people, including those who teach fractions, have never had a chance to think through the conceptual issues raised by rational numbers. This can be especially disconcerting for those who thought they already understood all there is to know about fractions. But once they get past that, teachers usually find the issues intriguing. Not only teachers! When I taught K–12 students, I quickly learned that if I wanted to spark their parents' excitement at open house, I should do some fractions work with them. Once parents got a glimmer of understanding why "invert and multiply" makes sense, they knew they wanted their children to have that kind of experience in math class.

That's still ahead of us in this seminar. By Session 7, I expect that these folks, too, will be intrigued and excited when they make new connections about dividing fractions. But now, for this session, we're thinking about dividing whole numbers where the answer "doesn't come out even" (a question Lori's first graders confront). And what happens when the divisor is greater than the dividend—that is, when you try to divide a number by a greater number? These are the questions that MaryAnn's students were asking in the cases we read.

Case discussion: When dividing gives an answer less than 1

In the first part of MaryAnn's case 13, her students are trying to find meaning for 5 ÷ 39. I pointed out that the students' discussion might be similar to some of what participants wrote about 5 ÷ 8 for their homework. Today in the seminar, small groups began their case discussions with focus questions 1–3, meant to draw attention to the ideas the students bring to this problem.

Small-group case discussion

As I visited groups, I noticed that by now most of the teachers had the idea that, in making up a division problem for 5 ÷ 39, it matters whether you're talking about things that can be divided. The first time MaryAnn's students met with 5 ÷ 39, they appeared to be thinking about items that couldn't be broken up. For example, it didn't occur to Alejandro to make change for dollar bills; it wouldn't make sense to cut up Deon's desks; and Cynthia seemed to be thinking of 5 pieces of hard candy for 39 principals. The following year, the same class returned to 5 ÷ 39, and when the students now talked about sharing candy bars that could be split evenly, this gave them access to new ideas about numbers.

Carol, Beatrice, and Iris were in a group discussing focus question 2, trying to figure out what could be going on in Darrell's head when he says "it's not a number." Beatrice asked, "Is it that he can't think about fractions? Or does he know what the answer would be but doesn't want to call it a number? I mean, does he think numbers have to be 1, 2, 3—numbers you count with? Like, $\frac{5}{39}$ can't be a number? Maybe he has ideas about fractions, but he needs to stretch his idea of what 'number' is."

On the other hand, Iris seemed to be arguing, in her group, for the position that Beatrice attributed to Darrell. "Fractions aren't numbers. Fractions tell you to do something. But a fraction isn't a number." Hmmm. I thought it was interesting that Iris was taking this view, but it was also disconcerting. Do I need to intervene here? But how?

Actually, Carol seemed to be handling the situation fairly well herself. "Why do you think fractions aren't numbers? I think they are numbers. They're different from whole numbers, but they're still numbers. They tell you how much of something is there."

There were other discussions about what fractions are, too. Camisha was saying, "It feels like cheating to say 5 ÷ 39 is $\frac{5}{39}$ or that 39 ÷ 5 = $\frac{39}{5}$. It never occurred to me that the fraction is the answer to the division—that's just what a fraction is."

Gaye added, "Isn't the division sign a fraction, except you put the numbers where the dots are, over and under the bar?"

These issues moved some teachers to pose their own questions to sort out the mathematics for themselves. For example, I came upon Marina and An-Chi having a debate about 3 ÷ 2. They explained to me that they went along with MaryAnn that 5 and 39 are hard numbers to think about here, and so they decided to pick smaller ones, 2 and 3. They each drew a diagram to solve 3 ÷ 2, and this is what they came up with:

An-Chi's diagram   Marina's diagram

An-Chi had divided each object into two halves and then took one half from each object: $\frac{3}{2} = 1\frac{1}{2}$. Marina said, "You draw three things and you sort of scrunch them together, and then you just divide the whole mess into two equal parts." Marina got $1\frac{1}{2}$, too.

As each explained her method, clearly convinced the other was wrong, they were shocked to see that they came up with the same answer. Now they were working hard to make sense of what the other was doing, and kept testing it on other numbers. They tried 2 ÷ 3, 4 ÷ 6, and 6 ÷ 4. They told me they wanted to see what it would be like if they had numbers in the same proportions. I was impressed at how they structured their own mathematical investigation.

When I sat down to listen in on another group, everyone stopped talking. At first I didn't know what that was about. They all had their casebooks open to the page with Leo and Cynthia's diagram, so I figured that's what they were working on. Then Amber turned to me and asked, "Is it more sophisticated to call that piece $\frac{1}{8}$ or $\frac{1}{40}$?" I was taken aback by the question. The difficult idea is that it is both $\frac{1}{8}$ and $\frac{1}{40}$! Amber went on: "If you're calling it $\frac{1}{40}$, you're looking at all the stuff. If you're calling it $\frac{1}{8}$, you have to be able to focus on one thing, on one of these blocks as being a whole." That told me that Amber did understand that the fraction depended on what your reference unit is, but why did she think one way of naming the part should be "more sophisticated" than the other?

Sometimes a question like *Which method is more sophisticated?* is useful. For example, those who participated in *Building a System of Tens* saw that grouping by tens, or breaking numbers apart by tens and ones, is frequently more powerful than counting by ones. And so we might say that children who fluently use the base ten structure of numbers employ "more sophisticated" methods than those who always rely on counting by ones. But sometimes the question of whether one method or one way of looking at things is more sophisticated than another—that seems like a trap, or a distraction.

I'm thinking back on the discussion we had in Session 1 about counting on versus starting at 1. There seemed to be consensus that counting on was better—more sophisticated?—than starting at 1, and so the discussion kept going back to, "How do I get my students to count on?" It was hard to get the teachers to think about the mathematical idea that a child has to have in place to be able to count on. What are children doing and learning when they start at 1?

I didn't want Amber to feel put down, but because I felt it was important to move the group off her question, I said, "You know, it might be that neither is more sophisticated. The sophisticated idea is to be able to see the meaning of both." And so I asked them to come up with two sentences that make the context clear, one that shows why you can call one of those pieces $\frac{1}{8}$ and the other showing why you can call it $\frac{1}{40}$.

Whole-group case discussion

When I brought the whole group together for discussion, I decided to start with An-Chi's and Marina's diagrams and asked them to come to the board to show the rest of us their thinking about 3 ÷ 2. An-Chi drew her diagram of 3 objects, each divided into 2 parts. Marina drew her 3 objects with one line drawn through the "middle of the whole mess." It's interesting that the whole group's response mirrored the discussion between An-Chi and Marina 30 minutes earlier.

Odette remarked, "I really understand what you're doing, An-Chi, but Marina, can you really do that?"

Labeeba commented, "I get what Marina's doing, but I don't think An-Chi's way would always work."

At this point, I decided to give them all 5 minutes to work this through. The teachers partnered up to explore with other numbers, one who saw it An-Chi's way with one who saw it Marina's. After a few minutes, most did seem satisfied that one could look at division problems either way. Some said they were still a bit confused, but would think about it at home. Carol said it reminded her of that time the two teachers were talking about division—that they both thought there was only one way to think about it, and then realized they could think about grouping or dealing, and both are right.

Next I asked the teachers to look at Cynthia and Leo's diagram in the casebook. "How can the same portion be both $\frac{1}{8}$ and $\frac{1}{40}$?" At first, they seemed to think that this was no problem, no big deal. And at first I thought that maybe it really wasn't an issue for them.

Amber told us that once she had been working on fractions with some children and kept asking them, "What's the whole?" They kept giving her wrong answers, pointing to the shaded regions when those regions were only parts. Finally, she realized that when she was asking for the whole, w-h-o-l-e, the children were thinking she was asking for the hole, h-o-l-e.

Then I asked, "What are your answers to the questions posed by MaryAnn's class?" Well, this got the discussion going, but within minutes, it seemed that there were so many ideas and so many questions and so much confusion, everything was a jumble.

I commented that we now had a lot of issues about fractions on the table, and that we would spend the next few sessions sorting them out. I suggested that instead of continuing with MaryAnn's case, it might be useful to work on the same ideas in another context. At this point I handed out "Math Activity: Comparing Fractions," and they got down to work on these questions.

Math activity: Comparing fractions

In this activity, participants compare fractions using diagrams and place the fractions on a number line. Certainly, almost everyone in the group has learned to compare fractions by finding common denominators or converting the fractions to decimals. Some also have a rule they call "cross multiplication" (but few can explain why it works). In this activity, participants are asked to set those methods aside and consider the reasoning suggested by their diagrams.

Small-group math work

I first sat down with Dofi, Iris, and Joseph, who had cut strips from graph paper and were folding them to mark off fractional parts. Dofi said, "It's hard to find fifths, sevenths, and ninths."

Iris concurred, "Yeah, eighths are easiest." Even so, they were finding close-enough approximations, and so I let them continue.

Spencer, Elspeth, and Maalika used graph paper and represented $\frac{4}{5}$ and $\frac{4}{7}$ like this:

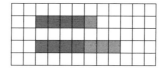

Spencer frowned and commented, "This doesn't help. It looks like $\frac{4}{5}$ equals $\frac{4}{7}$, but we know that's not true."

Elspeth said, "Well, actually, it could. If we took $\frac{4}{5}$ of a small candy bar and $\frac{4}{7}$ of a larger one, we might end up with the same amount."

Spencer agreed, "That's true. But that's not what we mean when we say that two fractions are equal. We know that $\frac{4}{5}$ is more than $\frac{4}{7}$."

Maalika said, "I think we need to make our candy bars the same size."

Elspeth suggested, "Let's get rid of the graph paper. I think that's what's messing us up."

Their redrawn representations looked like this:

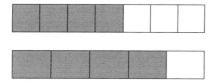

Maalika concluded, "Fifths are larger than sevenths, and 4 big pieces are more than 4 small pieces, so $\frac{4}{5}$ is greater than $\frac{4}{7}$."

Elspeth said, "We could state a rule here. The fractional piece gets smaller as you increase the denominator. The more pieces you have in the whole, the smaller the pieces."

In some of the small groups, participants could tell me which of a pair of fractions was greater, but they didn't seem to understand what it meant to write a "general statement about the relative sizes of fractions." This is what we would work on in whole group.

Whole-group math discussion

I began the whole-group discussion by illustrating what I meant by a general statement, writing out the following:

If the denominators of two fractions are the same, the fraction with the greater numerator is greater.

First I asked for some examples to illustrate this point. Participants offered $\frac{2}{5}$ and $\frac{3}{5}$; $\frac{1}{9}$ and $\frac{4}{9}$; $\frac{49}{100}$ and $\frac{51}{100}$.

Then I asked, "Can someone explain why this statement must be true for any pair of fractions that satisfy the condition?"

Gaye came forward. "Since the denominators are the same, all the pieces are the same size. So if the numerator is greater, you have more of those pieces, and the fraction is greater."

This was the kind of reasoning I was looking for. So we continued with the next idea. I asked, "What if the numerators are the same?"

Carol responded, "We talked about that one. If the numerators are the same, the fraction whose denominator is less is the greater fraction. We know that's true because if the denominator is less, the pieces are larger. So if you have the same number of pieces, but the pieces are greater, the fraction is greater."

I asked for a paraphrase, which Andrea offered. After I wrote out Carol's statement, I asked whether a generalization was suggested by the numbers $\frac{3}{8}$ and $\frac{2}{9}$.

Celeste said, "We were really stumped by that for a while, even though it was clear from our diagram that $\frac{2}{9}$ is less than $\frac{3}{8}$. But then it occurred to Andrea that we could compare both to $\frac{3}{9}$. We know $\frac{3}{9}$ is greater than $\frac{2}{9}$ by the first rule, and we know $\frac{3}{8}$ is greater than $\frac{3}{9}$ by the second rule, so that explains why $\frac{3}{8}$ has to be greater than $\frac{2}{9}$."

Andrea added, "We got the reasoning down, but we still didn't know how to state that as a rule."

Spencer suggested, "How about this: If one fraction has the greater numerator and the lesser denominator, then that fraction is greater than the other."

I looked around to see how others responded to the generalization Spencer stated. I said, "Let me write out this statement and then choose some numbers to which it applies." Once I wrote it down, participants suggested pairs of fractions: $\frac{3}{4}$ and $\frac{2}{5}$, $\frac{7}{9}$ and $\frac{6}{10}$, $\frac{99}{100}$ and $\frac{98}{101}$. Then we were ready to move on.

An-Chi said, "We know how to reason about $\frac{5}{6}$ and $\frac{7}{8}$, too, but it's hard to state a rule. Because 6 is less than 8, we know that $\frac{1}{6}$ is greater than $\frac{1}{8}$. If you look at the whole square, $\frac{5}{6}$ is $\frac{1}{6}$ away from the whole, and $\frac{7}{8}$ is $\frac{1}{8}$ away from the whole. That means $\frac{7}{8}$ is closer to the whole than $\frac{5}{6}$, and so $\frac{7}{8}$ is more."

Karran said, "I think I can state a rule. If for both fractions the difference between the numerator and denominator is 1, then the fraction with the greater denominator is the greater fraction."

Now we had four general statements on the board.
When comparing two fractions:

1. If the denominators are the same, the fraction with the greater numerator is greater.

2. If the numerators are the same, the fraction whose denominator is less is the greater fraction.

3. If one fraction has the greater numerator and the lesser denominator, then that fraction is greater than the other.

4. If for both fractions the difference between the numerator and denominator is 1, then the fraction with the greater denominator is the greater fraction.

I asked, "Could you use these generalization to help you place the fractions on a number line?"

Maalika said, "It was easy to order all those fractions on the number line until we got to $\frac{2}{5}$."

I wasn't sure it was so easy for everyone to place those six fractions on a number line, so I asked for more explanation, starting from the beginning. Dofi reported that, from the previous problems, we already know $\frac{7}{8}$ is greater than $\frac{5}{6}$, $\frac{4}{5}$ is greater than $\frac{4}{7}$, and $\frac{3}{8}$ is greater than $\frac{2}{9}$. Applying the fourth rule, we know that $\frac{5}{6}$ is greater than $\frac{4}{5}$. She also explained that $\frac{4}{7}$ is greater than $\frac{1}{2}$ and $\frac{3}{8}$ is less than $\frac{1}{2}$.

I first wrote out the order of these six numbers: $\frac{2}{9}$, $\frac{3}{8}$, $\frac{4}{7}$, $\frac{4}{5}$, $\frac{5}{6}$, $\frac{7}{8}$. Then I worked with the group to determine approximate placements on the number line. Spencer suggested I put tick marks at $\frac{1}{4}$, $\frac{1}{2}$, and $\frac{3}{4}$ as landmarks. Other participants guided me in placing the six fractions: $\frac{2}{9}$ is a little to the left of $\frac{1}{4}$; $\frac{3}{8}$ is halfway between $\frac{1}{4}$ and $\frac{1}{2}$; $\frac{4}{7}$ is a little to the right of $\frac{1}{2}$; $\frac{7}{8}$ is halfway between $\frac{3}{4}$ and 1; $\frac{4}{5}$ and $\frac{5}{6}$ are a little to the left of $\frac{7}{8}$.

Then I returned to Karran's point. "What's hard about $\frac{2}{5}$?"

Karran said, "We first drew a diagram, but $\frac{2}{5}$ is so close to $\frac{3}{8}$ that it's hard to tell. So then we went to common denominators."

I responded, "Yes, I know we can turn to common denominators, but let's see if we can reason about it some other way. What do you know about these two numbers?"

Gaye said, "We can't use any of our rules, because both the numerator and denominator of $\frac{2}{5}$ are less than the numerator and denominator of $\frac{3}{8}$."

Nadra said, "We do know they are both less than $\frac{1}{2}$."

I nodded, "Can you tell how much less than $\frac{1}{2}$?"

Joseph said, "It's easy to tell about $\frac{3}{8}$. Since $\frac{1}{2}$ is equal to $\frac{4}{8}$, $\frac{3}{8}$ is $\frac{1}{8}$ less than $\frac{1}{2}$."

I nodded and waited for someone to take on $\frac{2}{5}$. After a pause, Elspeth said, "You can think of $\frac{1}{2}$ as $\frac{2.5}{5}$. That means $\frac{2}{5}$ is $\frac{0.5}{5}$ less than $\frac{1}{2}$. Can you do that?"

I looked around to see what the group thought about Elspeth's thinking. Then Spencer said, "You don't really have to go to complex fractions. We can say $\frac{2}{5}$ is the same as $\frac{4}{10}$, and then it's easy, since $\frac{4}{10}$ is $\frac{1}{10}$ less than $\frac{5}{10}$. That means $\frac{2}{5}$ is $\frac{1}{10}$ less than $\frac{1}{2}$."

Elspeth asked, "Does that mean $\frac{0.5}{5}$ is equal to $\frac{1}{10}$?"

I nodded and said, "If we call that number 'one-half of one-fifth,' what does that mean to you?"

Elspeth smiled, "Oh, of course. If you have a whole divided into fifths, and then cut those fifths in half, your whole is now cut into tenths. One of those pieces would be $\frac{1}{10}$."

Then I took the group back to the main question we were trying to figure out. "Does this help us tell which is greater, $\frac{2}{5}$ or $\frac{3}{8}$?"

Marina suddenly had an insight, "Hey, it's not exactly our rule 4, but it's like it. Since $\frac{2}{5}$ is $\frac{1}{10}$ less than $\frac{1}{2}$, and $\frac{3}{8}$ is $\frac{1}{8}$ less than $\frac{1}{2}$, $\frac{2}{5}$ has to be the greater fraction."

There were some murmurs in the room, so I asked everyone to find a partner to go through the reasoning. When I brought the whole group together, I asked for a couple of paraphrases. After these were stated, Iris observed, "You really have to understand equivalent fractions to do this."

I nodded and then suggested, "Let's see what happens if we go for common denominators."

Gaye said, "That's what we did. $\frac{2}{5} = \frac{16}{40}$ and $\frac{3}{8} = \frac{15}{40}$. That tells us $\frac{2}{5}$ is greater than $\frac{3}{8}$ by $\frac{1}{40}$."

Karran chuckled, "No wonder we couldn't tell the difference from our diagrams."

To close the discussion, I said that we'll continue thinking about equivalent fractions and fraction comparison through the cases we'll read for next week. But now it was time to prepare for the written homework assignment.

Planning for the student-thinking assignment

For the next session, participants would collect and analyze the work of their students as they consider the brownie problem that Lori (in case 15) gave to her first graders or, for higher grades, a variation of it. I distributed the handout, asking participants to get into small groups to discuss case 15 and then look at the variations to the problem they might pose to their class.

As groups began talking about the case, they said they were surprised that the students didn't seem to be concerned about fair shares. "Don't they care that some of the kids got bigger brownies than others?"

Nadra said, "Lower-grade kids disregard remainders. They only deal with equal groups unless you give them materials or a context that gives them a way to deal with extra portions."

Camisha commented, "But these children cut the brownies in half."

Nadra responded, "They did that only after the teacher challenged them. First they said that each kid got 1 brownie—or 2 brownies, even though there weren't enough for that."

Elspeth said, "I think it's interesting that they cut up the brownies so that each child could get the same number of pieces, even though the pieces were different sizes. It's as if they don't notice that. When they cut one brownie into two parts, it's like now they have 8 brownies, and they can share 8 evenly among 4 children."

Camisha said, "Yeah. In MaryAnn's case, at first the students were thinking only in terms of whole numbers. The thing is, once they thought about cutting up the candy bar, they could think in terms of the size of the pieces."

Nadra said, "I'll be interested to see what my own students do."

Elspeth said, "I wonder if it would have been different if there were 6 brownies to share among 4 children. Kids can see halves pretty easily. I wonder if they would have been able to do that."

When I got to Joseph, Carol, and Odette's group, they were considering the actions of the teacher. Joseph said, "Lori knew it would be a difficult situation, so she worked with small groups. That's a good idea."

Odette observed, "She keeps bringing her students back to, 'Is it the same amount? Is it fair?' She doesn't tell them to do anything, but that's the question she wants them to think about."

Karran, Cathleen, and Spencer were working on the problem variation, 7 people sharing 4 brownies. Looking at the diagram, Cathleen asked, "Is this correct? Let's first look at this individually."

They took a couple of minutes and then agreed that it is correct. If each person gets $\frac{1}{2}$ and $\frac{1}{14}$ of a brownie, then you'll have divided 4 brownies equally among 7 people.

Spencer said, "What are the conceptual hurdles students will face as they think about this problem? Well, there's the idea of having to change the whole. You've got one-half cut into 7 pieces."

Cathleen said, "Students have a hard time cutting something into sevenths. They can easily do one-half and then one-fourth, one-eighth. But it's hard to cut something into an odd number of pieces."

I said, "Yes, that's true. We might think a little about why that's the case. But here, the students don't have to do the cutting. It's drawn for them."

Cathleen replied, "But we're thinking it will make more sense to the students if they have four brownies to cut up."

I nodded, "Yes, I see. It would be interesting to see how they do with that." Then I decided to tell a story to the group. "A few years ago, I was visiting a sixth-grade teacher, and when she got to the fractions unit, she felt it was important for her students to have manipulatives. But since she didn't have any manufactured manipulatives for fractions, she decided the class should make their own. She got out strips of oak tag, and told her students that they'd keep one whole, and then they would cut the strips to indicate $\frac{1}{2}, \frac{1}{3}, \frac{1}{4}, \frac{1}{5}, \frac{1}{6}, \frac{1}{7}, \frac{1}{8}, \frac{1}{9}, \frac{1}{10}, \frac{1}{12}$, and $\frac{1}{15}$. I saw them get to work on the first day, and they were struggling with thirds and fifths and sevenths. A week later, the teacher reported back to me the very interesting thinking her students engaged in as they were working to create their strips. And by then, they all had their fraction manipulatives that helped them solve problems.

"The thing is, because they made their own manipulatives and had struggled to make them precise, they knew that the manipulatives gave them only approximations. So when the students were working on addition problems, they'd get out their manipulatives and find an answer, but the manipulatives would be just a little bit off. So I would hear the kids say things like, 'It's a little bit off, so now I have to figure out if it's because my pieces are a little off, or if my answer isn't really exactly right.'"

Karran said, "Yeah, that's the way I felt when I was trying to compare $\frac{2}{5}$ and $\frac{3}{8}$! The diagrams helped us think about some things, but when it was just a little bit off, you couldn't really tell."

I appreciated that Karran was making a connection between my story and her experience. I added, "What we're really after is the reasoning. The diagrams and manipulatives aren't so much about helping us find the answer. We use them to help us reason about the numbers and operations."

Homework and exit cards

As I distributed the homework page, I told the group that I would be very interested to read about what their students do with the brownie questions. I clarified that teachers might adapt the problem slightly for their students' level: At the younger end, students might work on 4 students sharing 5 brownies or 4 students sharing 6 brownies; if students solve those problems, they can move on to 7 brownies shared among 4 people. At the older end, students should work on the variation on the planning sheet, 4 brownies shared among 7 people.

Then I posted exit-card questions:

1. What mathematics are you still wondering about from this session?

2. What was this session like for you as a learner?

On their exit cards, several participants wrote about feeling unsure of themselves in the realm of fractions and the work we did in Session 3.

IRIS: I'm still wondering about how to place fractions on a number line. I'm not sure I get that exactly.

LABEEBA: I understand the fractions I use a lot, but haven't done much with the ones I don't use and I didn't do well on these back in my "studying them" days.

On the other hand, several participants feel the world of fractions is opening up to them.

> GAYE: I learned a TON about fractions. I've always just converted to decimals or common denominators. Drawing pictures helped me to better visualize what was happening! This class has definitely stretched my math knowledge/thinking in a good way.
>
> ODETTE: This session made me feel confident as a learner. I was having trouble on the homework from last week and wasn't feeling very confident when I arrived. When we began with drawing the pictures of the fractions and comparing them, I felt more at ease.
>
> ANDREA: I feel like I understood much of what we talked about tonight, which was nice because I don't always feel like that.

I was pleased to read Nadra's card, since for the first two sessions she seemed so defensive.

> NADRA: I am now warming up as a learner in the group; more comfortable asking questions.

I was a little concerned by what Cathleen wrote.

> CATHLEEN: It was difficult to "ignore" my prior knowledge of common denominators and think of new strategies to compare fractions.

She seems not to understand that she is not expected to "ignore" her prior knowledge in order to investigate something new. I'll need to keep an eye on how she engages with the content in the coming sessions.

> BEATRICE: My fourth graders are just beginning a fractions unit and I am already sensing a great deal of confusion on their parts. I wonder how they will understand the rules we developed tonight.

Several participants asked about the content of Jayson's case, which we didn't have time to discuss in the session.

> DOFI: I'm wondering about the difference between $\frac{0}{7}$ and $\frac{7}{0}$. In the last case, they talked about zero and undefined, but reading this confused me.
>
> JOSEPH: $\frac{0}{9}, \frac{9}{0}, \frac{x}{9} = 0$???

Since we're not going to have time to discuss division by 0 in the sessions coming up, I'll address this in my written response to the homework.

Responding to the third homework

March 5

As I looked over the homework, I saw that several participants were still having difficulty making up story problems for 5 ÷ 8. In some cases, I had specific comments that addressed the particulars of what they had written. But on the whole, I wanted to use my written response as a way to convey some of the large mathematical issues we were working with. For that reason, I wrote a general response to the whole group.

Dear MMO seminar group,

For homework, you created story problems, all for 5 ÷ 8, but with contexts that resulted in different answers. I enjoyed reading about the thinking you put into this. Now I want to write about some of the mathematical issues that arise from this assignment.

Frequently story problems with numbers that are easy to think about may help us understand what is happening with numbers that are more difficult. For example, although it was challenging, as a group we came up with a set of story problems that involved 32 ÷ 5, some of whose answers are whole numbers, others that allowed fractional parts. Do you see that each of those problems could have been rewritten for 5 ÷ 8? That is, each of those story problems illustrated a context that involved a mathematical relationship independent of the particular numbers.

For example, consider the problem, *I have 32 yards of fabric and I'm making drapes that require 5 yards. How many drapes can I make?* The problem context involves division, no matter how many yards of fabric I have and no matter how many yards are needed for each item. The same problem can be adapted for 5 ÷ 8: *I have 5 yards of fabric and I'm making drapes that require 8 yards. How many drapes can I make?* In fact, since it doesn't make sense to make $\frac{5}{8}$ of a drape and there isn't enough fabric to make even one drape, the answer to that problem is 0.

We will be using this strategy from time to time in our upcoming work with fractions. We will, at times, think about a context in terms of whole numbers, or numbers that are easier to think about, in order to apply that context to fractions, or numbers that are harder to think about.

The problem about making drapes illustrates another issue: the importance of whether the context is discrete and allows only whole numbers or if it is continuous and allows fractional parts. As long as students are working with whole numbers, we don't have to pay attention to the distinction. However, if we want to create contexts for students to investigate fractions, we must select contexts that allow them to think about fractional parts.

As we continue with our investigations with fractions, we will find that sometimes our sense of the meaning of the operations relies on whole-number contexts. In order to create meaning for operating with fractions, we will need to revise these understandings to allow for fractional parts. For example, if we say that 3×4 means 3 groups of 4, what does $3 \times \frac{1}{2}$ mean? Can we talk about "groups" of $\frac{1}{2}$? If not, how can we revise our characterization of multiplication to include multiplying fractions? Does it help if we say that 3×4 means "3 portions of 4"? That would allow us to say that $3 \times \frac{1}{2}$ means "3 portions of $\frac{1}{2}$." This kind of thinking is in the work coming up for us in the seminar.

Another issue that arose with these problems has to do with the equal sign. If we want to write the result of division as an equation, it is correct to write $5 \div 8 = \frac{5}{8}$ or $5 \div 8 = 0.625$. These equations are independent of context. Remember that the equal sign is an expression of equivalence; it says that the quantities represented on either side of the equal sign are equal. We could also write $\frac{5}{8} = 5 \div 8$, $0.625 = 5 \div 8$, or $\frac{5}{8} = 0.625$.

Some of the word problems you have written involve division with the numbers 5 and 8, but because the context does not allow fractional parts, the answer may be 0 or 1. However, that does *not* mean $5 \div 8 = 1$ or $5 \div 8 = 0$. It is *always* the case that $5 \div 8 \neq 1$ and $5 \div 8 \neq 0$. The symbol = does not mean "this is the answer to the problem." If the context of a story problem requires a whole-number answer, we don't represent such a problem with an equation; rather, the whole-number answer comes from interpreting the value $\frac{5}{8}$ in this context.

I'd also like to use this message to write about the content of a case we didn't have a chance to discuss in our last session. That is, what happens when 0 appears in a division problem? Several of you asked about this in your exit cards.

To help us think about this, we might take on Matthew's insight from Georgia's case 11. When Matthew was asked to solve $63 \div 9$, he said "What number times 9 is 63? Seven." That is, in order to solve a division problem, he converted it to a multiplication problem with a missing factor. We can do the same thing with the problems students were working on in Jayson's case.

Let's take $0 \div 7 = ?$. To use Matthew's strategy, we can convert that to $7 \times ? = 0$. Since $7 \times 0 = 0$, we know that ? must equal 0; that is, $0 \div 7 = 0$.

But now, let's consider $7 \div 0 = ?$ When we convert that to a multiplication problem, it becomes $0 \times ? = 7$. But we know that anything multiplied by 0 equals 0, so there is no solution to this problem. There is no value for ? that makes the equation true.

Finally, let's consider $0 \div 0 = ?$ Converted to multiplication, we get $0 \times ? = 0$. In that case, ? can equal 1, but it can also equal 2, or 400, or $\frac{3}{5}$. That is, ? can take on any value and make the multiplication equation true. So we say that $0 \div 0$ is undefined; there is no single answer.

If you want to think about these issues in a context, try this one: I have a bag of 12 marbles. If I reach in and remove 3 at a time, how many times can I reach in until there are none left? That gives us a division context. The answer to that problem is 4. Now, try replacing the numbers 12 and 3 with 0 and 7. What if I have 0 marbles? How many times can I reach in and remove 7 until the bag is empty? The bag is already empty when I've reached in 0 times, and I can't remove 7 any more than 0 times.

What if I have 7 marbles, but each time I reach in and pull out 0? How many times can I reach in until the bag will be empty? There's no solution. I can keep reaching in forever and the bag will never empty.

What if I have 0 marbles in the bag. How many times can I reach in and remove 0 marbles, resulting in an empty bag? I can reach in any number of times; the bag will always be empty.

This story context may sound convoluted to you. Of course, nobody is going to keep reaching into a bag forever. But the point of the context isn't to be realistic. Rather, it's to allow us to think about the meaning of division. This particular image of grouping helps us think about what's going on when we say that you can't divide with a divisor of 0. For the same reason, a fraction with a denominator of 0 is undefined.

By the time you read this message, we will be well into our study of fractions. There's a lot to think about. Enjoy the ride!

Maxine

S E S S I O N

4

MAKING MEANING FOR OPERATIONS

Greater Than, Less Than, Equal To

Mathematical Themes

- The numerator and denominator, taken together, determine the value of a fraction.

- Multiplying the numerator and the denominator by the same constant yields an equivalent fraction.

- Changing the unit results in different fractional names for the same quantity.

- To determine which of two fractions is greater, one may find common denominators and compare numerators, find common numerators and compare denominators, or compare the two fractions to a third number.

- In addition, the addends and the sum refer to the same unit.

Sharing student work: The brownie problem	Small groups Whole group	20 minutes 15 minutes
Chapter 4 case discussion	Small groups Whole group	30 minutes 30 minutes
Break		15 minutes
Math activity: Adding fractional amounts	Small groups Whole group	25 minutes 25 minutes
DVD for Session 4	Whole group	10 minutes
Homework and exit cards	Whole group	10 minutes

Background Preparation

Read

- the casebook, chapter 4
- the detailed agenda for Session 4
- "Maxine's Journal" for Session 4

Work through

- the focus questions for Session 4
- the math activity: Adding fractional amounts

Preview

- the DVD, Session 4

Materials

Duplicate

- "Focus Questions: Chapter 4"
- "Math Activity: Adding Fractional Amounts"
- "Fifth Homework"
- "Examining Curriculum Activities"

Obtain

- graph paper
- DVD player
- index cards

Choose

Curriculum materials for Session 5 (from the NCTM *Navigations* options, page 129, or another curriculum); duplicate as needed

What Is (and What Is Not) Addition of Fractions?

Addition of whole numbers is usually quite clear. Two quantities are joined. A group of 3 apples and a group of 2 apples, when combined, make a single group of 5 apples. To combine 2 apples and 3 bananas, we identify some common characteristic, such as pieces of fruit, and call the total 5 pieces of fruit.

Similarly, in sorting out addition of fractions, it is important to be clear on the whole or the unit that is referred to by each fraction in the sum. Consider these two story situations:

- Mary ate $\frac{1}{5}$ of a bag of chips for lunch and $\frac{2}{5}$ of the bag for an after-school snack. What fraction of the bag of chips did Mary eat?

- In Mary's class, $\frac{1}{5}$ of the girls are absent and $\frac{2}{5}$ of the boys are absent. What fraction of the class is absent?

One of these represents a situation for adding fractions and one does not. Consider a diagram illustrating the bag of chips problem. The first box represents a bag of chips. The second box shows the situation after Mary has had lunch. The third box represents the situation after Mary has had her after-school snack. By combining the shaded amounts, the answer is seen to be $\frac{3}{5}$, the sum of $\frac{1}{5}$ and $\frac{2}{5}$.

Whole bag of chips

$\frac{1}{5}$ of the bag eaten

$\frac{1}{5} + \frac{2}{5}$ of the bag eaten

This is an addition of fraction situation because both the $\frac{1}{5}$ and the $\frac{2}{5}$ are fractional amounts of the same unit.

In the second problem, the first fraction refers to the number of girls and the second fraction refers to the number of boys. Since each fraction refers to a different whole, this does not represent $\frac{1}{5} + \frac{2}{5} = \frac{3}{5}$.

These two situations illustrate a major aspect of addition of fractions: When two fractions are added, there is an implied assumption that the two fractions are both in reference to the same unit, and the fraction that represents the sum is in reference to the same unit. Notice that this same assumption is in place for whole-number addition: Given a context including 2 elephants and 3 pints of juice, it is unlikely that 2 + 3 will arise as a relevant computation. For additional information on Mary's class problem, see "Maxine's Journal," lines 239–257.

In some situations, it is not so easy to see this distinction. For instance, consider this variation on the bag of chips situation:

- Mary ate $\frac{1}{5}$ of a bag of chips for lunch and gave the rest to her friend. After school, her friend bought a similar bag of chips, and Mary ate $\frac{2}{5}$ of that bag for an after-school snack. What fraction represents how much Mary ate?

A diagram solution might look like this:

$\frac{1}{5}$ of the lunch bag of chips $\frac{2}{5}$ of the after-school bag of chips

But the question arises: Did Mary eat $\frac{3}{5}$ ($\frac{1}{5} + \frac{2}{5}$) or $\frac{3}{10}$ ($\frac{1}{10} + \frac{2}{10}$)? To resolve this confusion, we must examine the question, "What fraction represents how much Mary ate?" The question is ambiguous, because it does not indicate what unit the fractional answer is to refer to. If the unit is taken to be a bag of chips, then the answer is $\frac{3}{5}$ of a bag of chips. If the unit is taken to be both bags of chips, then the answer is $\frac{3}{10}$ of all the chips.

In a similar problem situation, the unit is clearly identified and not implied:

- Mary ran $\frac{1}{5}$ of a mile at lunchtime and $\frac{2}{5}$ of a mile after school. How far did Mary run?

Since the size of a mile is a known quantity, the fact that Mary ran $\frac{1}{5}$ of a mile at lunch and $\frac{2}{5}$ of a different mile after school does not lead to confusion, because the unit whole (1 mile) applies to both fractions in the addition ($\frac{1}{5} + \frac{2}{5}$) and to the fraction in the sum ($\frac{3}{5}$). This is clearly an addition of fractions situation.

S E S S I O N 4

Detailed Agenda

Sharing student work: The brownie problem (35 minutes)

Small groups (20 minutes)

Whole group (15 minutes)

Small-group sharing (20 minutes)

In this first activity, participants read and discuss what they wrote about the thinking of their own students. In the last session, participants met in small groups to plan for this assignment. Place them into the same small groups so they may share the results of their planning. Remind them to examine each other's student work and read all of their colleagues' analyses of the work before beginning any discussion. In that way, their conversation can include the similarities and differences they noted. Let them know they will have 20 minutes for this conversation.

Whole-group discussion (15 minutes)

Everyone in the seminar posed essentially the same question to their students, no matter what the grade level (with some modification of the numbers). This provides a chance to gather ideas about how students' thinking about fractions develops over time. Focus the conversation on two questions:

- What understandings do the students draw on to make sense of these ideas?

- What ideas about fractions do you see in their work?

Begin by asking, "I'd like to hear first what the teachers of young students noted." Ask for comments from teachers of grades K–2, and then continue by asking for comments from grades 3–4, and so on.

Case discussion: Less than, greater than, equal to (60 minutes)

Small groups (30 minutes)

Whole group (30 minutes)

The cases in chapter 4 present students in grades 2–5 working on how to order fractions and how to determine whether two fractions are equivalent.

They frequently use diagrams as a tool for their reasoning. The main ideas in the cases include these:

- In order to compare fractions with a diagram, both fractions have to be represented as parts of the same-size whole.

- Diagrams comparing fractions with different denominators can support the development of the idea of common denominators.

- Two different-looking fractions may be equivalent; that is, they can refer to the same point on the number line.

- The equivalence of two fractions may be determined by reasoning about a diagram or by comparing the relationship of the numerators and denominators.

Small-group work (30 minutes)

Distribute "Focus Questions: Chapter 4." Question 1, based on Faith's case 17, asks about the thinking of fourth graders working to compare fractions. Participants will likely notice the similarity between the work they did last session and the thinking of Faith's students. Once this idea arises, let groups know they need not spend a lot of time on this question.

Question 2, based on Nelly's case 18, continues the analysis of how fourth-grade students compare fractions. It includes an example of how a student comparing fractions created common denominators based on her diagram. Question 3, based on Malik's case 19 and Zura's case 20, prompts participants to make connections between a diagram illustrating equivalent fractions and the numerical procedure for producing them.

Questions 4 and 5, based on Kate's case 21, examine the thinking of second graders as they work with ideas of equivalent fractions. Question 6 invites participants to analyze the actions and questions of the teachers in two of the cases.

After 15 minutes, announce that the whole-group discussion will concentrate on focus questions 2 and 3.

As you interact with the small groups, ask questions to help them connect their own thinking about common denominators and equivalent fractions with their analysis of the student thinking in the cases. Consider questions such as these: "How does your way of thinking about common denominators compare with what Bibiana does in case 18? We say that equivalent fractions are formed by multiplying the numerator and the denominator by the same number; how can you connect this to the ideas in the diagrams offered in cases 19 and 20?"

Whole-group case discussion   (30 minutes)

The main points to come up in the whole-group discussion should include these:

- How did common denominators arise in Bibiana's work, and what does that indicate about the procedure for finding common denominators?

- How can the diagrams in the cases be used to support understanding of the procedure for finding equivalent fractions?

Begin the discussion by asking for comments on the work of Bibiana. Participants might note that the diagram allowed both fractions to be represented easily; the whole could be visually partitioned into both fourths and sixths.

Once these ideas have been explored, turn to the related questions about equivalent fractions. While participants may have procedural methods and formal math arguments (for instance, multiplying the fraction by 1) to justify the procedure, also ask for an argument based on reasoning from the diagram. For example: If you multiply the denominator by 2 or 3 or n, you are making each part that proportion smaller; therefore you need double or triple or n times the number of pieces in order to have the same amount.

If there is time remaining, ask participants what they noticed in case 21, where Kate's second graders are working on similar ideas.

See "Maxine's Journal," lines 120–148, for an example of this discussion.

Break   (15 minutes)

Math activity: Adding fractional amounts   (50 minutes)

Small groups (25 minutes)

Whole group (25 minutes)

While the math activity for this session continues the focus on fractions begun in the case discussion, it also points to the issues that participants will be grappling with as they work on the cases in the next session. These are the main ideas examined through the math activity:

- The same amount can be expressed as a sum of fractions or written as a single fraction.

- The same amount can be described by different and nonequivalent fractions if the whole to which the fraction refers changes.

- In addition of fractions (as in any addition), the necessary assumption is that both fractions refer to the same unit.

Some participants in the seminar may teach this content and some may not, depending on their grade level. In order to put primary teachers at ease, you may want to make small groups according to grade level. Even among participants who are familiar with these ideas, however, it is likely that few have examined the concepts underlying the procedures for operating with fractions. It may be disconcerting for these participants to realize that their knowledge is incomplete. If you sense uneasiness, acknowledge that several seminar sessions and activities will be devoted to fractions and that few adults, no matter how educated, have had opportunities to think through all of these concepts.

Small-group math work (25 minutes)

Organize participants into small groups and distribute the handout "Math Activity: Adding Fractional Parts." Question 1 presents a situation in which a student expresses the answer to a fraction problem with a sum of fractional parts, without actually doing the addition and condensing the answer into a single fraction. This question foreshadows some of the cases in the next chapter. It is not likely to be challenging to participants.

On the other hand, question 2, based on Jorge's pizza eating, raises the idea that slight differences in the wording of a question will affect the answer. How many slices of pizza did Jorge eat? How much of a pizza did he eat? How much of the pizza did he eat? These three questions require different responses. In the first, the reference whole is a slice; in the second, the whole is a pizza, and in the third, the whole is all of the pizza available.

As you work with small groups, ask them which story problem was easiest for them to conceive. Many will likely say the problem for $\frac{3}{16}$ (How much of the pizza did he eat?). Point out that while this version of the problem is easy to think of, it does not map onto the addition of fractions problem $\frac{1}{8} + \frac{2}{8} = \frac{3}{8}$; rather, it might be tempting to represent it as $\frac{1}{8} + \frac{2}{8} = \frac{3}{16}$. Let groups puzzle over this confusion and then suggest they work on question 3.

Question 3 presents another case where the two fractions refer to different wholes. "$\frac{1}{5}$ of the girls" assumes a whole that is the number of girls, and "$\frac{2}{5}$ of the boys" assumes a whole that is the number of boys. If the number of girls and the number of boys are equal, then $\frac{1}{5}$ of the girls represent $\frac{1}{10}$ of the class. Similarly, $\frac{2}{5}$ of the boys represent $\frac{2}{10}$ of the class. So if the number of girls and number of boys is equal, this situation can be correctly represented as an addition of fractions, where the whole for all fractions involved is the entire class: $\frac{1}{10} + \frac{2}{10} = \frac{3}{10}$.

Focus the small-group work on questions 2 and 3. Ask participants to write out their story situations for the Jorge's pizza and Mary's class problem in complete sentences. Take note of confusions that get expressed and sorted out. It will be useful to include these in the whole group discussion.

Whole-group math discussion (25 minutes)

Start the whole-group discussion with the pizza problem, soliciting possible questions for each given answer. Even if it appears that everyone in the group has sorted this out, ask one or two people to explain what was confusing at first and how they came to see the issue. Ask, "What did you need to think through in order to arrive at this solution?" It is useful to have stated explicitly the need to clarify what the whole is when writing a fraction.

Then turn to the problem about Mary's class and ask for explanations of that situation. If some groups went beyond what happens when the number of boys and the number of girls are equal to consider other possibilities, defer that discussion until the situation involving the same number of girls and boys is fully detailed. Again, the main point of the discussion is that when adding fractions, it is important that both fractions refer to the same whole.

Viewing the DVD: Adding fractions (10 minutes)

Whole group

Remind participants of the thinking they did in the math activity on Jorge's pizza problem and the class absentee problem. Let them know that in this DVD clip, they will be looking at a seventh grader working on similar ideas. Explain that this clip is not from a class, but is an exceprt from an interview. The student, Nadja, who is in seventh grade, is asked to create a story problem that would be appropriate for $\frac{1}{5} + \frac{2}{5} = \frac{3}{5}$.

Ask participants to consider these questions as they watch the DVD and solicit their responses after the clip:

- What does Nadja understand?

- What are the assumptions she seems to be operating under but hasn't explicitly stated?

- What would you want her to clarify?

The discussion might include these ideas:

- In addition of fractions, the two fractions have to refer to the same whole.

- There are situations that appear to be represented by the same symbols, but which are not addition of fractions.

This discussion is one more step in a process for participants to sort out these ideas. After gathering a few comments, let the group know they will have further opportunity to clarify these ideas in their homework and will be continuing to work on them in the next session.

Homework and exit cards (10 minutes)

Whole group

One part of the homework assignment begins an activity in which participants analyze a lesson from a designated curriculum. In the process, they consider how they can use curriculum materials to engage their own students in the ideas of the seminar. This homework can support participants' use of their local district curriculum, or you may wish to introduce a different curriculum, or use the resources of *Navigations,* published by the National Council of Teachers of Mathematics (NCTM). If you choose the *Navigations* material as a focus, suggestions for lessons by grade level appear on page 129.

The questions on the "Examining Curriculum Activities" worksheet will support participants in using curriculum with intention. Participants are asked to identify the mathematical ideas they would expect their students to encounter and to develop some questions they could ask to keep their students focused on the central mathematical themes. The work of examining curriculum activities begins with this homework and continues in the next session, when participants will meet in small groups to compare what they have written and to revise their thinking. After Session 5, participants will complete a homework assignment on student thinking, which they might base on the lesson they have just analyzed with their colleagues.

Distribute the handouts "Fifth Homework" and "Examining Curriculum Activities." Provide a time for participants to read these assignments. Point out that there are three kinds of homework for next session: to read the next chapter; to write about the mathematics they have been working on in this session; and to prepare for a discussion of a curriculum lesson designed for students.

Announce that in the next session, they will use the writing they do for the curriculum activity as the basis for discussion with a small group of colleagues, and they will turn in to you the writing they do about the mathematics they are working on in the seminar:

"At the next session, Session 5, you will meet in grade-level groups to discuss the lesson you have analyzed. As homework for Session 6, you will present a lesson to students and write about what happens. It will be up to you to decide what lesson to present: either the one you have just discussed with colleagues or a different lesson."

If you decided to assign the reading of chapter 8, "Highlights of Related Research," in sections throughout the seminar, rather than all at once at the end of Session 7, it is appropriate to assign sections 3 and 4 for reading homework now. Let participants know that although they will not be discussing this reading at the next meeting, these sections are pertinent to the work of the past two sessions and thus make useful reading at this point in the seminar.

As the session ends, distribute index cards and pose these exit-card questions:

1. What ideas about fractions are clear to you? What is still confusing?

2. Anything else you would like to tell the facilitators about your experience in the seminar?

Before the next session...

In preparation for the next session, read participants' written homework on the "sharing brownies" student-thinking assignment and write a response to each participant. For more information, see the section in "Maxine's Journal" on responding to the fourth homework. Make copies of both the papers and your response for your files before returning the work.

DVD Summary

Session 4: Adding Fractions

Seventh-grade student Nadja with interviewer Dee Watson (3 minutes 30 seconds)

The clip begins when Dee askes Nadja to write a story problem for $\frac{1}{5} + \frac{2}{5} = \frac{3}{5}$.

Nadja writes:

> Amira has $\frac{1}{5}$ of a cookie. Victory gives her $\frac{2}{5}$ of another cookie. How much out of 1 cookie does Amira have?

Dee asks Nadja to read the story and say what the answer is.

Nadja gives an answer of "three-fifths of one cookie."

Dee asks if the answer would still be $\frac{3}{5}$ if it were $\frac{2}{5}$ of *two* cookies and suggests that Nadja draw something to show that situation.

Nadja draws some circles and divides them into five parts. She has trouble making equal parts and says she isn't good at drawing. Dee establishes that Nadja means the parts to be the same size.

Nadja colors in $\frac{1}{5}$ of a single cookie and $\frac{2}{5}$ of each of the other two cookies, and says the person would get five-fifths or a whole cookie in this situation.

Dee asks Nadja what the difference is between the two situations.

Nadja says that in *her* story, $\frac{1}{5} + \frac{2}{5}$ is $\frac{3}{5}$, but in the other scenario, you get a whole cookie.

Dee asks, "What does that tell you about adding $\frac{1}{5}$ to $\frac{2}{5}$?"

Nadja replies, "Depending on what the situation is, is how you get the answer."

Examining Curriculum Activities: Choices

Choose lessons from the local district curriculum, from a published curriculum you would like your group to explore, or from this list of suggested activities from the *Navigations* series, published by NCTM.

Each participant should have a lesson from his or her own grade level or grade band to consider. Participants at the same grade level should select the same lesson for ease of discussion, in groups of three or four, during Session 5.

From *Navigating through Number and Operations in PreKindergarten–Grade 2* (NCTM, 2003)

    Kindergarten: "Frump's Fashions" (pages 41–45)
    Grades 1–2: "Park Your Car" (pages 49–51)

From *Navigating through Number and Operations in Grades 3–5* (NCTM, 2007)

    Grades 3–5: "Actions on Fractions" (pages 34–40 and 163)

From *Navigating through Number and Operations in Grades 6–8* (NCTM, 2006)

    Grades 6–8: "Science Fair" (pages 20–23 and 115–116)

SESSION 4

MAKING MEANING FOR OPERATIONS

Focus Questions: Chapter 4

1. Consider Faith's case 17.

   (a) In the beginning of the case, Harry and Annie use diagrams to explain why $\frac{2}{3}$ is greater than $\frac{1}{2}$. What ideas about fractions are present in their explanations? What ideas about fractions are left unstated in their explanations?

   (b) Explain the method for comparing fractions used by each of these students: Chuck (lines 44–61), Gary (lines 69–76), Ami (lines 101–108), and Jesse (lines 145–156). What ideas about fractions does each method depend on?

2. Consider Nelly's case 18.

   (a) Explain the ideas about fractions that you can see in the work of these students: Eli, Rebecca, Matt, and Bibiana.

   (b) Trace the class discussion after Bibiana's poster is shared. Consider the ideas of Matt, Max, and Jillian. What does each student add to the discussion? What ideas does each student figure out? What is still missing?

   (c) What is Kalina's conjecture toward the end of the case (line 262)? Find a fraction that disproves her conjecture.

3. In Malik's case 19 and Zura's case 20, the students work to explain how they know two fractions are equivalent. Use the diagrams in Malik's case to explain why multiplying the numerator and denominator by the same amount produces an equivalent fraction.

4. In Kate's case 21, Reed makes a connection between the word *quarter* as used in money contexts and in fractions. Colin adds to this idea by proposing ways to make $1.00. What are the connections between money and fractions that this class is working on?

5. Near the end of case 21, Sadie proposes that they test the idea of quarters as four parts with the flag of Nigeria. What ideas about fractions does the class work on in this part of the discussion?

6. The teachers in these cases make a number of decisions and strategic moves to draw students' attention to particular mathematical issues. Look over cases 18 and 21 to identify and discuss specific actions taken, or specific questions posed, by the teachers Nelly and Kate. What is the impact of each teacher's move on the students?

SESSION 4

MAKING MEANING FOR OPERATIONS

Math Activity: Adding Fractional Amounts

1. Consider this problem:

   There are 14 sandwiches to be shared equally among 8 people. How much will each person get?

   One student wrote this as a solution: Each person will get 1 sandwich plus half a sandwich plus a quarter of a sandwich. So $1 + \frac{1}{2} + \frac{1}{4}$.

   What is your analysis of this solution?

2. Consider this situation:

   Jorge has two pizzas, one pepperoni and one cheese. Each pizza is the same size, and each is cut into 8 equal slices. Jorge eats two slices of the pepperoni pizza and 1 slice of the cheese pizza.

   Use these facts to write three different story problems about Jorge's pizza eating, one for each of the following three answers:

   (a) 3   (b) $\frac{3}{8}$ (c) $\frac{3}{16}$

3. Consider this problem:

   In Mary's class, $\frac{1}{5}$ of the girls are absent and $\frac{2}{5}$ of the boys are absent. What fraction of the class is absent?

   (a) Explain why the answer to this is not $\frac{3}{5}$.

   (b) Write a story problem that would be solved by $\frac{1}{5} + \frac{2}{5}$.

   (c) What is the difference between your story problem and the situation in Mary's class?

Session 4 Detailed Agenda

SESSION 4

MAKING MEANING FOR OPERATIONS

Fifth Homework

Reading assignment: Casebook chapter 5

In the casebook, read chapter 5, "Combining Shares, or Adding Fractions," including the introductory text and cases 22–24. Use the questions in the introduction to the chapter to guide your reading.

Writing assignment 1: Thinking about mathematics

This assignment is about the math *you* are learning, not about the math learning of your students. Reflect on the mathematics you have been thinking about in this seminar. Choose one topic to write about. Explain how you thought about this originally, what makes sense to you now, and what aspect of the idea are you still working on. This is an opportunity to share your thinking and questions with the seminar facilitator(s), who will respond to your writing.

Writing assignment 2: An activity from curriculum designed for students

In Session 5, there will be time to work with colleagues to consider how to engage students in ideas similar to those in this seminar. In order to prepare for that discussion, please read over the assigned curriculum activity. Do the math activity yourself. DO NOT DO THE LESSON WITH STUDENTS AT THIS TIME.

You will have an opportunity to discuss the mathematical ideas of this lesson with colleagues in Session 5. You may want to work on this material with your own students AFTER that discussion.

In preparation for your discussion with colleagues at the next session, write answers to the questions on the "Examining Curriculum Activity" worksheet for the particular activity you are examining.

Bring three copies of your writing to the next session so that you may share and discuss these ideas with your colleagues.

SESSION 4

MAKING MEANING FOR OPERATIONS

Examining Curriculum Activities

1. What mathematical ideas might students develop as they work on this activity?

2. How do the math ideas of this lesson connect with math ideas your students have already worked with?

3. What questions might you ask students to keep them engaged in the central idea of the lesson? What is it that you want each question to bring out?

4. If you encounter students for whom this activity is too hard, how might you modify it, and why might that modification be useful?

5. If you encounter students for whom this activity is too easy, how might you modify it, and why might that modification be useful?

Session 4 Detailed Agenda

Session 4
Greater than, less than, equal to

Maxine's Journal

March 12

As participants entered the room, there was very high energy about sharing their students' work on the brownie problem. The session began there, and then moved on to the discussion of the chapter 4 cases, in which students worked on comparing fractions and equivalent fractions. Finally, we worked on a math activity involving addition of fractions and watched video of a middle school student responding to similar problems.

Sharing student work: The brownie problem

I said that participants were, on the whole, very excited to share their students' work on the brownie problem. Actually, teachers of the youngest students were very excited, but as we went up in the grades, the energy seemed more muted. In fact, some of the middle school teachers were quite disconcerted by what they had discovered. Many of their students didn't immediately recognize that the problems involve division, or that the result of $4 \div 7$ is $\frac{4}{7}$. Cathleen, in particular, was disturbed that many of her students didn't have any idea where to start. When given the most basic problem—7 brownies to share among 4 people—they asked whether they should add, subtract, multiply, or divide, and couldn't draw a diagram of the situation. She was coming to see that, although her students might memorize calculation procedures, they didn't have any sense of what those procedures might mean; they didn't have any tools for approaching a story problem without having been told what operation to use.

Although students of the other middle school teachers fared better, Spencer, Celeste, and Karran were also surprised by the results. They asked their students to solve the problem about 7 people sharing 4 brownies, but did not provide the diagram solution on the activity sheet for students to analyze. However, at least one student in each class solved it that way.

Karran had changed the problem slightly to 7 people sharing 5 brownies. She showed how one of her students cut the 5 brownies into thirds and gave each of the 7 people $\frac{2}{3}$ of a brownie. The student then cut the remaining $\frac{1}{3}$ into sevenths, and said that each person got $\frac{2}{3} + \frac{1}{7}$ of $\frac{1}{3}$. Karran said, "I did the math, and it comes out right: $\frac{2}{3} + (\frac{1}{7} \times \frac{1}{3}) = \frac{5}{7}$. But, wow…"

Spencer said that one of his students, working on 4 brownies shared among 7 people, did the same thing as the students in MaryAnn's case. "This student first gave everyone half a brownie. Then, instead of cutting the remaining half into sevenths, he cut it into eighths. So everyone got $\frac{1}{2} + \frac{1}{8}$ of $\frac{1}{2}$, and then there was $\frac{1}{8}$ of $\frac{1}{2}$ left over. He said you can keep cutting the remaining piece into eighths, and the pieces will get smaller and smaller, but it can go on forever."

The lower-grade teachers were also engaged in discussion of their students' work. They were fascinated that some of the students distributed pieces of brownie but weren't concerned about the size of the pieces.

In our short whole-group discussion, three main points came out:

- There is a transition from counting pieces without caring about the size of the pieces to making sure each person gets the same amount of brownie.

- Teachers can create an opportunity for learning when students' work gives different representations for the same amount. For example, if one method results in $1 + \frac{1}{2} + \frac{1}{4}$ and another in $1 + \frac{1}{4} + \frac{1}{4} + \frac{1}{4}$ (or if one student says the answer is $\frac{4}{7}$ and another says it's $\frac{1}{2} + \frac{1}{14}$), the teacher can ask, "Which of these is correct, or are they both correct? How do we know?"

- It is crucial that students expect to make sense of problems in math class.

Case discussion: Less than, greater than, equal to

The math activity we did in Session 3 had helped teachers read the cases in chapter 4. However, they were surprised that the fourth graders could notice the same generalizations participants had devised in the previous session. Gaye said, "I had never thought about how to compare $\frac{3}{4}$ and $\frac{5}{6}$ before—that you can look at the distance from 1 to see which is longer. But these fourth graders see it right away."

Small-group discussion

Some of the groups debated what actually happened in Nelly's case when Bibiana created her diagram to show that $\frac{5}{6} - \frac{3}{4} = \frac{1}{12}$. Nadra was saying, "Obviously, Bibiana knew how to subtract with common denominators and drew a diagram to show it."

But Elspeth wasn't so sure. "Maybe you're right, but I don't think that's clear in the case. Many of the students had drawn the fractions on 6-by-6 squares. The way Bibiana drew her picture, when she wanted to compare $\frac{3}{4}$ and $\frac{5}{6}$, she could see the difference was that one strip of 3 squares."

Odette asked, "So why didn't she say the difference is $\frac{3}{36}$?"

Joseph said, "I'm not so concerned about whether Bibiana already knew the algorithm for subtracting fractions. I'm interested that she could draw this diagram for it and that her classmates found it so fascinating."

Elspeth said, "You're right. We can't know what was in Bibiana's head other than what is written here. But it certainly seemed to be satisfying to some of the students in the class who were making the connections."

Maxine's Journal, Session 4

Joseph added, "I was especially interested in Matt, who described Bibiana's diagram twice. The first time, he tried to describe it the way he had been thinking about his own drawing. The second time, he elaborated on Bibiana's language."

Spencer's group spent some time on Zura's case 20. He said, "I thought it would be obvious to fourth graders that when the numerator and denominator are equal, the fraction is 1."

Beatrice responded, "I think if you give them any fraction, like $\frac{36}{36}$, they'll get it right. The issue here is that they are making a general claim. Is it true for all numbers? Lili is asking an important question: Does it still work if the numbers are negative? She doesn't have any images for $\frac{-36}{-36}$ the way she does for $\frac{36}{36}$, so she can't really say."

Celeste added, "And, in fact, the claim isn't true when the numerator and denominator are equal to 0."

When I got to Iris, Maalika, and An-Chi, they were discussing Kalina's conjecture—that if the numerator and denominator of one fraction are greater than those of another, then the first fraction is greater. Iris said, "That sounds right to me."

Maalika said, "Yes, but the focus question [2c] says it's not. Let's try some fractions and see what's going on."

Iris wrote down some pairs of fractions and said, "Look, $\frac{1}{5}$ is less than $\frac{7}{12}$, and $\frac{3}{4}$ is less than $\frac{5}{6}$. The fraction with the greater denominator and numerator is greater."

An-Chi said, "But remember, if we start increasing the denominator, the value of the fraction decreases. So let's start with $\frac{3}{4}$ and keep 5 in the numerator. What happens if the denominator increases? Like, what about $\frac{3}{4}$ and $\frac{5}{10}$?"

Maalika said, "Oh, yeah; $\frac{5}{10}$ is $\frac{1}{2}$, and that's less than $\frac{3}{4}$."

Iris said, "But maybe the problem is that $\frac{5}{10}$ isn't in simplest form $\frac{3}{4}$ and $\frac{1}{2}$ fit Kalina's conjecture."

An-Chi said, "But then we can just pick a different denominator. Like what if we compare $\frac{3}{4}$ and $\frac{5}{11}$? We know $\frac{5}{11}$ is less than $\frac{1}{2}$, so it's less than $\frac{3}{4}$. So we found a pair of fractions that disproves Kalina's conjecture."

Iris said, "But look, there were lots of fractions that made it work."

I had listened to this conversation without intervening, but at this point decided to speak up. I said, "Iris, it might seem like you were collecting evidence in support of Kalina's conjecture, but for a general claim to be true, it has to be true for all pairs of numbers that satisfy the conditions. All we need is one counterexample for us to know that it's not true. But I bet now that you've found one counterexample, you could find lots of others. I suggest that you look for five more."

I moved to different groups for a while, and then came back to check in with Maalika, An-Chi, and Iris. They said that once they had found one pair of numbers, it was easy to find others. Maalika said, "Take any pair of fractions and then start really increasing one of the denominators. That's how you get to the counterexamples."

Whole-group discussion

Several groups had spent some time thinking about how to use diagrams to explain the rule for finding equivalent fractions, and that's where I chose to begin the whole-group discussion. I said, "Let's start with Ida's picture at the end of Malik's case. Let's say we have a picture of thirds." I drew a rectangle divided into thirds and shaded one part.

I asked, "So how did Ida show that $\frac{1}{3} = \frac{2}{6}$?"

Marina said, "You cut each of the thirds into two parts. That gives you six parts all together, and two are shaded."

Gaye called out, "Oh, I see! If you double the denominator, it's like you're cutting each part into two. And when you do that, you automatically also cut the parts of the numerator into two. It really happens in just one step."

Dofi said, "It doesn't have to be just doubling, either. You can cut each part into three parts or four parts or five. That's the same as multiplying the denominator and numerator by that number of parts. The shaded amount stays the same."

Carol added, "It can go in the other direction, too." When I asked what she meant, she said, "You can group the parts. That's like dividing the numerator and denominator by the same number. I was thinking back at Bibiana's picture and how she saw twelfths when she began with thirty-sixths."

We all turned back to Bibiana's diagram to make sense of what Carol was saying. She explained that Bibiana had drawn a 6-by-6 square, with 36 internal squares, and divided the whole thing into fourths by drawing a vertical and a horizontal line. "But you can see that each of the fourths is made up of 9 squares. So, even though Bibiana didn't say it, we can see that $\frac{3}{4}$ is equal to $\frac{27}{36}$. But Bibiana didn't focus on thirty-sixths. She looked at pieces by grouping 3 squares together. By looking at those strips of 3 squares, we can see that $\frac{27}{36}$ is the same as $\frac{9}{12}$." Carol concluded, "You can divide the 27 and the 36 by 3 and get an equivalent fraction."

With a few minutes left before break, I said that I had heard some interesting comments in small groups about what the teacher, Nelly, did in case 18. Joseph began that discussion. "I was fascinated about what she described in the beginning of the case. She looked at an assessment and was disappointed in her students' work. But when she returned to the problem with her class, she didn't tell them she was disappointed. She told them they all thought about the problem in different ways and said, 'I'm sure that you will find a lot to talk about in your groups.' She set up that expectation, and they did have a lot to talk about."

Marina added, "That's right. Then in their groups, they all figured out that $\frac{5}{6}$ is more than $\frac{3}{4}$. But that wasn't the climax. The interesting work came from how they drew their pictures and reasoned about them."

Dofi said, "I underlined what the teacher said when she started the discussion of the posters. She said, 'Isn't it fascinating that we can all agree on an answer and still find it so interesting to talk about the different ways we have to prove it?' She is telling them that the way they are thinking is interesting and that they should be interested in what other students have to say. But she doesn't say it that way. She sets the expectation by telling them how interested *she* is. And she speaks with the assumption that, of course, they find it all as fascinating as she does."

An-Chi added, "And it seems like the kids in her class are interested in it, too."

Math activity: Adding fractional amounts

After break, we worked on a math activity that involved addition of fractions. Small groups began with the problem of sharing 14 sandwiches among 8 people. I sat down to watch Dofi, Labeeba, and Nadra. "OK, first everyone gets 1 sandwich. Now there are 6 sandwiches left. Next, everyone gets another $\frac{1}{2}$, leaving 2 sandwiches. Finally, everyone gets $\frac{1}{4}$, so each person gets a whole, a half, and a quarter. That makes $1\frac{3}{4}$."

Labeeba said, "I know this isn't the way you would do it with real sandwiches, but what if we did it by cutting each sandwich into 8 pieces?" This group seemed to be in a worthwhile exploration, so I moved on.

Odette, Maalika, and Andrea were working on the second problem and were having difficulty. "Jorge eats 2 slices of the pepperoni pizza and 1 slice of the cheese," so it was easy to see that he had eaten 3 slices. They had also come up with a question whose answer is $\frac{3}{16}$. They showed me drawings of 2 pizzas, each cut into 8 pieces. One pizza had 2 slices shaded; the other 1.

Odette said, "See, he eats $\frac{3}{16}$ of the pizza."

Maalika added quietly, "There's no way to look at that picture and get $\frac{3}{8}$."

Andrea said, "Maybe you need to look at just one pizza."

Puzzled, Odette responded, "Why would you do that?"

Andrea went over to the snack table and came back with two paper plates. She drew lines to mark off the 8 slices, shaded in 2 slices on one plate and 1 on the other, and then went through the demonstration. "Look, like we said, if you talk about slices, the answer is 3. If you talk about both pizzas at once, you can see the $\frac{3}{16}$. But if you think about how much pizza he ate, and think about how much in ate in terms of one pizza, it's $\frac{3}{8}$. It's as though you take the 1 cheese slice and put it here with the 2 pepperoni slices, and you see it's $\frac{3}{8}$ of a pizza."

I continued to move from group to group, following the discussions, and soon it was time to bring everyone together. I started by asking Andrea to show us her demonstration.

It turned out that most of the groups had struggled to come up with a question whose answer would be $\frac{3}{8}$. (This is interesting to me, because $\frac{3}{8}$ is the answer to the addition problem $\frac{2}{8} + \frac{1}{8}$.) When Andrea had finished her demonstration, Iris said, "I can see the $\frac{3}{8}$ when you move that one piece over to join the other two, but as long as that slice of cheese pizza stays on that other plate, I don't think it's $\frac{3}{8}$. Then you have to talk about sixteenths. At least this is how it seems to me." Iris paused and then ventured, "Is there anything right in what I'm saying?"

I think Iris was saying that she sees a difference between "$\frac{3}{8}$ of a pizza" and "the same amount as $\frac{3}{8}$ of a pizza." If you eat $\frac{2}{8}$ of one pizza and $\frac{1}{8}$ of another, it's the same amount as if you eat $\frac{3}{8}$ of a single pizza, but to her, that's not the same as eating $\frac{3}{8}$ of a single pizza. Now "pizza" becomes a unit of measure, rather than the physical object that you would eat. I asked Iris whether this is what she meant, and she nodded. That seemed to give her the resolution she was asking for, but I'm not sure if anyone else got her point.

I was ready to leave it at that until Odette blurted out, "Wait a minute. I'm just thinking about what that whole pizza problem is saying. Does this mean $\frac{1}{8} + \frac{2}{8} = \frac{3}{16}$?"

I certainly didn't want participants to leave with that incorrect idea, so if that was what they were thinking, we needed to think some more. I looked questioningly at the group.

Then Karran stepped up to the board. She wrote:

$$1 + 2 = 3$$

$$\frac{1}{8} + \frac{2}{8} = \frac{3}{8}$$

$$\frac{1}{16} + \frac{2}{16} = \frac{3}{16}$$

Karran explained, "You can't mix up what you're talking about in the middle of the equation. If you're talking about slices of pizza, then the equation is $1 + 2 = 3$. If you're talking about how much of all the pizza, then it's $\frac{1}{16} + \frac{2}{16} = \frac{3}{16}$. And if you're talking about how much of 'one' pizza, like what Andrea was showing, then it's $\frac{1}{8} + \frac{2}{8} = \frac{3}{8}$."

Karran clarified that in addition, the units have to stay the same. I looked back at Odette, who was nodding thoughtfully.

Spencer said, "In our group, we were trying to figure out the problem about Mary's class. That's what the issue was. The fraction of girls that are absent is based on a different unit than the fraction of the whole class that is absent—unless there are no boys in the class, that is."

I said, "Spencer is getting to the heart of the problem about Mary's class, but most of the small groups didn't get a chance to dig into it. For homework, you'll get a chance to write about what you're learning about fractions and the questions you have. You might choose to write about that problem and explain how you understand that issue or specify the questions you have."

Then I added, "Before we finish up, I want to give you a DVD image of a seventh grader thinking about adding fractions."

DVD: Nadja adds fractions

The DVD clip shows a seventh grader, Nadja, who creates story problems for $\frac{1}{5} + \frac{2}{5}$. When the interviewer changes the problem by changing the unit to which $\frac{2}{5}$ refers, Nadja is clear that the new problem cannot be solved by $\frac{1}{5} + \frac{2}{5} = \frac{3}{5}$.

When the clip ended, Odette commented, "It was pretty easy for her to come up with her own story problem."

Karran added, "And she clearly understood that the problem was different when the unit changed."

Joseph said, "She still needs to feel more confident that the revised problem cannot be thought of as $\frac{1}{5} + \frac{2}{5}$."

Karran said, "Right. The revised problem is $\frac{1}{5} + (\frac{2}{5} \times 2)$."

Homework and exit cards

As I distributed the homework pages, including lessons from the *Navigations* series, I explained that there were two writing assignments. For assignment 1, participants would select one mathematics topic they have been working on, write about how their understanding of that topic has changed, and pose questions they are still thinking about. I reminded participants that they might want to use this assignment to work on the problem about Mary's class, problem 3 of the math activity.

For assignment 2, they would review an activity from the *Navigations* series and answer the questions on the "Examining Curriculum Activities" sheet. I explained that, in the next session, they will hand in assignment 1 to me. Assignment 2 will be shared in small groups, and they will use it to prepare for the next homework assignment.

I alerted them to the fact that they were not to do the *Navigations* lesson with their students yet. They would have an opportunity to do that later.

Then I posted the following exit-card questions.

1. What ideas about fractions are clear to you? What is still confusing?

2. Anything else you would like to tell the facilitators about your experience in the seminar?

The exit-card responses were informative. Among the lower-grade teachers, a few still wanted to tell me how insecure they feel about fractions, although they did quite well in today's session.

LABEEBA: I think I am pretty clear on equivalent fractions and comparing fractions, but beyond that, it's beyond me at this point. I don't understand (or remember) how to multiply fractions—and definitely not how to divide them!

IRIS: I feel like I'm getting clearer on ideas about fractions. Sometimes I'm not clear about fraction rules. Maybe I should continue to focus on the context of the story problems and think about those instead of worrying about the rules.

CAMISHA: Fractions have always been challenging for me. I see many ideas coming together—making sense—in my mind, but am really tripped up easily as any new fraction problem is presented to me. I'm working on it.

Amber's card brought my attention to the fact that some participants—or at least one—left the session with incorrect ideas about one of the main points about addition.

AMBER: I have a clearer understanding of how to compare fractions but am now struggling to think about how to add fractions. I was sure that $\frac{1}{5} + \frac{2}{5} = \frac{3}{5}$. It's still hard to see it as $\frac{3}{10}$.

I'm hoping participants will write about the problem about Mary's class for homework, and so I'll have a chance to see where they are in the next session. In the meantime, when I respond to Amber's student-thinking assignment, I'll add a note about this.

Quite a few participants wrote enthusiastically about how much they are learning about fractions. I've been particularly paying attention to the teachers in the upper grades who have been responsible for teaching fractions for years. Are they prepared to delve into this content and see that they have more to learn? Clearly Karran, who had taken a DMI seminar with me last fall, is ready to learn.

KARRAN: The idea of equivalency made a lot more sense after seeing the visual pictures in the cases (instead of just saying, multiply the numerator and denominator by ___).

I'm pleased that Karran is not ashamed of having new insights into familiar content. Spencer and Celeste referred to their work with students.

SPENCER: It's interesting to think how students can naturally start thinking about common denominators without even being introduced to it.

CELESTE: I found homework for today *really* interesting to do with my students and watch them problem solve.

I'm still concerned about Cathleen.

CATHLEEN: I don't see why you would give students a problem like the one about Jorge's pizza or Mary's class. It just confuses them and brings people to wrong conclusions, like $\frac{1}{5} + \frac{2}{5} = \frac{3}{10}$. That's just wrong.

I'll need to be careful in my responses to Cathleen and I will try to be attentive to her, in particular, in our next session.

Responding to the third homework

March 15

I found it fascinating to read through the set of homework in which teachers from kindergarten to grade 9 asked their students the same or similar questions. It was also very interesting to see what many of the teachers learned from the assignment. For example, Gaye wrote, "I used to look at my students and evaluate and judge them based on how fast and accurate they were. But there is such value in slowing down to talk about the way they do everything."

I'll include Odette's assignment in my journal, particularly because of the whole-group discussion she describes, as well as the interesting written work of her students.

Odette

Background Information:

I had my children work on the brownie problem with 7 brownies divided among 4 friends. I thought the students would try to give away whole brownies first. Then they would realize that there are only 3 left and you can't give out any more wholes. I thought they would draw on basic knowledge of trying to split things evenly. But I thought they would struggle with drawing equal pieces and naming the fraction pieces.

During the Activity:

I gave out the activity and automatically some of the students said that it couldn't be done. They said, "It can't be done because there are an odd number of brownies and an even number of people." I told them that there was a way to figure out the problems so everyone gets the same amount and there is none left over. Most of the students read the problem again. Some still looked confused while others tried to split the pieces up.

7 students answered $1\frac{3}{4}$.

4 students answered $1 + \frac{1}{2} + \frac{1}{4}$.

3 students got the picture correct but couldn't explain the number fractions.

3 students answered incorrectly.

After the students finished the activity individually, we talked about how they approached the problem. All students agreed that they gave one whole brownie to each friend first. Then they had 3 brownies left over. One students offered this explanation: "I know that there were 3 brownies left for 4 children so I broke each of the 3 brownies into fourths and then each person got $\frac{1}{4}$ from each of the remaining brownies." We agreed that this was a great strategy.

I offered this idea: "What if we wanted to give our friends bigger pieces than 3 one-quarter pieces? Is there a way to do that?" Four of the students who had answered with $1 + \frac{1}{2} + \frac{1}{4}$ raised their hands to give their explanation. They offered the explanation, "I took 2 of the leftover brownies and broke them up in halves. So then everyone would get 1 whole plus $\frac{1}{2}$. Then there would be 1 brownie left over, and we could cut that into fourths, and everyone would get $\frac{1}{4}$."

I asked, "So is this the same answer as saying $1\frac{3}{4}$, like we got when we split the brownies into fourths?"

Some of the kids looked confused, so I drew some brownies on the board. I colored in 1 whole and split the second brownie into fourths. I colored in 3. I asked, "What fraction does this show me?" The students agreed that it was $1\frac{3}{4}$ because it was one whole, and 3 out of 4 pieces were colored in.

Then I colored in another whole brownie and split the second one in half. I colored in $\frac{1}{2}$. I asked, "What fraction does this show me?" The students knew that it was $1\frac{1}{2}$. "But I still have one quarter to add to have $1 + \frac{1}{2} + \frac{1}{4}$. What can represent that last quarter?" One student said that we could cut the remaining $\frac{1}{2}$ in half and that would be $\frac{1}{4}$. Then it would look the same as the other answer we got.

So I asked, "Is $1\frac{3}{4}$ the same as $1 + \frac{1}{2} + \frac{1}{4}$?" We all agreed that it was.

Odette's write-up was followed by the written work of her 17 students. I've selected a few to include here.

Kimberly's work

Derrick's work

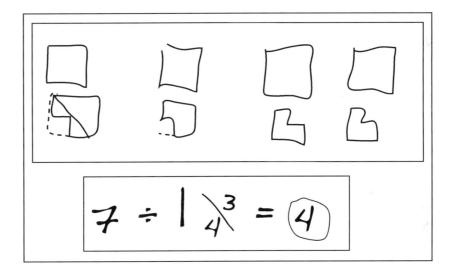

Brian's work

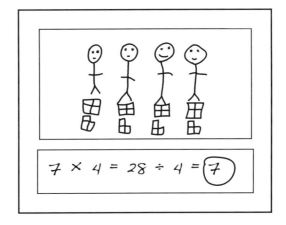

Mandy's work

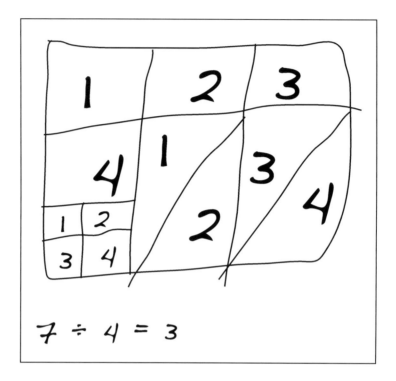

In my response to Odette, I wanted to applaud the whole-group discussion she'd had with her students. Her question, "Is $1 + \frac{1}{2} + \frac{1}{4}$ the same amount as $1\frac{3}{4}$?" is a great one. I also wanted to comment on some of the ideas I see in her students' work.

Dear Odette,

What a fascinating lesson you had with your students! I loved reading about the discussion you led, and I found it very interesting to look at your students' written work.

"Is $1 + \frac{1}{2} + \frac{1}{4}$ the same amount as $1\frac{3}{4}$?" Your question is such a good one, it's worth keeping in your pocket for other occasions. That is, whenever your students get different answers to a problem, it's worthwhile to ask if all of the different answers are correct. Do all answers represent the same quantity? If not, which are correct, which are incorrect, and how do they know? Frequently there is important mathematics to be unearthed with such questions. In this lesson, your third graders had an opportunity to begin thinking about adding fractions with unlike denominators. As you read the cases coming up, particularly those in chapter 5, you might consider what could be learned if the teachers in the cases asked their students a similar question.

The fact that your students immediately recognized that this is a division problem is significant. They have this kind of context to rely on whenever they are trying to figure out something about division. I also found interesting the initial response of some students that the division couldn't be done because there are an odd number of brownies and an even number of people. Clearly, they were thinking that their answer needed to be a whole number with no remainder. It seems they were answering the question, "Is 4 a factor of 7?" Might we infer from their comment that they already recognize that an even number is never a factor of an odd number? Or, in language that might be more familiar to them, an odd number divided by an even number never results in a whole number without remainder.

As I looked through your students' written work, I was struck by a few things. You placed Kimberly's work first, and it certainly is impressive. She has a clear way of structuring her work, keeping track of the number of brownies used as she distributes pieces to four people.

We don't have as clear an image of Derrick's process, but we do see that he gave each person $1\frac{3}{4}$ brownies. His number sentence reads $7 \div 1\frac{3}{4} = 4$. This is correct, but I'm curious about why he wrote it this way as opposed to the way most of his classmates wrote it: $7 \div 4 = 1\frac{3}{4}$. If there's another opportunity, it might be interesting to share these two number sentences with the class. How do they interpret each of them?

Similarly, we don't have a clear image of Brian's process, but his picture shows that he distributed $1\frac{3}{4}$ brownies to each of four people. Then he wrote "$7 \times 4 = 28 \div 4 = 7$." The first thing I want to comment on is what is *correct* in Brian's number sentence. It seems that he multiplied the number of brownies by the number of pieces each brownie provided: there are 7×4, or 28 fourths. Then he distributed those 28 pieces among 4 people, and each person got $28 \div 4$, or 7 fourths. At least, I am inferring that he started to think of each fourth as one piece, and so his number sentence is about those pieces. By counting each fourth as 1, he has converted the problem to one that entails only whole numbers.

One thing Brian still needs to learn is what the equal sign means. The error he has made is very common; many people interpret the equal sign to mean something like "the answer is." But actually, = is a symbol that indicates the equivalence of the two expressions on either side of it. When Brian's sentence is read with the correct meaning of =, it means that 7×4 has the same value as $28 \div 4$ and that $7 \times 4 = 7$. In order to represent his thinking with correct notation, he would need to write two equations: $4 \times 7 = 28$ and $28 \div 4 = 7$.

Finally, I want to comment on Mandy's work. One question I have for her is that the brownies seem to be of different sizes. Does that matter? But setting that issue aside, her diagram indicates that each person got 1 whole brownie plus $\frac{1}{2}$ and $\frac{1}{4}$. Then she counted the number of pieces each person got: 3. So now, the fact that she didn't start with 7 brownies of equal size seems to be more critical.

When we looked at some of the work of younger students in the cases, they made sure that each person got the same number of pieces without paying attention to the size of the pieces. For example, many young students cut one brownie in half and, in that way, make 8 chunks of brownie to distribute. We would say that each person gets either 2 whole brownies or $1\frac{1}{2}$ brownies. But these young students say each person gets 2.

Like Brian, and like many younger students, Mandy converted the problem to one that entails only whole numbers. Unlike the younger students, Mandy seems to have cared about giving each person the same amount of brownie. But unlike Brian, when she converts to whole numbers, she counts pieces of different sizes to equal 1.

Thanks for sharing such interesting work. You will have a fascinating time once your third graders get to their fractions unit.

Maxine

SESSION 5

MAKING MEANING FOR OPERATIONS

Combining Shares, or Adding Fractions

Mathematical Themes

- Students' solutions for sharing situations may result in different additive expressions with fractions. Teachers can help students develop ideas about addition of fractions by challenging them to determine which of their classmates' answers are equivalent and which are incorrect.

- The meaning of multiplication or division may need to be extended when the numbers to be operated on shift from whole numbers to fractions.

- The equivalence of $a \div (\frac{b}{c})$ and $a \times (\frac{c}{b})$ can be seen by considering different interpretations of a single diagram.

Chapter 5 case discussion	Small groups	30 minutes
	Whole group	30 minutes
Math activity: Multiplying and dividing with fractions	Groups of four	25 minutes
Break		15 minutes
Math activity discussion	Different groups of four	20 minutes
	Whole group	15 minutes
DVD for Session 5	Whole group	15 minutes
Examining curriculum activities	Small groups	25 minutes
Homework and exit cards	Whole group	5 minutes

Background Preparation

Read

- the casebook, chapter 5
- the detailed agenda for Session 5
- "Maxine's Journal" for Session 5
- the casebook, chapter 8, section 7

Work through

- the focus questions for Session 5
- the math activity: Multiplying and dividing with fractions

Materials

Duplicate

- "Focus Questions: Chapter 5"
- "Math Activity: Multiplying and Dividing with Fractions"
- "Sixth Homework"

Obtain

- graph paper
- interlocking cubes
- index cards

Representing the Same Story Situation with Two Different Expressions:
How is $6 \div (\frac{1}{2})$ the Same as 6×2?
How is $(\frac{5}{6}) \div (\frac{1}{2})$ the Same as $(\frac{5}{6}) \times 2$?

A key understanding about the relationship between multiplication and division is that the same situation can be modeled by two different expressions, one involving multiplication and one involving division. Consider the following story context from problem set A of the math activity in this session:

> Maura has 6 cups of flour. Each batch of cookies requires $\frac{1}{2}$ cup of flour.
> How many batches can Maura make?

A diagram solution might look like this:

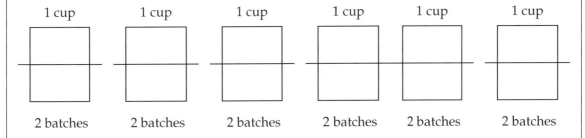

Each box represents both 1 cup of flour and 2 batches of cookies.

The diagram can be interpreted in different ways. Each of the smaller rectangles represents a unit that can be named "a half-cup." The diagram shows each cup is 2 half-cups. Using multiplication, 6 cups is equal to 6×2 half-cups. 12 half-cups represent 12 batches.

However, the diagram also illustrates that each cup of flour is split into 2 equal parts. Each half-cup can make one batch. The question then becomes, "How many half-cups are there in 6 cups?" This matches a division interpretation: 6 cups $\div \frac{1}{2}$ cup per batch = 12 batches.

The inverse relationship, "If 1 cup corresponds to 2 batches, then 1 batch corresponds to $\frac{1}{2}$ cup," is key to understanding how the same problem can be solved by either a multiplication or a division expression.

The same reasoning applies when the initial amount is not a whole number. Consider the following story context from problem set B of the math activity in this session:

> Maura has $\frac{5}{6}$ of a cup of flour. Each batch of cookies requires $\frac{1}{2}$ cup of flour.
> How many batches can Maura make?

The principle remains the same: 1 cup makes 2 batches of cookies, and $\frac{1}{2}$ cup makes 1 batch of cookies.

In the whole-number problem, the first step is to draw 6 cups. In this problem, the first step is to draw $\frac{5}{6}$ of a cup.

Session 5 Detailed Agenda

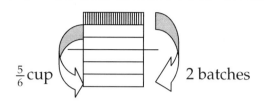

1 cup corresponds to 2 batches or 2 half-cups.

$\frac{5}{6}$ cup corresponds to $\frac{5}{6}$ (of 2 batches) or $\frac{5}{6}$ (of 2 half-cups).

Using multiplication, $\frac{5}{6}$ cup is equal to $\frac{5}{6} \times 2$ half-cups would give an answer in half-cups; $\frac{5}{6} \times 2$ half-cups is the same as $\frac{5}{6} \times 2$ batches, ... or $\frac{10}{6} = \frac{5}{3}$ batches.

As with the previous example, the diagram can also be interpreted as a division situation. The question is, how many half-cups are there in $\frac{5}{6}$ cup?

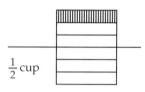

There is one half-cup plus $\frac{2}{3}$ of a half-cup, or $\frac{5}{3}$ half-cups.

Since each half-cup represents 1 batch, this represents $\frac{5}{3}$ batches.

The same problem can be solved using $\frac{5}{6} \div \frac{1}{2}$ and $\frac{5}{6} \times 2$. Both arithmetic expressions fit the problem situation. These two examples illustrate the general principle $a \div (\frac{b}{c}) = a \times (\frac{c}{b})$. This equivalence can also be derived using more formal approaches. Consult the facilitator note in the agenda for Session 6 for an examination of the formal approach.

SESSION 5

Detailed Agenda

Case discussion: Different views of fractions (60 minutes)

Small groups (30 minutes)

Whole group (30 minutes)

In the cases in chapter 5, students encounter problems we recognize as addition of fractions, but they often express the answer in terms of its parts (for instance, $\frac{1}{2} + \frac{1}{4}$) instead of completing the addition and expressing the result as a single fraction (in this instance, $\frac{3}{4}$). As participants work with the cases, they should consider these paired questions: What do these students understand? What have they yet to learn?

In their case discussion, participants should address this question:

- What is the difference between using fractions as labels (e.g., labeling a portion as $\frac{1}{2} + \frac{1}{4}$) and understanding how to combine fractions (e.g., realizing that $\frac{1}{2} + \frac{1}{4}$ can be expressed as the number $\frac{3}{4}$)?

Some participants will find this idea unfamiliar; others might refer to the question posed in Session 1, about the difference between counting and adding with whole numbers, and see this question as a variation of that idea, but with the number set expanded to include fractions.

Some participants might be excited by the students' incomplete solutions and express satisfaction, noting that the solutions are literally correct and pointing out how they match the diagram or situation. Other participants might express concern and wonder if the students know what it means to add fractions, or if they even have the idea that fractional amounts can be rewritten as a single fraction.

Differences among how participants view the student work can provide a way for all to deepen their ideas. If you encounter a small group that has focused only on one point of view, you may want to interject the other. Also, you might ask participants to consider what questions they might ask students in order to bring out these ideas.

Consider grouping participants by grade level for this discussion and for the math activity that follows. This may help primary-grade teachers who do not regularly work with these ideas to feel more comfortable working on this content.

Small-group case discussion
(30 minutes)

Distribute "Focus Questions: Session 5" and let the group know they will have 30 minutes to work in their small groups. Focus question 1, based on MaryAnn's case 22, engages participants in analyzing the thinking of three students: Maribel, Alejandro, and Jackson. In particular, suggest that participants examine the thinking of Jackson on Day 3, as represented in the last figure in this case, and the conversation Jackson has with MaryAnn near the end of the case (lines 165 to 175).

Question 2, based on Greta's case 24, focuses on Dominic's solution of $\frac{1}{4} + \frac{1}{12}$ for a problem with an answer of $\frac{1}{3}$. Encourage participants to discuss both what is correct in his thinking and what is missing. Keep participants focused on what Dominic did, rather than let them propose a different or better way to solve the original problem.

In discussing question 3, based on Henry's case 23, participants will explore their own thinking about the arithmetic sentences that match a given diagram. Encourage them to explore the logic of both Tanya and Ramón.

Whole-group case discussion
(30 minutes)

Spend the first 15 minutes of whole-group discussion clarifying ideas about Jackson and Dominic, asking what the students understood and what was missing. You might want to record comments on a poster so they will be visible to all.

Once the analysis feels complete and the group has identified ideas the students seem to grasp and ideas that are still confusing or missing, ask the participants to examine this list, consider the thinking the students offer, and pose this question: "How can the teachers in these two cases, MaryAnn and Greta, build on the thinking of the students to pose questions that will move the whole class forward?"

Math activity: Multiplying and dividing with fractions
(60 minutes)

Groups of 4 (20 minutes)

Different groups of 4 (25 minutes, after the break)

Whole group (15 minutes)

This math activity shifts the focus from addition of fractions to multiplication and division. It is complicated to sort out these operations when the numbers involved already appear to have the operation of division embedded in them.

Call attention to the directions to first *draw diagrams to solve* each of the story problems. Remind the participants of the math activity they did with 7 − 2, when modeling the problems with cubes or number lines helped reveal the mathematical structure of the problem. Let them know that that same kind of thinking will be helpful in this math activity.

For many participants, this activity makes sense when they can reinterpret a single diagram to be both $6 \div \frac{1}{2}$ and also 6×2. Emphasize that even though the activity appears to be a matching exercise, they can choose more than one arithmetic phrase for each word problem.

Small-group math work (20 minutes)

Initial groups of 4

Distribute the handout "Math Activity: Multiplying and Dividing Fractions." Organize participants into groups of four and assign each group a set of four problems, two from Set A and two from Set B. Assign half of the groups problems 1, 2, 5, and 6, and assign the remaining groups problems 3, 4, 7, and 8.

Provide poster paper to each group. Ask participants to draw diagrams and write explanations that can be seen easily by all in the seminar. Tell each group to make two identical posters, so that pairs can take them along to new groups for the follow-up discussion.

As you work with the groups, ask questions to help them articulate the connections between their diagrams, the story context, and the operations. Ask, "How do you see division represented in this diagram? How do you see multiplication? What part of the diagram illustrates $\frac{1}{2}$ or 2?"

If some groups complete their poster of the four problems before time is over, suggest they turn to the remaining problems, but let them know not to make a poster for those.

Break (15 minutes)

Small-group discussion of the math activity (20 minutes)

Different groups of four

Rearrange the groups into new groups of four so that each group includes pairs of participants who worked on different sets of problems. Tell the new groups that they should discuss all eight problems by examining the two posters together.

Whole-group discussion of the math activity (15 minutes)

Begin the whole-group discussion by asking, "What did you notice while working on these problems?" After participants have had the chance to discuss how multiplying by 2 and dividing by $\frac{1}{2}$ can represent the same problem situation, ask how their thinking changed when they turned to the problems in Set B, focused on $\frac{5}{6}$ rather than 12.

Finally, turn the conversation to the summary question, "What is the same and what is different about these two sets of problems?"

Viewing the DVD: Is It Multiplication or Division? (15 minutes)

Whole group

The DVD segment shows seventh-grade students explaining how they did one of the same problems participants worked out in the math activity: *Maura has to travel 6 miles. When she walks, she covers $\frac{1}{2}$ mile in an hour. How many hours will it take her?*

Ask participants to examine the diagrams of the students in the class to identify their approaches, and to compare the student approaches with their own way of working on the problem. Ask questions such as, "What mathematical ideas do you see in the work of the students? How is this the same or different from the way you worked on the problem?"

Examining Curriculum Activities (25 minutes)

Small groups, grade band grouping

Organize participants according to the lesson they took on as homework for Session 4. One goal of the activity is to help participants become more analytical users of published curriculum. The discussion should include these two main points:

- What are the mathematical ideas that students might explore with the activity?

- As students work on the activity, what questions can teachers ask to focus attention on these mathematical ideas?

Suggest they begin by sharing in their small groups the mathematics they noted as they examined the activity in preparation for this discussion. Then they can turn to question 3, to share and refine the kinds of questions they might ask to keep their students engaged with the central mathematical ideas.

You might use the last 5 minutes in whole-group discussion so that participants can share some of the questions they posed. When questions are offered, ask them to articulate what they would expect to learn from their students by asking that question.

Homework and exit cards (5 minutes)

Whole group

Distribute the "Sixth Homework" sheet. Let the group know they may choose the curriculum activity they have just analyzed as a basis for this student-thinking assignment. In this case, they might choose to revise their responses to the questions they worked on for homework.

If they prefer to use a different lesson, they should write responses to the questions posed on the "Examining Curriculum Activities" sheet as part of their planning for that lesson.

As the session ends, distribute index cards and pose these exit-card questions:

1. What was significant for you in today's session?

2. What questions is this seminar bringing up for you?

Before the next session…

In preparation for the next session, read what participants wrote in their homework about a mathematical issue they are working on. For more information, see the section in "Maxine's Journal" on responding to the fifth homework. Make copies of both the papers and your response for your files before returning the work.

DVD Summary

Session 5: Is It Multiplication or Division?

Seventh-grade class with teacher Bruce Kamerer (9 minutes 10 seconds)

This seventh-grade class is working on related problems about multiplying and dividing by 2 and by $\frac{1}{2}$. The problems they were given are the same as those in problem Set A of the math activity for Session 5, but we see only the students' work on problem 3. They have been asked to represent each problem using a picture or diagram and to decide which among four arithmetic expressions correspond to each problem (more than one may apply):

$6 \div 2 \quad 6 \div \frac{1}{2} \quad 6 \times 2 \quad 6 \times \frac{1}{2}$

After working on the problems in small groups, students present their work. Three different groups present their work on the following problem:

> Maura has to travel 6 miles. She walks $\frac{1}{2}$ mile in an hour. How many hours will it take her?

The first pair of students shows a number line that goes from 0 to 6, marked in intervals of $\frac{1}{2}$, to represent 6 miles. Each half-mile is marked with a bracket showing "1 h." They have written $6 \div \frac{1}{2} = 12$ as their first number sentence. The teacher asks them why this problem is division. They explain: "You have to take 6 miles and divide them equally by the half because that's how far she went in an hour." They have also written $6 \times 2 = 12$. They explain, with help from the teacher, that the 2 means 2 hours for each mile, and 6×2 means 6 groups of 2 hours.

The second pair of students uses six squares, each divided in half horizontally. They have also written:

$\frac{1}{2}$ mile per hour

1 mile = 2 h
2 miles = 4 h
3 miles = 6 h
4 miles = 8 h
5 miles = 10 h
6 miles = 12 h

Like the first pair of students, they have chosen both $6 \div \frac{1}{2} = 12$ and $6 \times 2 = 12$. They explain that each box represents both 1 mile and 2 hours, and that they divided each box in half to show how many half miles are in 6 miles; this corresponds to the number sentence $6 \div \frac{1}{2}$. The teacher helps them explain how their picture also represents 6×2.

Finally, one boy shows how he represented the problem with a graph. He draws a graph that shows hours along the horizontal axis and distance in miles along the vertical axis. He draws in points at each hour along the x-axis corresponding to each $\frac{1}{2}$ mile along the y-axis.

SESSION 5

MAKING MEANING FOR OPERATIONS

Focus Questions: Chapter 5

1. MaryAnn in case 22 presents the work of three students: Maribel, Alejandro, and Jackson.

    (a) Study Maribel's solutions in Figures 5.1 and 5.2. Explain her method. What ideas about addition of fractions can you see in her work? What ideas appear to be missing?

    (b) Study Alejandro's solution in Figure 5.3. Explain his method. What ideas about addition of fractions can you see in his work? What ideas appear to be missing?

    (c) Study Jackson's work in Figures 5.4, 5.5, and 5.6. What ideas about addition of fractions can you see in his work? What ideas appear to be missing?

2. In Greta's case 24, Dominic answers the problem about three children sharing one stick of gum by saying that each gets $\frac{1}{4}$ and $\frac{1}{12}$. What is right about his solution? What is worrisome about it? What does this illuminate about fractions and adding fractional parts?

3. In Henry's case 23, Ramón represented $\frac{1}{3} + \frac{1}{3}$ this way:

This drawing led him to believe that $\frac{1}{3} + \frac{1}{3} = \frac{2}{3}$, but Tanya thought it showed $\frac{1}{3} + \frac{1}{3} = \frac{2}{6} = \frac{1}{3}$. Explain the thinking of Ramón and of Tanya. Make up a word problem that is appropriate for each of these answers. What does this illuminate about fractions and adding fractions?

Session 5 Detailed Agenda

SESSION 5

MAKING MEANING FOR OPERATIONS

Math Activity: Multiplying and Dividing with Fractions

Draw diagrams to solve each of the following word problems. Write an arithmetic sentence that matches your diagram solution for each. Then examine the boxed arithmetic sentences at the left to determine which of these correspond to each problem. You may list more than one for each problem. Explain the connections between the problem situation, the diagram solution and the arithmetic sentence.

Problem Set A

(a) $6 \div 2$	1. Maura has 6 cups of flour. Each batch of cookies requires $\frac{1}{2}$ cup of flour. How many batches of cookies can she make?
(b) $6 \div \frac{1}{2}$	2. Maura has 6 batches of cookies. She plans to share them equally with her friend, Jamilla. How many batches will each of them get?
(c) 6×2	3. Maura walks $\frac{1}{2}$ mile in an hour. At this rate, how many hours will it take her to walk 6 miles?
(d) $6 \times \frac{1}{2}$	4. Maura has to travel 6 miles. She plans to walk halfway and run halfway. How far will she run?

SESSION 5

MAKING MEANING FOR OPERATIONS

Problem Set B

(a) $\frac{5}{6} \div 2$	5. Maura has $\frac{5}{6}$ of a cup of flour. Each batch of cookies requires $\frac{1}{2}$ cup of flour. How many batches of cookies can she make?
(b) $\frac{5}{6} \div \frac{1}{2}$	6. Maura has $\frac{5}{6}$ of a batch of cookies. She plans to share them equally with her friend, Jamilla. How many batches will each of them get?
(c) $\frac{5}{6} \times 2$	7. Maura walks $\frac{1}{2}$ mile in an hour. At this rate, how many hours will it take her to walk $\frac{5}{6}$ mile?
(d) $\frac{5}{6} \times \frac{1}{2}$	8. Maura has to travel $\frac{5}{6}$ of a mile. She plans to walk halfway and run halfway. How far will she run?

Summary question

What is the same and what is different about working on these two sets of problems?

Session 5 Detailed Agenda

SESSION 5

MAKING MEANING FOR OPERATIONS

Sixth Homework

Reading assignment: Casebook chapter 6

In the casebook, read chapter 6, "Taking Portions of Portions, or Multiplying Fractions," including the introductory text and cases 25–27. Consider the questions posed in the introduction as you read the cases.

Writing assignment: Writing about student thinking

Pose a mathematics task to your students related to the work of this seminar. You might pose a question taken directly from one of the cases, the math activities we have been doing, or from the curriculum activity you examined in this session.

First consider why you want your students to work on this question or task, using questions 1 and 2 from the "Examining Curriculum Activities" sheet. What mathematical ideas do you want them to explore?

Then develop questions you might ask as the students are working in order to bring that mathematics to their attention (question 3). Also explore how you might modify the lesson to meet the needs of individual students (questions 4 and 5). Include your responses to these questions in your write-up.

After the session, think about what happened. What did you learn? What surprised you? Write up your questions, how your students responded, and what you make of their responses (your expectations, your surprises, and what you learned). Include specific examples of student work or dialogue. Examining the work of just a few students in depth is very helpful.

At our next session, you will have the opportunity to share this writing with the colleagues from your small-group planning session. Please bring four copies of your writing to share.

Session 5
Combining shares, or adding fractions

Maxine's Journal

March 26

The session last night was packed with ideas. In fact, some of the issues that came up got me so stimulated, I want to get right into the description of what happened so I can use my writing to work them through.

Case discussion: Different views of fractions

Opening with the case discussions, participants, as usual, got into small groups, and I, as usual, listened in for the issues that came up. Since I had heard several different perspectives on MaryAnn's case 22 being voiced, I began our whole-group discussion there: "MaryAnn had given her students a problem intended for work on adding fractions with unlike denominators [the "Sharing Brownies" problem]. Yet few of the students, if any (and this is arguable), used addition of fractions to solve the problems. So what did that mean?"

I was somewhat taken aback when Odette and Carol responded, almost angrily. Odette said, "I disagree with the way you are even saying this. I'm familiar with the materials MaryAnn is using, and it's not the intent of the problem to teach addition of fractions."

Carol added, "The point of the material is really to let you see, as a teacher, what the students already know. There isn't an agenda behind the problem."

At the time, and even now, I had mixed feelings about what Odette and Carol were saying. For one thing, it felt good that they were responding to my question with such passion. I was glad they felt free enough to object to what I said and argue their own ideas so vigorously. It was also good to see that they could treat the curriculum materials as a tool to help them learn about their students' thinking—a major goal of the course. This, too, felt related to last session's discussion.

My concern is this: Do they think that having a learning agenda for their students is inconsistent with finding out what those students understand? Do they think that the elementary mathematics curriculum materials are designed to lead the class from activity to activity, the teacher learning about what students are thinking, but never working to move students through an idea? And from one idea to the next?

What Odette and Carol are now talking about is a far cry from pages of drill. However, if their goal has become simply to find out about student thinking, with no concern for what students are learning, then how do children get beyond what they already know?

Then again, it might be that Odette and Carol really mean something different from how I interpret their responses. As we are moving to develop new teaching practices, we don't yet have a common vocabulary to describe them. But this seems to be a difficult idea for many teachers: Being responsive to student thinking is *not* in conflict with having a mathematical agenda. In fact, later in the session we worked precisely on that idea.

I've been flipping through my journal to find examples of this in my own practice. For the last two sessions, one of the main goals on my agenda was to have the teachers look at how the same quantity can be represented by different fractions, depending on what the reference unit is. This was an issue I expected they would confront when they worked on MaryAnn's second case in chapter 3—that the same piece could be called $\frac{1}{8}$ or $\frac{1}{40}$. And that was exactly the reason why, in the last session, Jorge's pizza problem was on the math activity sheet—so they could think about how 3 slices could be called either $\frac{3}{16}$ of the pizza or $\frac{3}{8}$ of a pizza.

But as the group worked on that case of MaryAnn's in Session 3, and then on the problem, they brought their own ideas to it. When Amber asked, "Is it more sophisticated to call that piece $\frac{1}{8}$ or $\frac{1}{40}$?" I tried to move her off the question of relative sophistication in order to call attention to the idea of reference unit. And in Session 4, when Andrea found it useful to represent the pizza problem with two paper plates, I encouraged her to share her ideas with other members of the seminar because I expected it would help them think about the mathematics, too.

I guess one way to say it is, I enter class with a set of goals or issues we should work on, and I pay attention to how the activities center on those issues. Thus, as I listen for the teachers' ideas, the things I say and the interventions I make are intended to keep bringing them back to these issues, precisely by having them work through their own ideas. My goals—an expression of my agenda—shape my responses to what the teachers say. But the teachers' ideas are the medium through which we move toward those goals and realize that agenda.

Anyway, to return to Session 5, I didn't get into a deep exploration of what having an agenda means. Instead, I responded to Odette and Carol by saying, "According to the text, MaryAnn saw this problem as addition of fractions. When she gave it to her class, she probably did not expect all her fourth graders to write $\frac{3}{8} + \frac{1}{4} = \frac{5}{8}$. If that's what you thought I meant by 'working on adding fractions with unlike denominators' and you disagree with that, then I really do agree with you."

Then I asked that together we first examine the work of the students in the case. I began, "As I listened in on the small groups, I heard different interpretations of what Maribel had done. Labeeba, perhaps you can tell us what your group was thinking."

Labeeba explained, "Well, we disagreed with MaryAnn's judgment that Maribel wasn't adding. When we looked at her pages, we thought that she was showing how each person got 3 pieces from the first round of sharing and 2 pieces from the second. She used what she had done in the first two parts of the problem adding 3 + 2, and, since the pieces are all eighths, she knew it was $\frac{5}{8}$."

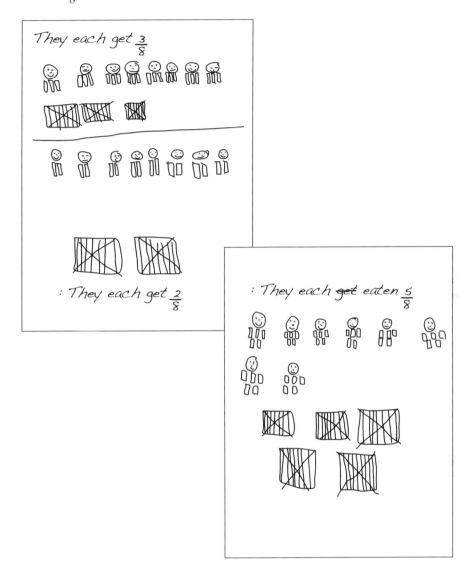

Andrea began, "When we looked at it, it seemed that what MaryAnn said was true. Maribel did the third question the way she did the first two. She added up all the whole brownies, so there she's adding. But then she took 5 brownies and split them up 8 ways."

Dofi exclaimed, "We can all have different ideas about what Maribel did, but we won't know because we can't ask her."

I asked, "Is that a problem for the work we are doing here in our seminar?"

To which Joseph replied, "I don't think so. Maribel is a child we'll never meet. For all we know, this is something that happened years ago, and by now she has figured out addition of fractions—and multiplication and division, and even algebra! But when we think about what Maribel did on this problem, it helps us think about ways our own students solve problems. If one of our kids hands in a paper like this, then we could ask her."

Karran said, "I want to talk about Alejandro's work. It looked to me as though he had names like $\frac{1}{4}$ and $\frac{1}{8}$ as individual items, but he didn't see the relationship between them. There's a thing he calls $\frac{1}{4}$ and a thing he calls $\frac{1}{8}$, but he doesn't see $\frac{1}{8}$ as a part of $\frac{1}{4}$."

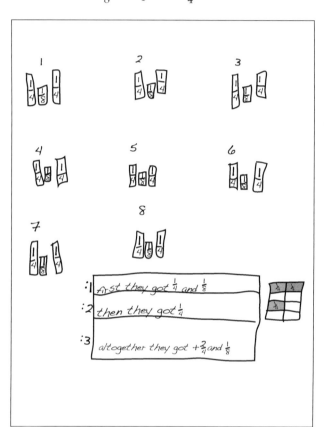

Celeste said, "But he has that other drawing over there. It looks like he cut the fourths in half to make eighths."

"Yes, he has that picture there," Karran agreed. "But he doesn't use it to say that everyone got $\frac{3}{8}$. He said, for the first question, that everyone got $\frac{1}{4}$ and $\frac{1}{8}$. He needs to see how the amounts $\frac{1}{4}$ and $\frac{1}{8}$ are related to each other in order to be able to say they add up to $\frac{3}{8}$."

This seemed to be such an important idea! I told the group, "I want to pause to think about what Karran is saying. As she has studied Alejandro's work, she's been thinking about an idea that needs to be in place in order to understand addition of fractions. She realizes that children might think about *one-fourth* or *one-eighth* as names or labels, but not see how they represent quantities that have a relation to each other. And so, as we examine student thinking, we are also formulating a goal—that they should come to understand fractions as representing quantity. That doesn't mean that, in one day, you try to get your students to say '$\frac{1}{4}$ is twice as much as $\frac{1}{8}$,' but that is something you would like them to come to see."

Elspeth added, "But it's not necessarily bad if children think about fractions in terms of labels. There's a time when that might be an appropriate thing to do."

Joseph responded, "If I know there are these different ways kids might be thinking about fractions, then I can understand better what my students are doing. It's not the same as saying one way of looking at fractions is bad and the other is good. Younger children might use *halves* and *fourths* and *thirds* as labels, and in that way they would get some experience with those things as numbers. Then later, they'll have something to build on when they need to learn that two of these things make one of those. You can't just jump in at the level of relationships."

Next Amber spoke up. "When you work with students who have language disabilities, you see that they have more trouble with relationship words like *between*, *above*, *before*, and *after*. Nouns and verbs don't cause the same trouble. I think fractions are like relationship words. It's not as simple as just saying '3.' You have to pay attention to 3 out of 4, or $\frac{3}{4}$ of something. It's the relationship between the two numbers that you have to consider. For instance, when a child is having a hard time understanding the word *between*, it's because he or she has to pay attention to two things. It's not the two things you see but the abstract relationship between them."

An-Chi went to the board and drew this picture:

An-Chi suggested, "It's the same as when a child thinks that $\frac{3}{4}$ means it's a shape like that. He's thinking about *three-fourths* as a noun. But when he sees the whole square and thinks about the relationship between the 3 squares shaded in and the 4 squares that make up the whole, then he's getting what a fraction is."

These were important issues, so I paused to let the ideas sink in before I went on. Then I suggested we talk about Jackson.

Idris said, "I am Jackson. Look at my paper. It's all over the place."

Joseph said, "We spent a long time looking at Jackson's work. It's messy, and it takes some effort to see what he's doing, but it seems like he has some good ideas. He was the only student who used addition signs in his work and tried to add fractions with unlike denominators."

Celeste added, "In our group, we had a special fondness for Jackson. We have seen so many children who have organizational problems like his. But consider what he was thinking about. He tried to add $\frac{1}{4} + \frac{1}{4} + \frac{1}{8}$. I know so many students who, when trying to add fractions, add the numerators and add the denominators. Jackson said he looked at that but knew the answer couldn't be right; it didn't make sense to have an answer in sixteenths."

Beatrice said, "Jackson tried to add and wrote down $\frac{3}{8}$. But Maribel got an answer of $\frac{5}{8}$. I wonder what Jackson thought about that."

I said, "That's a good question. In the case, the teacher describes how students presented their different methods for finding an answer. They might follow each of their classmates' solutions and see that it makes sense. But I wonder if there's a question the teacher might pose that would help them look across solutions. Do you know what I mean?"

Odette said, "Oh, this is like what happened when my class worked on sharing 7 brownies. Some students wrote $1 + \frac{1}{2} + \frac{1}{4}$, and some students wrote $1\frac{3}{4}$. I asked if these are both the same answers. Maybe MaryAnn could do that here."

Beatrice caught on to what Odette was saying, "Look at the different answers students got. Jackson had three correct answers $\frac{1}{4} + \frac{1}{4} + \frac{1}{8} = \frac{3}{8}, \frac{1}{4}$ and $\frac{3}{8}$, and $\frac{1}{2}$ and $\frac{1}{8}$. Then Alejandro got $\frac{2}{4}$ and $\frac{1}{8}$, and Maribel got $\frac{5}{8}$. MaryAnn could ask the class if all of these stand for the same amount of brownie or if they are different."

Joseph said, "I would include Jackson's answer of $\frac{3}{8}$, too. They might not see right away that $\frac{3}{8}$ is incorrect, but I would want the students to work that out—to be able to say why $\frac{3}{8}$ is not correct."

Dofi said, "I wonder if Alejandro would be able to see that $\frac{2}{4}$ and $\frac{1}{8}$ could be written as $\frac{2}{4} + \frac{1}{8}$."

Spencer said, "It also seems important for the students to see that all those expressions—except $\frac{3}{8}$—are equal to $\frac{5}{8}$."

Beatrice added, "It might be important for MaryAnn to point the class to Alejandro's picture, even though we don't really know what Alejandro saw in it. It seems as if that diagram is the key to seeing which of the expressions are equivalent."

These were important points, and it all seemed to harken back to Odette and Carol's outcry in the beginning. By the end of the discussion, participants were using the case to think about how to use students' ideas to move one's teaching goals forward. They saw that, based on the work of the students, the teacher could ask a question to help the class think about addition of fractions with unlike denominators. Having seen their work, she would have an idea of what ideas were in place, what ideas were missing, and how to steer her students in ways that would allow them to make new connections.

Before we ended the case discussion, I wanted to tell a story. "In general, when we read a case, all we know is what was written in that case. As Joseph said earlier, we can't ask Maribel any questions, and for all we know, she may have graduated from high school by now. Although that's mostly true for me, too, I actually did know MaryAnn the year she taught the class in this case. Something she told me was that at the end of the year, Jackson's father came to her and said that she had changed Jackson's life. He explained that, until Jackson came to MaryAnn's class, all that his teachers could see was how scattered and disorganized he was. MaryAnn could look past that to see that he was actually a strong thinker. Once MaryAnn saw it, then Jackson could see it in himself. He said that Jackson now has a self-confidence he never had before."

Celeste said, "I like to hear that story. My group liked Jackson."

Math activity: Multiplying and dividing with fractions

I handed out the math activity sheet, and within a few minutes I became very aware that it presented a difficult task for the teachers. The sheet asked them to match up given pieces of arithmetic—expressions showing multiplication and division of both whole numbers and fractions—with several word problems. I asked participants to pay attention to the first sentence of the directions: to draw diagrams for each of the word problems. I said that even if they think they know which expression goes with each word problem, drawing the diagram first is likely to lead to greater insights.

I had assigned half the problems to each group: One set of groups had problems 1, 2, 5, and 6; the other set, problems 3, 4, 7, and 8. That meant one group worked on problems about batches of cookies, the other on walking or running some distance. It also meant that everyone worked on pairs of problems with identical wording, but different numbers; so, for example, if $6 \div \frac{1}{2}$ matched a problem, then $\frac{5}{6} \div \frac{1}{2}$ matched its partner.

One of the struggles many individuals had, whether they were starting with 6 or $\frac{5}{6}$, was what it means to divide by $\frac{1}{2}$. To many of them, dividing by $\frac{1}{2}$ was the same as dividing by 2. It turned out, though, that each group had someone who challenged that notion. These participants went back to our discussion of whole-number division to make their case: "Look, you can think about dividing by 2 as seeing how many groups of 2 you can get from the amount you start with. So now you think about how many portions of $\frac{1}{2}$ you can get from the amount you start with."

Some of the groups debated about which arithmetic expression matched the context of the problem. For example, Camisha, Gaye, Celeste, and Joseph had created the following diagram for this problem: *Maura has 6 cups of flour. Each batch of cookies requires $\frac{1}{2}$ cup of flour. How many batches of cookies can she make?*

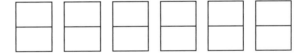

Gaye said, "Each large rectangle stands for 1 cup of flour. The problem asks, how many $\frac{1}{2}$ cups can we get from 6 cups? We can count them up and we get 12. That means $6 \div \frac{1}{2} = 12$."

Everyone in the group agreed. Then Joseph said, "I can look at that diagram and see that each cup of flour gives me 2 batches of cookies. Right? Each $\frac{1}{2}$ cup is one batch, so each cup gives me 2 batches. So the diagram shows me $6 \times 2 = 12$."

Camisha said, "But Gaye said the problem is $6 \div \frac{1}{2}$. The problem doesn't have a 2 in it."

Maxine's Journal, Session 5

Gaye said, "Yeah, I think $6 \div \frac{1}{2}$ is right."

Joseph then pointed to the directions. "It says you may list more than one arithmetic statement for each."

Celeste was listening and now exclaimed, "This is so cool! You can see in the diagram that $6 \div \frac{1}{2} = 6 \times 2$. It just depends on how you look at it. You can divide the number of cups of flour by $\frac{1}{2}$ cup, or you can multiply by batches per cup. Both ways of thinking about it rely on the same information and give the same answer."

Other members of the group weren't quite following Celeste. I left them to continue working on their problems.

The group with Cathleen, Dofi, Karran, and Carol wasn't working as well. Cathleen ignored the directions to draw diagrams and was stating what she already knew: "Dividing by a number is the same as multiplying by the reciprocal, so you already know that $6 \div \frac{1}{2}$ and 6×2 are the same." Karran was going along with Cathleen, but Dofi and Carol were feeling frustrated and had separated themselves from the other two. I saw that they were making headway with their diagrams, so I left them alone. I directed my comments to Cathleen and Karran. "I know that you are already familiar with some of the mathematics, but there are opportunities for new insights here. If you work out some of these diagrams, it might help you see why that reciprocal relationship works here."

Cathleen responded, "My kids hate *why* questions."

But now Karran had started drawing and then looked over to see what Carol and Dofi were doing. Then she turned back to Cathleen and said, "Look, this is kind of neat."

After 25 minutes, I rearranged the groups: two participants who had worked on problems 1, 2, 5, and 6 were now grouped with two who had worked on problems 3, 4, 7, and 8. I said, "You may not feel that you finished all your problems, but you can continue working with your new group. I just want to make sure everyone gets to all of the first four problems."

When I came to Spencer, An-Chi, Beatrice, and Marina, they were happy to tell me what they had discovered. Spencer spoke first: "Marina and I had worked on 3, 4, 7, and 8. When we started working with An-Chi and Beatrice's problems, we realized they were the same. Like 1 and 3 are the same problem: How many $\frac{1}{2}$s are in 6? But our diagram is a straight line, and their diagram is rectangles."

Marina continued, "The same with 2 and 4. They're both $\frac{1}{2}$ of 6, but they drew rectangles and we drew a straight line."

Amidst these insights, many groups struggled with this set of problems. But they were also doing more than the specifics of the task. By the time we were ready for whole-group discussion, they had formulated some questions they had about fractions.

Whole-group discussion of the math

Gaye started us off. "In my group, we had two diagrams for $6 \times \frac{1}{2}$ that look completely different." She came to the board to show us. "This is the way Labeeba and I did it."

"And this is the way Maalika and Nadra did it."

"Ours [the first diagram] shows $\frac{1}{2}$ of 6. Maalika and Nadra's shows 6 halves. I think they're both right, but it seems so weird. The two diagrams look so different, but they both show $6 \times \frac{1}{2} = 3$."

Cathleen said, "The first one shows $\frac{1}{2} \times 6$."

Elspeth responded, "Isn't that the same thing?"

Andrea interjected, "I don't know. It's hard for me to believe $\frac{1}{2} \times 6$ and $6 \times \frac{1}{2}$ are the same thing. They just seem so totally different. They say something different to me. It's surprising that they both come out to 3."

An-Chi took us deeper. "So what about $\frac{5}{6} \times \frac{1}{2}$? I'll show you my way—I drew $\frac{1}{2}$ and took $\frac{5}{6}$ of it." An-Chi came to the board and drew the following diagram:

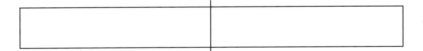

"That shows $\frac{1}{2}$."

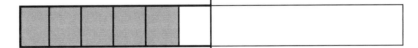

"And that shows $\frac{5}{6}$ of the half."

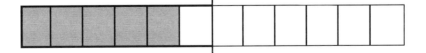

"And you can see that it turns out to be $\frac{5}{12}$ of the whole thing."

"I don't get it," Andrea said. "Why do you say it's $\frac{5}{12}$ of the whole thing?"

An-Chi was quick to respond. "Let's say you made a cake and then next day there's half the cake left. Then your daughter comes home from school with some friends; there are five of them total, and they want to eat the cake. But you say they have to leave a piece for your other daughter. So they cut six slices and each eat a portion of cake. You can say they ate $\frac{5}{6}$ of half a cake. That's $\frac{5}{12}$ of the whole cake."

It seemed clear that An-Chi had a handle on this, but I knew her explanation was going by too fast for many of the others. However, before I could open up the space for everyone to take in An-Chi's story problem, Carol jumped in.

"I have a different diagram. It looks like this."

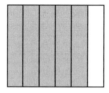

"See, that shows $\frac{5}{6}$, and then you take $\frac{1}{2}$ of it."

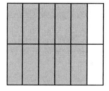

"And $\frac{1}{2}$ of it makes $\frac{5}{12}$."

Now there was a pause, until An-Chi spoke again. "You know, Carol's diagram is different from mine, but I can look at hers and see my way of doing it, too. You start with the whole rectangle and first draw the horizontal line to show $\frac{1}{2}$. Then you draw in her vertical lines, to show $\frac{5}{6}$ of $\frac{1}{2}$. You end up with the same thing."

Nadra slammed her hand on her desk and declared, "I've never gotten multiplication of fractions. I always thought that multiplying meant you were making things bigger. So multiplication of fractions wasn't really multiplying. You use the same word, but it's a totally different thing."

Marina said, "Yeah, multiplying fractions seems really different. But you know, for the first time, it's starting to feel like it means something."

By now it was time to end this activity, but I was aware of having left Cathleen's earlier comment hanging. Especially since Cathleen was having such a hard time engaging with this content, I felt I needed to get back to her. And so I said, "We have to stop here. I mean, stop this whole-group discussion for today—we're certainly not going to stop thinking about these ideas. But before we end, I just want to return to a comment of Cathleen's, that the diagram Gaye drew in the beginning of the discussion must be seen as $\frac{1}{2} \times 6$ and not $6 \times \frac{1}{2}$."

I pointed to Gaye's diagram that was left on the board.

I continued, "One of the things we have been looking at is that we can reverse the factors of a multiplication problem and get the same result. We know that's true with whole numbers: 3 × 4 = 4 × 3 and 10 × 24 = 24 × 10. This fact, that we can switch the order of factors in a multiplication problem, is called the *commutative property of multiplication*. Today we've been exploring the commutative property when multiplying fractions.

"Now Cathleen raised an interesting question, which we can consider first with whole numbers. Does 3 × 4 mean 3 groups of 4, or does it mean 3 taken 4 times?" I drew two pictures to illustrate what I meant.

OOOO OOOO OOOO   OOO OOO OOO OOO

"There isn't anything inherent in 3 × 4 that tells us which way to interpret it. But if it's important to distinguish the two, there needs to be a convention, an agreement, about which diagram matches 3 × 4 and which matches 4 × 3. The thing is, different communities have different conventions. For example, the Japanese say 3 × 4 corresponds to the second drawing. But many (not all) textbooks in the United States say that 3 × 4 corresponds to the first drawing.

"In this seminar, we can be on the lookout to see if it matters—if we have to make a decision. For now—especially since we've seen that even with fractions, $\frac{1}{2}$ of $\frac{5}{6}$ = $\frac{5}{6}$ of $\frac{1}{2}$—we can assume that $\frac{1}{2} \times \frac{5}{6}$ can be thought of both ways."

Viewing the DVD: Is it multiplication or division?

I said, "We're going to spend the last part of the session discussing the curriculum activities you looked at for homework. But before we do, I want to spend a few minutes showing you a video of seventh-grade students doing the same problems you just worked on."

I didn't want to spend a lot of time on this video. The students solved the problems in ways quite similar to what the participants had done. But I chose to show the video so that participants would have images of students working on these same problems.

Examining curriculum activities

For homework in preparation for this session, participants had been given an activity for their grade level from NCTM's *Navigations* series. They were to read through the lesson, list the mathematical ideas they would choose to highlight through this activity, and formulate some questions they might pose to students as they worked in order to bring their attention to those ideas. I now put participants into groups according to the lesson they had worked on.

I said, "The materials, themselves, identify the main mathematical goals of the lesson that the authors had in mind. But any lesson can be tweaked to shift the goal. I want you to think about where your students are with regard to the ideas in the lesson, and then imagine that you will give them this lesson in the coming week. What would be the main goal you would have in mind for your students? This is what I want you to discuss in your small groups. You might start by sharing the ideas you listed for homework."

Although I had given K–2 teachers a choice of two activities (one for kindergarten, the other for grades 1–2), Andrea, the only kindergarten teacher, had chosen to work on the activity for older students. She explained that her main motivation was to make sure she would be able to discuss her work with colleagues: "They said that 'Park Your Car' is designed for grades 1 and 2, but I figured I could adapt it to make it work with my kindergarteners. Besides, it's almost April, and my students will soon be in first grade, anyway. I got so much from asking my students to do the brownie problem and then comparing their work with that brought in by teachers of other grades, I want to do the same thing again."

In fact, all of the K–2 teachers were intrigued by the "Park Your Car" activity, particularly with the questions about the relationship between addition and subtraction.

The groups working on the grades 3–5 activity discussed how they wanted to adapt the activity for their own students.

ODETTE: My students have just begun their work on fractions. The *Navigations* activity suggests that we have a discussion about which fractions are less than or greater than $\frac{1}{3}$. I think I want to start with a discussion about which fractions are less than or greater than $\frac{1}{2}$.

CAROL: My class has already been doing some activities around comparing fractions. But I like the suggestions in the book to think about these four categories: (1) fractions with the same denominators, (2) fractions with a numerator of 1, (3) fractions with the same numerators (other than 1), and (4) fractions with different numerators and different denominators.

BEATRICE: My students have done a lot of work with area models of fractions. Now I want them to think more about length. I want to give them the parallel number lines and see how they use those.

JOSEPH: I also like that the page includes decimal representations. Sometimes when I do this work, I wonder whether my students really understand that decimals are just a different way to represent fractions. I'd like to use "Parallel Number Lines" to investigate that.

When I got to the grade 6–9 group, they were examining the student work included in the handout of the activity.

CATHLEEN: The book said that students who solve the problem the way Jamal did then do the next part of the problem wrong. So how do you get them to not do it Jamal's way?

SPENCER: But Jamal's work so far is correct. You can't tell if he would solve the rest of the problem correctly or not. After all, his work looks quite similar to Kara's. It's just that Kara had an additional diagram that showed more detail.

CELESTE: It seems to me that if students make an error like the one they describe in the book, that provides an opportunity for the class to discuss it. Same with what Robert did. He drew a correct diagram, but had trouble with the second part of the problem where he identifies what fraction each part represents. That could lead to an interesting discussion.

KARRAN: Before bringing his work to the whole class, I would want to have a discussion with Robert. I'd want to understand his thinking first and see what threw him off, where his thinking went wrong. Then I could decide if it would be useful for the whole class to consider that conceptual issue together.

Homework and exit cards

I distributed the homework sheet. In addition to reading the next chapter of the casebook, participants would give their students a task related to the content of this seminar and write up another student-thinking assignment. Then I posted the exit-card questions.

1. What was significant for you in today's session?
2. What questions is this seminar bringing up for you?

The exit cards were reassuring. Every single person wrote about a new insight. Some expressed that it was hard or indicated that there were areas of confusion, but they all conveyed satisfaction with the work.

GAYE: I feel clearer about the inversion idea—the idea that $6 \div 2$ is the same as $6 \times \frac{1}{2}$. It was helpful to be reminded of what the division and multiplication signs mean.

ODETTE: I will be more confident going into the fractions unit with my class—especially with modeling ideas of equivalency: why $\frac{4}{6} = \frac{2}{3}$.

MARINA: The drawing of some of the models—although very hard—helped me to think about what actually happens with fractions when multiplying and dividing. Why we were taught to invert and multiply. The relationship of fractions to those operations. Ugh—not sure I'm making sense.

KARRAN: I'm thinking about fractions in terms of story problems. I used to think about fractions as manipulating numbers. Fractions make more sense in a context.

BEATRICE: Tough class, but it made me think.

SPENCER: It really does help to think about challenging fraction problems in terms of whole numbers in order to determine which operation you need to use.

ANDREA: Multiplying/dividing fractions has always been a challenge for me. I am (believe it or not) enjoying "stretching my thinking" to consider the relationship between the two. I'm learning the *why*.

NADRA: So many questions arise as I think about these problems. Thanks for being patient.

CATHLEEN: Word problems. I never even thought of using fractional word problems until this seminar. They do word problems with whole numbers, but we do fractions with just the numbers.

Responding to the fifth homework

March 29

For their homework, participants had been asked to write about a mathematical issue they have been working on in the seminar. Many chose to discuss why the answer to the following problem is not $\frac{3}{5}$: *In Mary's class, $\frac{1}{5}$ of the girls are absent and $\frac{2}{5}$ of the boys are absent. What fraction of the class is absent?*

I liked having this question in the Session 4 math activity because of an event that happened some years ago. I was working as a math coach for a fifth-grade teacher who was working on a fractions unit with her class. One day when I visited her, we stepped out into the hall for just a few minutes before the lesson so that she could tell me what would happen that day. She showed me the problem she had made up to introduce addition of fractions, and it was the Mary's class problem. When I saw this problem, I had just those few minutes to alert her to the fact that the answer to her problem was not $\frac{3}{5}$, and we quickly made up a problem that could be solved by addition.

I suspect that fifth-grade teacher wasn't alone in making this kind of mistake. It might *seem* like it should be addition since you are combining the girls and boys. After all, if the problem were "1 girl is absent and 2 boys are absent," we would add 1 + 2 to answer the question, "How many children are absent?" What makes the fraction problem different?

In the homework, I saw that many participants were thinking about the issues very clearly. However, some incorrectly stated that we need to know the number of boys and the number of girls to answer the question. For example, Amber wrote:

> If the class had 10 boys and 10 girls, the answer of $\frac{3}{5}$ would be correct. Without knowing their individual totals, the answer cannot be correct.

Because the issues of this problem were so closely tied to our work about addition of fractions, I decided to write a message to the whole seminar group in which I describe the correct reasoning of different participants. For some participants, I added individual notes that addressed the different content they wrote about.

Dear MMO seminar group,

I was very interested in the different ways of thinking about the question I posed about the absent children in Mary's class, and so I want to share with you some of these ideas that I drew from your homework.

The main idea is captured by this sentence: "Each fraction ($\frac{1}{5}$ and $\frac{2}{5}$) is part of a different whole, so you can't simply add the two fractions together." This is an important issue that characterizes addition: the units to which the two addends and the sum refer must be the same. In this problem, there are three reference units: the number of girls in the class, the number of boys in the class, and the total number of children in the class.

Consider an alternative problem about Mary's class: $\frac{1}{5}$ *of the girls are wearing short-sleeved sweaters, and* $\frac{2}{5}$ *of the girls are wearing long sleeved sweaters. What fraction of the girls are wearing sweaters?* In this case, all three numbers of the addition refer to the same unit—the girls in the class. The answer to the question is found by adding $\frac{1}{5} + \frac{2}{5}$, so $\frac{3}{5}$ of the girls are wearing sweaters. We don't have to know how many girls are in the class to answer the question.

Some of you explored what was happening in the absent-children problem by assigning different values to the number of girls and the number of boys. One person actually set up a table.

Number of girls in the class	Number of boys in the class	$\frac{1}{5}$ of the girls	$\frac{2}{5}$ of the boys	Fraction of the class that is absent
10	10	2	4	$\frac{6}{20} = \frac{3}{10}$
10	20	2	8	$\frac{10}{30} = \frac{1}{3}$
20	10	4	4	$\frac{8}{30} = \frac{4}{15}$
15	15	3	6	$\frac{9}{30} = \frac{3}{10}$
20	20	4	8	$\frac{12}{40} = \frac{3}{10}$

The table gives us some interesting information. For one thing, notice that whenever the number of boys and the number of girls is the same, the answer is $\frac{3}{10}$. We don't need to know the exact number of boys and girls to know when the answer will be $\frac{3}{10}$.

Some of you used diagrams to see what is going on. If the number of boys and the number of girls are equal, then the diagram might look like this:

From this picture, we can see that $\frac{3}{10}$ of the class is absent.

Now assume there are twice as many boys as girls in the class.

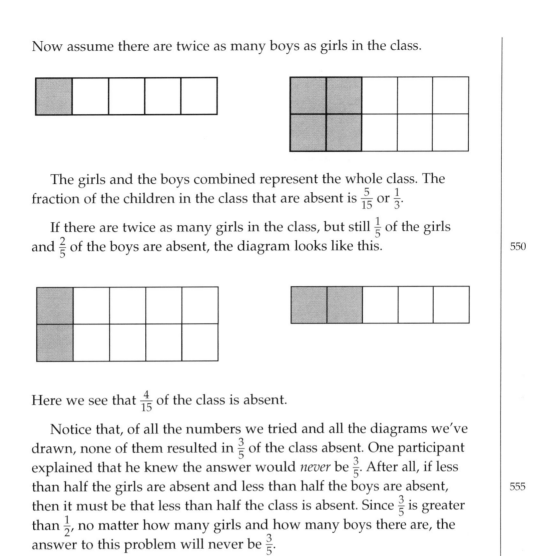

The girls and the boys combined represent the whole class. The fraction of the children in the class that are absent is $\frac{5}{15}$ or $\frac{1}{3}$.

If there are twice as many girls in the class, but still $\frac{1}{5}$ of the girls and $\frac{2}{5}$ of the boys are absent, the diagram looks like this.

Here we see that $\frac{4}{15}$ of the class is absent.

Notice that, of all the numbers we tried and all the diagrams we've drawn, none of them resulted in $\frac{3}{5}$ of the class absent. One participant explained that he knew the answer would *never* be $\frac{3}{5}$. After all, if less than half the girls are absent and less than half the boys are absent, then it must be that less than half the class is absent. Since $\frac{3}{5}$ is greater than $\frac{1}{2}$, no matter how many girls and how many boys there are, the answer to this problem will never be $\frac{3}{5}$.

Maxine

SESSION 6

MAKING MEANING FOR OPERATIONS

Taking Portions of Portions, or Multiplying Fractions

Mathematical Themes

- It may be necessary to expand ideas about multiplication of whole numbers in order to develop meaning for multiplication involving numbers less than 1.

- Just as multiplication of whole numbers can be represented with a rectangle, so can multiplication involving fractions and mixed numbers.

- Mapping a diagram solution for a division of fractions problem to the arithmetic procedures for the calculation provides access to understanding why $a \times \frac{b}{c}$ produces the same answer as $a \div \frac{c}{b}$.

Sharing student-thinking assignments	Small groups	30 minutes
Chapter 6 case discussion	Small groups	30 minutes
	Whole group	25 minutes
Break		15 minutes
Math activity: Fractions in division	Small groups	25 minutes
	Whole group	25 minutes
	Small groups	25 minutes
Homework and exit cards	Whole group	5 minutes

Background Preparation

Read

- the casebook, chapter 6
- the detailed agenda for Session 6
- "Maxine's Journal" for Session 6

Work through

- the focus questions for Session 6
- the math activity: Fractions in division

Materials

Duplicate

- "Focus Questions: Chapter 6"
- "Math Activity: Fractions in Division"
- "Seventh Homework"

Obtain

- graph paper
- interlocking cubes
- index cards

Dividing Fractions

Most adults learned a rule for dividing fractions: Multiply the dividend by the reciprocal of the divisor, a rule commonly referred to as "invert and multiply." The justification for why this rule produces the answer to a division problem is not usually remembered. One way to examine the rule is to consider a diagram solution to a division problem.

Consider the problem posed in the math activity of this session:

Wanda really likes cake. She decides that one serving should be $\frac{3}{5}$ of a cake. She has 4 cakes, all the same size. How many servings does she have?

One way to determine a solution is to draw rectangles representing the cakes, break each rectangle (one cake) into fifths, shade three of the fifths to represent a serving, and count the number of servings ($\frac{3}{5}$ of a cake).

The diagram shows there are 6 full servings and 2 slices of cake left.

The amount of cake left can be expressed in different ways, depending on what is referenced as a whole. Relative to a single cake, the amount left is $\frac{2}{5}$; that is, 2 slices as compared to 5 slices in 1 cake. Relative to a serving, the amount left is $\frac{2}{3}$; that is, 2 slices as compared to 3 slices in 1 serving. Since the answer to the question is stated in terms of servings, the fractional part of the answer will be $\frac{2}{3}$.

This diagram solution to the problem offers a visual image that can be connected to each step of the traditional arithmetic solution: $4 \div \frac{3}{5} = 4 \times \frac{5}{3} = \frac{20}{3} = 6\frac{2}{3}$

$4 \div \frac{3}{5}$ or "How many $\frac{3}{5}$s are there in 4?" matches problem situation and is the basis for the diagram solution above.

$4 \times \frac{5}{3}$ Consider one of the cakes drawn above. 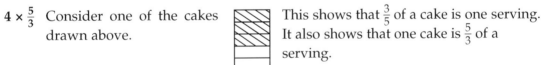 This shows that $\frac{3}{5}$ of a cake is one serving. It also shows that one cake is $\frac{5}{3}$ of a serving.

If each cake is $\frac{5}{3}$ of a serving, and there are 4 cakes, it is a multiplication (or repeated addition) process to show that $4 \times \frac{5}{3}$ produces the number of servings in 4 cakes.

In the diagram solution, each of the 4 cakes is divided into 5 slices and then grouped 3 slices at a time. This can be represented by $(4 \times 5) \div 3 = \frac{20}{3}$ or $6\frac{2}{3}$ servings.

The key idea that underlies the connection between the diagram and the procedure is that the sentence "One serving is $\frac{3}{5}$ of a cake" expresses a relationship between cakes and servings which can also be expressed as "One cake is $\frac{5}{3}$ servings."

It is also possible to justify the commonly taught procedure by calling upon the formal properties of operations.

Consider the set of steps transforming $4 \div \frac{3}{5}$ into $4 \times \frac{5}{3}$:

$$\frac{4}{1} \div \frac{3}{5} = \frac{\frac{4}{1}}{\frac{3}{5}} = \frac{\frac{4}{1} \times \frac{5}{3}}{\frac{3}{5} \times \frac{5}{3}} = \frac{\frac{4}{1} \times \frac{5}{3}}{1} = \frac{4}{1} \times \frac{5}{3}$$

The key idea in the sequence is that multiplying both the numerator ($\frac{4}{1}$) and the denominator ($\frac{3}{5}$) by the same quantity ($\frac{5}{3}$) does not change the value of the expression. Since $\frac{3}{5} \times \frac{5}{3} = 1$, the denominator in the new expression is 1, and so the value of the original division expression is exactly what is in the numerator of the transformed expression $4 \times (\frac{5}{3})$.

SESSION 6

Detailed Agenda

Sharing student-thinking assignments (30 minutes)

Small groups

In the first activity of this session, participants share their writing that describes the mathematical thinking of their own students. Group together participants who used the same curriculum activity. Remind them to read the papers of everyone in their group before discussing any. They should look not just at the particulars of a single classroom, but for ideas that come up in more than one class. Make the groups responsible for timing, being sure that each paper receives attention in the allotted half hour.

Case discussion: Multiplying fractions (55 minutes)

Small groups (30 minutes)

Whole group (25 minutes)

The cases in chapter 6 present issues that arise as students begin to make sense of the operation of multiplication as it applies to fractions. Since their concepts have been developed in the context of whole numbers, students (as well as many teachers) must reconsider the meanings and actions associated with multiplication in this new domain of rational numbers (fractions and decimals). Ideas such as "multiplication makes things bigger" or "multiplication is repeated addition" must be challenged or expanded.

Additionally, the tools participants use to represent multiplication must expand from groups or arrays of discrete objects to representations that allow for non-whole number factors. As participants work on the ideas in this chapter, they will likely find that they must reconsider some of their own assumptions about the nature of multiplication in order to think through what it means to apply this operation to fractions.

Small-group case discussion (30 minutes)

Distribute "Focus Questions: Session 6" and let the group know they will have 30 minutes to work in their small groups.

Focus questions 1 and 2 are based on Henry's case 27. The first question invites participants to examine the idea that with fractions, multiplication cannot be interpreted as repeated addition. Question 2 engages participants in creating story contexts that accommodate multiplication of fractions and decimals. In discussing question 3, based on Ann's case 25, participants will explore the thinking of students as they describe various spans on a clock as a fraction of a fraction, one context for the multiplication of two numbers less than 1.

Focus question 4, based on Sarita's case 26, is a math exploration for participants in which they examine the use of diagrams to represent multiplication of mixed numbers. This foreshadows work that will be the basis for the math activity in Session 8, so if your participants feel their work on this problem is incomplete, let them know there will be another opportunity to work on this concept.

Whole-group case discussion (25 minutes)

Begin the whole-group discussion by having participants share some of the story contexts they created for multiplying two fractions or two decimals. After a few have been offered, ask "How are these different from story contexts that you considered for 3 × 4?" Also ask how their ideas of multiplication have been expanded as a result of thinking about multiplication of fractions and decimals.

If several groups worked with Sarita's case, you may choose to have someone from one of those groups say what they noticed about the connection between the diagrams they drew and multiplication of mixed numbers. If most participants did not work on this question, defer any discussion until Session 8.

Break (15 minutes)

Math activity: Fractions in division (75 minutes)

Small groups (25 minutes)

Whole group (25 minutes)

Small groups (25 minutes)

The math activity for this session focuses on the division of fractions. For most adults this is associated with the phrase "invert and multiply," which describes a procedure for obtaining the answer to a division problem but offers little basis for understanding.

As the participants work through the problems, they should examine how the problem situations fit their conceptions of division and then make the connections between their diagram solutions and the computational procedure. In the discussion of part 1(f), participants should work to resolve the dilemma,

"Why is the answer to the question $6\frac{2}{3}$ when you can see $\frac{2}{5}$ so clearly in the diagram?"

Small-group work (25 minutes)

Distribute "Math Activity: Fractions in Division." Let participants know you will call them together for a whole-group discussion of problem 1, after which they will return to their small groups to work on the remaining problems. As you interact with small groups, ask questions about the connections between the diagram, the operations, and the solution. Possible questions include these:

- How does your diagram represent division by $\frac{3}{5}$?
- What in the diagram corresponds to $\frac{5}{3}$?
- Where is $\frac{20}{3}$ in the diagram?

You should also ask questions to focus attention on the changing unit in this problem:

- What is the name of those two pieces?
- Is there another name you can give them?
- How can the same amount of cake represent 2 different numbers?

Check with the groups to be sure all have discussed Wanda's cake before you begin the whole-group discussion. If some groups need more time to resolve the issues, other groups can go on to the remaining problems.

As you watch the groups work, choose one to present their solution to the whole group. Choose a group whose diagram and solution is representative of most groups' work. If you have seen interesting but idiosyncratic approaches, display and discuss them after the more common solution is articulated.

Whole-group discussion (25 minutes)

Even if it seems most people have an answer to Wanda's cake problem in their small groups, it is worth having a solution displayed and discussed in the whole group. Choose a participant to draw his or her solution on a poster in front of the group, talking through the solution while drawing. Once this solution is explained, ask for additional comments.

The following points should be included in this discussion. These points are not independent of each other, but are different ways to say the same thing:

- If one serving is $\frac{3}{5}$ of a cake, then one cake is $\frac{5}{3}$ of a serving.
- The diagram can be interpreted as $4 \times \frac{5}{3}$ and also $4 \div \frac{3}{5}$.

- In doing the arithmetic $4 \div \frac{3}{5}$, $\frac{20}{3}$ appears. $\frac{20}{3}$ can also be seen in the diagram.

- The "invert and multiply" rule can also be justified by properties of the operations: $4 \div \frac{3}{5}$ can be transformed to a problem with a divisor of 1 by multiplying both 4 and $\frac{3}{5}$ by $\frac{5}{3}$; that is, the problem can be rewritten as $4 \div \frac{3}{5} = (4 \times \frac{5}{3}) \div (\frac{3}{5} \times \frac{5}{3}) = 4 \times \frac{5}{3} \div 1$.

- Examining the units is another way to justify the answer. 4 cakes $\div \frac{3}{5}$ cake/serving means 4 cakes $\times \frac{5}{3}$ servings/cake yields $\frac{20}{3}$ or $6\frac{2}{3}$ serving.

Small groups, continuing work (25 minutes)

Have participants return to their small groups and continue working with the remaining problems in the math activity. Problems 2 and 3 are similar in structure to Wanda's cake problem. Problem 2, taken from a case in chapter 7, has a whole-number answer, and problem 3, like Wanda's cake problem, does not have a whole-number answer.

Questions 4 and 5 are linked together because they both represent $2\frac{2}{3} \div \frac{2}{3}$; however, they offer very different division contexts. Frequently, participants solve problem 5 without reference to division, and they have to work to see it as an example of division. Question 6 invites participants to examine the similarities and differences between problems 4 and 5. See "Maxine's Journal," lines 208 to 256, for an example of this discussion.

As the end of the time approaches, let participants know they will be writing about their own mathematical ideas for homework and suggest they use that opportunity to explore these problems further. If many of the groups completed their work on the remaining problems and time permits, you might have each group display one problem and their solution on a poster. Then suggest that everyone use the last few minutes of class to look at the range of posters.

Homework and exit cards (5 minutes)

Whole group

If you decided to assign the reading of chapter 8, "Highlights of Related Research," in sections throughout the seminar, rather than all at once at the end of Session 7, it is appropriate to assign sections 5 and 6 for reading homework now. Remind participants that although they will not be discussing this reading at the next meeting, these sections are pertinent to the work of the past two sessions and thus make useful reading at this point in the seminar.

As the first session ends, distribute index cards and pose these exit-card questions:

1. What has it been like to receive responses to your writing?

2. Is there anything you would like to tell the facilitators about this session?

Before the next session...

In preparation for the next session, read participants' writing about their students' thinking and write a response to each participant. For more information, see the section in "Maxine's Journal" on responding to the sixth homework. Make copies of both the papers and your response for your files before returning the work.

SESSION 6

MAKING MEANING FOR OPERATIONS

Focus Questions: Chapter 6

1. In his case 27, Henry states that "multiplication is not just repeated addition." What does he mean? What else is it?

2. Henry also indicates that it is difficult for his students to make sense of $\frac{1}{2} \times \frac{1}{4}$ or 0.6×0.5. We have been exploring the use of contexts and story situations to interpret arithmetic expressions. What problem situations would match these arithmetic expressions? Can you make more than one for each expression?

3. In Ann's case 25, Ferris, Liam, and Midori all use expressions containing what Ann calls "a portion of a portion equivalency." Explain the thinking of each student. What is correct about it? How does it connect with multiplication of fractions?

4. In the seminar, you have been drawing diagrams to represent multiplication involving fractions between 0 and 1. Sarita's students in case 26 also approach multiplication of mixed numbers with a diagram solution. What does Basimah figure out and show Sarita in the diagram after line 193? Try the same approach with some other pairs of numbers. Will it always work?

SESSION 6

MAKING MEANING FOR OPERATIONS

Math Activity: Fractions in Division

1. Wanda really likes cake. She decides that one serving should be $\frac{3}{5}$ of a cake. She has 4 cakes, all the same size. How many servings does she have?

   (a) Draw a diagram to model this situation.

   (b) What answer does your diagram indicate?

   (c) Solve the problem using an arithmetic sentence.

   (d) How does your arithmetic sentence match your diagram?

   (e) After 6 servings are eaten, how much cake is left?

   (f) For the division problem $4 \div \frac{3}{5}$, why is the answer $6\frac{2}{3}$ rather than $6\frac{2}{5}$?

Solve each of the following problems with a diagram. Write an arithmetic sentence that matches the situation. What connections do you see between the diagram and the arithmetic?

2. You are giving a party. You have 6 pints of ice cream for the party. If you serve $\frac{3}{4}$ pint of ice cream to each person, how many people can you serve?

3. I am making a soup that requires $\frac{5}{6}$ cup of green beans per person. If I have picked 3 cups of green beans from my garden, how many people will I be able to serve?

4. I eat $\frac{2}{3}$ cup of cottage cheese for lunch each day. I have $2\frac{2}{3}$ cups of cottage cheese in my refrigerator. How long will it last me?

5. I put $2\frac{2}{3}$ gallons of gas into my empty lawn mower. I notice it is now $\frac{2}{3}$ full. What is the capacity of the gas tank?

6. How are problems 4 and 5 the same? How are they different?

Session 6 Detailed Agenda

SESSION 6

MAKING MEANING FOR OPERATIONS

Seventh Homework

Reading assignment: Casebook chapter 7

In the casebook, read chapter 7, "Expanding Ideas About Division in the Context of Fractions," including the introductory text and cases 28 and 29. Use the questions posed in the introduction of the casebook to guide your reading.

Writing assignment: Pursuing a mathematical question

This assignment is about the math you are learning in the seminar, not about the math learning of your students. Think about the math work you have done and choose a topic to write about.

You may wish to continue thinking about the same topic you wrote about at the end of Session 4. If you choose to do that, reread both what you wrote then and the response you received from your facilitator, then explain how you are thinking about this topic now. Include examples to show what you have figured out and what you are still trying to sort out.

You may also choose to write about a different math idea. In that case, explain how you thought about this idea previously, what makes sense to you now, and what aspect of the idea are you still working on.

Session 6
Taking portions of portions, or multiplying fractions

Maxine's Journal

April 9

We started the sixth session by sharing the student-thinking assignments participants had written for homework and then returned to our work on fractions. Although the remainder of the session was presented as two different activities, it really seemed that we spent the entire time on the same thing. Whether we were discussing the cases in chapter 6 or exploring the math activity, everyone was working on her or his own understanding of fractions. And there was hardly a lull. The energy was high the entire time.

Sharing student-thinking assignments

Several teachers had based their assignments on the activity from the *Navigations* series that they had analyzed in the last session; others gave their students an activity from one of the cases, or something from their own curriculum. If participants used the same activity, I grouped them together; otherwise I grouped them by grade level. After half an hour, I collected their work and we regrouped for the case discussion. I'm looking forward to reading their assignments.

Case discussion: Multiplying fractions

As participants began discussing the chapter 6 cases in their small groups, I saw that some of the issues from last session's math activity were reemerging in this context. Nadra immediately brought her group to Henry's case 27, "What I Want My Students to Understand About Multiplication." She focused on his statement, "Multiplication does not always make things bigger."

"OK," Nadra was saying to her partners, "why do you say that $\frac{1}{4}$ of $\frac{1}{2}$ is multiplication? What makes it multiplication?"

Camisha said, "What about this for a word problem? *A board measures $\frac{1}{2}$ meter, and needs to be cut into 4 equal pieces. How long is each piece?* Is that $\frac{1}{4} \times \frac{1}{2}$?"

Nadra said, "That seems like $\frac{1}{2} \div 4$ to me."

Beatrice said, "But I think that's the point. $\frac{1}{4}$ of $\frac{1}{2}$ is the same as $\frac{1}{2} \div 4$. Each piece is one-fourth of the whole board. So it's $\frac{1}{4} \times \frac{1}{2}$."

In response to focus question 2, Elspeth, Marina, and Dofi showed me the word problems they made for 0.6 × 0.5. Dofi said, "I walk half a mile, and for six-tenths of the walk I listen to music. For what distance do I listen to music?"

Elspeth added, "We also thought about what it was like with the numbers reversed: I walk six-tenths of a mile and listen to music half the way. We drew it both ways on the number line. They really seem different, even though the answer is the same."

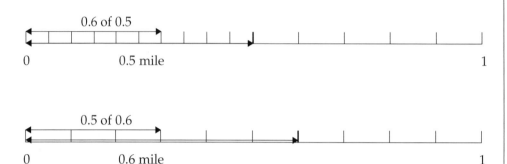

In another group, Maalika, An-Chi, and Gaye were looking at Sarita's case 26, "Multiplication of Mixed Numbers," and discussing the rectangle the students had used to solve $2\frac{3}{4} \times 3\frac{2}{3}$. Maalika said, "Let's go back to the other diagrams we've drawn. What if we used rectangles this way, instead? Would our diagrams look so different?"

Joseph, Labeeba, and Odette were looking at Ann's case 25, with the clock faces. They worked through the arithmetic expressions that represented each of the ways the students saw the portions. Odette said, "Let's look at 3 o'clock. Liam said it shows $\frac{1}{6}$ plus $\frac{1}{2}$ of $\frac{1}{6}$." She wrote down $\frac{1}{6} + (\frac{1}{2} \times \frac{1}{6})$. Then she continued, "Ferris calls it $\frac{1}{2}$ of $\frac{1}{2}$," and she wrote out $\frac{1}{2} \times \frac{1}{2}$. Odette concluded, "So that means $\frac{1}{6} + (\frac{1}{2} \times \frac{1}{6}) = \frac{1}{2} \times \frac{1}{2}$." She quickly did the arithmetic: $\frac{1}{6} + \frac{1}{12} = \frac{2}{12} + \frac{1}{12} = \frac{3}{12} = \frac{1}{4}$. "Yep, it comes out right."

Sarita's case in particular also captured the attention of the middle school teachers. Spencer said, "You can see that you need to multiply the whole numbers (2×3), then each whole number times a fraction ($2 \times \frac{2}{3}$ and $3 \times \frac{3}{4}$), then multiply the fractions ($\frac{3}{4} \times \frac{2}{3}$), and then add them all up."

Celeste commented, "It's like multiplying binomials. You can see in the diagram how the distributive property is applied."

Cathleen said, "If your kids can't multiply fractions but they can add the pieces, they could solve problems this way."

Karran asked, "But is it really efficient?"

Celeste said, "It might not be efficient if students never get past it. But it seems to me that these diagrams can help students figure out what's going on. That's what Sarita says, too. On line 197, she says, 'My goal is that the students, at some point, will develop an arithmetic algorithm from their picture.' Then she shows two algorithms you can derive from it."

Spencer said, "Right. There's the way I was just talking about, finding partial products. But you can also see what happens when you convert the mixed numerals to improper fractions. You can see why it works to multiply the numerators and multiply the denominators."

Whole-group case discussion

When I brought the whole group together, I wanted to examine the diagram from Sarita's case, but I first wanted to do some preliminary work. I reminded participants of some of the representations of multiplication we saw back in Session 2. "Remember, we saw how rectangles can represent multiplication of whole numbers. For example, this rectangle illustrates $3 \times 4 = 12$ and $4 \times 3 = 12$."

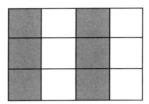

Then I said, "Let's look together at a rectangle that would illustrate $\frac{1}{2} \times \frac{1}{2}$. Just take a minute to draw it yourself."

After a moment, Beatrice volunteered to come to the board to show us. She drew this picture:

She explained, "In order to show $\frac{1}{2}$, I drew a line and marked off half, and then I drew a line perpendicular and marked off half of that. So now I have a square that's $\frac{1}{2} \times \frac{1}{2}$. But I looked at that and realized it doesn't show $\frac{1}{4}$. So I then drew in the square that's 1×1."

Beatrice then finished her diagram and concluded, "The small square is $\frac{1}{4}$ of the large square, which is 1×1. So this shows that $\frac{1}{2}$ unit × $\frac{1}{2}$ unit = $\frac{1}{4}$ square unit."

Nadra let out a long, "Ohhhhh." When I asked her what she had seen, she said, "I need to think about this some more. But I'm starting to get why this is multiplication."

After that, we worked through the fractional part of Sarita's problem: $\frac{3}{4} \times \frac{2}{3}$. Based on what Beatrice had done, we soon came up with a diagram that looked like this:

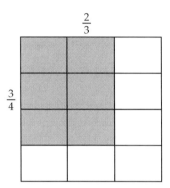

Spencer said, "Right. Let's say each side of the large square is 1 inch. The picture shows that $\frac{2}{3}$ of an inch times $\frac{3}{4}$ of an inch is $\frac{6}{12}$ of a square inch."

Then we worked through the original problem: $3\frac{2}{3} \times 2\frac{3}{4}$.

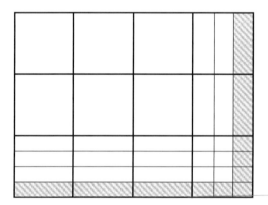

Together, we first found the four subproducts:

3×2 yields 6 square units

$\frac{2}{3} \times 2$ yields 4 parts, each $\frac{1}{3}$ of a square unit, or $\frac{4}{3}$ square units

$3 \times \frac{3}{4}$ yields 9 parts, each part $\frac{1}{4}$ of a square unit, or $\frac{9}{4}$ square units

$\frac{2}{3} \times \frac{3}{4}$ yields 6 parts, each part $\frac{1}{12}$ of a square unit, or $\frac{6}{12}$ square unit

Then we added the subproducts:

$6 + \frac{4}{3} + \frac{9}{4} + \frac{6}{12} = 9 + \frac{1}{3} + \frac{1}{4} + \frac{6}{12} = 9\frac{13}{12} = 10\frac{1}{12}$ square units

Finally, we looked at the figure on page 115 of the casebook to see how it illustrates another strategy for multiplying mixed numbers: $\frac{11}{3} \times \frac{11}{4} = \frac{121}{12} = 10\frac{1}{12}$.

Math activity: Fractions in division

When participants sat down to work on the math activity sheet after break, they quickly became involved in the problems. The feeling in the room was one of confidence. As I chatted with small groups, they said that they were working on the same issues they had been struggling with in the last session, but now they felt in control. And that made me feel good.

Some groups did every problem; others stayed with the first. But all of them knew they were learning something important about fractions.

However, there was a bit of tension with Cathleen. For example, her group had drawn a picture to illustrate $4 \div \frac{3}{5}$, based on Wanda's cake problem. Cathleen had already done the arithmetic: $4 \div \frac{3}{5} = 4 \times \frac{5}{3} = \frac{20}{3} = 6\frac{2}{3}$. She rankled when I asked her to find $\frac{5}{3}$ in the diagram. She said, "I am too frustrated. I can't do it now." As I walked away, I heard her tell the rest of the group, "There is no $\frac{5}{3}$ in the drawing; it's just in the math!"

I've come to the conclusion that Cathleen is so anxious about being exposed as not knowing that it's hard for her to let much in. Or maybe she is letting things in, but not when I first pose a question. After all, she did seem pretty intrigued by Sarita's diagram in case 26 and thought about what diagrams like that might offer her students. Maybe I just shouldn't push her.

Throughout the seminar, though, I've felt that I needed to be watchful that Cathleen wasn't disrupting other participants' learning. Especially since many elementary school teachers cede authority to middle school teachers, I've been careful about who is placed with Cathleen in small groups. Today she was with the other middle school teachers, and by now Karran, Spencer, and Celeste can work around Cathleen.

After everyone had worked on the first problem, I called a whole-group discussion. That problem tells us that Wanda has 4 cakes, and she considers a serving to be $\frac{3}{5}$ of a cake. The question is, How many servings are there? Everyone had been able to solve the problem, but they were surprised to discover that they had different ways to explain it.

The feel of this discussion was actually quite amazing—there was so much excitement, there were times I felt that I needed to control the mob! Other teachers would start talking before the current speaker was finished, rushing to the front to draw pictures on the board.

As I sit here now, I can't write down everything that was said, nor can I recapture the way everyone was talking at once. But I'll try to set out some of the major points.

Labeeba started the conversation, drawing the following diagram:

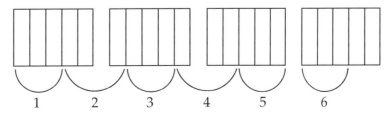

She explained, "Wanda has 4 cakes, and a serving is $\frac{3}{5}$ of a cake. Now, to think about this problem, my group said that a slice of cake is $\frac{1}{5}$, and a serving is $\frac{3}{5}$. We needed to do that so we could keep straight what we were talking about. We cut each cake into 5 slices, so now we have 20 slices. Since a serving is 3 slices, we took out groups of 3, and got 6 servings."

Odette, who had been in Labeeba's group, finished the problem for her. "Once you take out those 6 servings, there are 2 slices of cake left. You can call that amount 2 slices, or $\frac{2}{5}$ of a cake, or $\frac{2}{3}$ of a serving!"

Andrea said her group created a different diagram but came to the same conclusions. Her diagram looked like this:

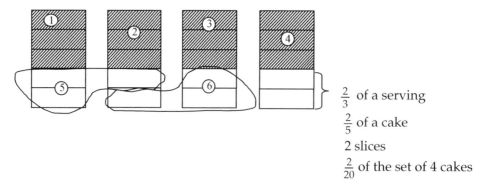

$\frac{2}{3}$ of a serving

$\frac{2}{5}$ of a cake

2 slices

$\frac{2}{20}$ of the set of 4 cakes

I wasn't sure what they saw as the difference between Andrea's and Labeeba's diagrams, but some participants felt that Andrea's was clearer.

Karran then came to the board and said, "My group did it that way, too. When I look at that, for the first time I can make sense of 'invert and multiply'! Look, to do $4 \div \frac{3}{5}$, you say $4 \times \frac{5}{3}$, and that's $\frac{20}{3}$ or $20 \div 3$. You take the 4 cakes and multiply by 5 servings each, and that gives you 20. In other words, you take the 4 and multiply it by the denominator. Then you divide by the numerator, you divide by 3, to see how many servings."

Carol said, "When you just do it with numbers, you get $6\frac{2}{3}$. Why is it $6\frac{2}{3}$ instead of $6\frac{2}{5}$?"

Odette came back to her point. "When you look at the leftovers, you can name it 2 or $\frac{2}{3}$ or $\frac{2}{5}$, depending on what you're counting. The answer $6\frac{2}{3}$ means 6 whole servings and $\frac{2}{3}$ of a serving. That's what the numbers give you. But you could say 6 whole servings and $\frac{2}{5}$ of a cake left over, or 6 whole servings and 2 slices left over."

The discussion continued, and I remember that most of the teachers (even Cathleen) spoke up at one time or another, though I can't remember exactly what was said. There were also lots of times when someone was up at the board talking to about half the groups, while the rest were talking to partners, working on some other point that had come up, or themselves running to the board to share an insight.

Near the end of the discussion, An-Chi looked as if she were about to burst. "I just saw something. Oh, my gosh. Earlier, in my small group, we talked a lot about how $10 \times \frac{1}{2}$ and $10 \div 2$ are the same thing. And then we talked about how 10×2 and $10 \div \frac{1}{2}$ are the same thing, too. So now I'm looking at this and thinking, what about $4 \div \frac{3}{5}$? Is it the same as $4 \times \frac{5}{3}$? Well, we know it gives you the same answer because of 'invert and multiply.' But when we go back to Labeeba's and Andrea's diagrams, we see it. You ask, how many servings are in each cake? There's a whole serving and $\frac{2}{3}$ of a serving, so there are $\frac{5}{3}$ servings in each cake. To find out how many servings there are if you have 4 cakes, you multiply 4 times the number of servings in a cake: $4 \times \frac{5}{3}$."

One satisfying aspect of this discussion was that the teachers were not content merely to find the answer to the problem. They used the problem as a context to explore mathematical connections, including the general algorithms for solving problems like these. Another was that they were also bringing into play many mathematical issues they had been working on in the last few sessions.

At this point, I asked participants to get back into their small groups. I said, "We've had a lot of new insights from working on Wanda's cake problem. Now I want you to look at some other problems to see how the same ideas appear with different numbers."

As participants got to work, many of them felt satisfied—and powerful—to be able to make sense of "invert and multiply" in the different contexts. In problem 2, where each person gets $\frac{3}{4}$ pint of ice cream, Dofi said, "OK, that means each pint serves $\frac{4}{3}$ portions."

Their diagram for problem 3 (3 cups of green beans, each portion is $\frac{5}{6}$ cup) showed that there are 3 whole portions and $\frac{3}{6}$ of a cup remaining. Mariana declared, "That's enough for $\frac{3}{5}$ of a portion. And that's what the arithmetic says: $3 \div \frac{5}{6} = 3\frac{3}{5}$."

Two of the small groups got to problems 4 and 5:

4. I eat $\frac{2}{3}$ cup of cottage cheese for lunch each day. I have $2\frac{2}{3}$ cups of cottage cheese in my refrigerator. How long will it last me?

5. I put $2\frac{2}{3}$ gallons of gas into my empty lawn mower. I notice that it is now $\frac{2}{3}$ full. What is the capacity of the gas tank?

They reached the same answer, 4, for both problems, but it was driving them crazy. The two problems used all the same numbers, but the problems were so different! What was going on?

The two groups were sitting next to each other, and as they dug into the dilemma, they essentially became a group of eight, sometimes breaking apart into pairs, threes, or fours as they worked.

The issue with these problems is that they represent the rational number analog to dealing and grouping. I suggested that the participants try changing the numbers in the problem to whole numbers to see what it feels like then:

4. I eat 2 cups of cottage cheese for lunch each day. I have 6 cups of cottage cheese in my refrigerator. How long will that last me?

5. I have several identical lawn mowers and have 6 gallons of gas. That fills 2 tanks. What is the capacity of one tank?

Unfortunately, it didn't help that they had to change the wording of problem 5 to make it make sense for whole numbers.

After a while, Spencer declared that he saw problem 5 as multiplication with a missing factor. "It says $\frac{2}{3}$ of the gas tank is $2\frac{2}{3}$ gallons. That means $\frac{2}{3}x$ equals $2\frac{2}{3}$, which is $\frac{8}{3}$." He wrote down $\frac{2}{3}x = \frac{8}{3}$. Then he used the steps he knew to solve for x: $\frac{8}{3} \times \frac{3}{2} = 4$.

Celeste pointed out that whether you initially write the equation as $\frac{2}{3}x = \frac{8}{3}$ or $\frac{8}{3} \div \frac{2}{3} = x$, the next step is to multiply $\frac{8}{3} \times \frac{3}{2}$. She said, "I wonder if that's a way to think about why this is a division problem." Celeste had been thinking alone, drawing a diagram, which she now shared with her group.

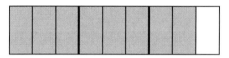

She explained, "Since the shaded parts represent $\frac{2}{3}$ of the tank, I can see how much $\frac{1}{3}$ of the tank."

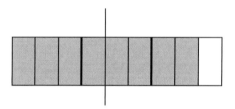

Celeste explained, "That shows me $\frac{1}{3}$ of the tank is $1\frac{1}{3}$ gallons."

Gaye said, "That makes sense. We know that $\frac{1}{2}$ of $2\frac{2}{3}$ is $1\frac{1}{3}$."

Celeste continued, "So to make up a whole tank, I have to add on $\frac{1}{3}$ of the tank. Add $1\frac{1}{3}$ gallons to $2\frac{2}{3}$ gallon. I can combine that $\frac{2}{3}$ of a gallon with the $\frac{1}{3}$. That gives me another whole gallon."

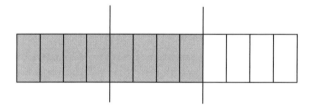

Celeste concluded, "This diagram shows me how I start with $2\frac{2}{3}$ gallons, divide by the numerator of $\frac{2}{3}$ to find how many gallons are in $\frac{1}{3}$ of the tank, and then multiply by the denominator of $\frac{2}{3}$ to find out the capacity of the whole tank."

Other members of the group of eight were watching intently as Celeste went through her explanation.

I asked, "Does that help you see this problem as $2\frac{2}{3} \div \frac{2}{3}$?"

Celeste said, "I need to think about this some more."

Spencer said, "No. I still see it as multiplication with a missing factor."

Then Celeste asked, "Isn't that one way to think about what division is—multiplication with a missing factor?"

Elspeth said, "I don't yet follow everything Celeste did. I'm going to have to work on this at home."

When it was time to leave, I told the whole seminar group that this session had been a joy. I also acknowledged that even though everyone felt good about the progress we had all made, I wasn't assuming that everyone had "gotten it all." I wanted to communicate that the experience of "getting it" is important in doing mathematics, but it's often a temporary feeling. The ideas build, and so if you stay with an idea, no matter how much you feel you've got it, after a while you'll discover more questions. And even with a single idea, "getting it" can come and go; it can be a tenuous grip. Besides, I'm sure everyone in the room knows that even though they had made progress, they hadn't been able to think through every idea that had been presented. In particular, they might want to spend some more time thinking about the connections between problems 4 and 5.

Homework and exit cards

I distributed the homework assignment and explained to participants that, for the next session, they would write about the mathematics *they* are learning. I emphasized that I didn't want them to write about their students' learning, about their teaching, or their overall reflections of the course.

I explained, "After the final session, I will ask about what this course has meant to you. For now, I want you to write about a specific mathematical issue you've been working on. Has there been a math activity you found particularly challenging? What did you learn from it? Is there a case for which you had to work especially hard to think through the mathematics? You might write about how your understanding of multiplication of fractions has changed—or even, what multiplication means. What have you learned from writing word problems or drawing diagrams? What are you still trying to figure out about division?"

I gave these examples of what participants might write about because, when I have taught this seminar before, some participants interpreted the task as writing general reflections on what they have learned about mathematics or about the teaching and learning of mathematics. I want this homework assignment to be an opportunity to think through a particular mathematical idea.

Because I allowed the last math activity to run over the allotted time, we didn't have time for exit cards. I am sorry not to have them. I always like to have some indication of how each participant is leaving the session—even if my impression is that all is going well. After all, there may have been one or two individuals who felt left out of the enthusiasm.

Responding to the sixth homework

April 12

For this student-thinking assignment, many of the lower-grade teachers looked at their students' ideas about subtraction. A major theme was that some of the problems they gave their students could be solved by subtraction or by finding a missing addend. Some teachers had their students work on the "Parking Lot" problem from *Navigations*; others gave the stickers problem from Jody's case 5, back in chapter 1 of the casebook.

Most of the higher-grade teachers gave their students a fractions problem. Three of them, including Cathleen, asked their students to work on a problem from the Session 5 math activity. I'm including Cathleen's writing in my journal.

Cathleen

I posed this question: "Maura walks $\frac{1}{2}$ mile in an hour. How many hours will it take her to walk 6 miles?" My students looked at me with very puzzled expressions.

I had my students work independently on the problem, allowing them to think and draw for a while. I noticed that the majority of them multiplied the 6 (from the 6 miles) by 2 (they told me that they took 2 from the $\frac{1}{2}$ mile) to get 12 hours. With their pictures, this made sense to them. But several other students had different thoughts.

Tamara stated that $\frac{1}{2}$ of 6 is 3, so it would take 3 hours for Maura to travel. Her logic was incorrect, but she is right that $\frac{1}{2}$ of 6 is 3. To Tamara, this made good sense.

Cindy drew the following picture.

Cindy wrote under her picture that she took half of the 6 miles (drawing 6 stars to represent the 6 miles) and then divided them in half. She said that it would take Maura 3 hours to walk the 6 miles.

Matt wrote "$6 \times \frac{1}{2} = 3$" at the top of his paper. Matt struggles in math and has even more difficulty explaining his work. He seems to either know it or not know it. I asked how he knew to multiply, and he said that he didn't know, except that it just felt right.

When looking back on this assignment, I see that my students are still having great difficulty in thinking through their process. I don't believe that it's just because they haven't had to think like this in math. They don't want to think on their own. I'm not sure at this point how to get them to think outside the box.

Especially since Cathleen has been very touchy in the seminar, I needed to be careful in my response to her. First, it's important to praise her. Second, I wanted to address her question and point her in a productive direction. And third, I want her to understand better how diagrams can serve us as we work on mathematics problems, especially those involving fractions.

Dear Cathleen,

I am pleased that you are trying out problems from the seminar with your students. This problem about someone walking 6 miles at $\frac{1}{2}$ mile per hour is a good one. Do I understand correctly that most of your students determined correctly that it would take 12 hours, but three of your students said it would take 3 hours? They came to that conclusion by taking $\frac{1}{2}$ of 6.

Did your students have an opportunity to talk to one another? Sometimes if students are asked to discuss their thinking in small groups, it gets them past the impulse to rush to an answer and, instead, to actually think about what the problem is asking and reason about it. Certainly your three students know that $\frac{1}{2}$ of 6 equals 3. Is there a way that their classmates can help them recognize that this doesn't address the question they were asked?

At times it's useful to pose questions that help students recognize a contradiction. For example, what would they say if Maura has to walk 6 miles and it takes 1 hour for her to walk 2 miles? Can they see that the answer to that question is 3 hours? Does it make sense for the same trip to take the same amount of time, whether she walks slowly or more quickly?

Often, by the time students get to middle school, they have dropped the expectation that mathematics should make sense. That gives the teacher an additional challenge: to help students reconnect with their capacity—and expectation—to apply their own reasoning in math class.

One of the things we have seen in our MMO seminar is that visual representations—often in the form of diagrams that map out the relationships in a problem—help people to reason about those relationships to solve the problem. In the process, they also come to recognize how the operations behave, including why the calculation algorithms work the way they do.

But in order to use diagrams effectively, we need to be able to think about how a diagram matches the problem. Whereas Cindy has drawn a diagram of $\frac{1}{2}$ of 6, her diagram does not show how the 6 miles and $\frac{1}{2}$ mile in the problem are related.

You didn't include in your paper much about the thinking of the students who correctly solved the problem. I imagine that some of them made a diagram that looked something like this.

```
 2 hours  2 hours  2 hours  2 hours  2 hours  2 hours
├────┬────┬────┬────┬────┬────┤
 1 mile   1 mile   1 mile   1 mile   1 mile   1 mile
```

This diagram shows a line that represents 6 miles, divided into lengths of $\frac{1}{2}$ mile. The diagram also shows that since it takes 1 hour to go $\frac{1}{2}$ mile, it takes 2 hours to go 1 mile. Once these relationships are established, it becomes clear that the trip will take 12 hours.

Spencer also gave the same problem to his class, and one of his students drew a diagram that looked like this to represent $6 \div \frac{1}{2} = 12$:

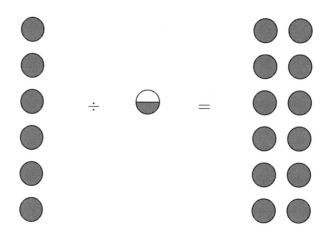

Although this student has come up with an appropriate arithmetic sentence to match the problem, the diagram does not capture the relationships of the problem. It doesn't demonstrate how any of the quantities relate to each other; nor does it give any information about what the operation of division does. If each circle is supposed to stand for 1 mile, then it seems that the answer is 12 miles, which is not related to the problem.

What I'm trying to say is that drawing diagrams is not merely a crutch to solving problems. Rather, in creating a diagram, one must think through how the different quantities in a problem relate. That relationship leads to the solution to the problem. The diagram can also help us understand more generally the relationships implied by the operation. Eventually, we can apply the operation with a sense of those relationships, without having to actually draw a diagram. Sometimes we hold those pictures in our head.

Cathleen, I appreciate the challenges you face in your teaching, and I appreciate your willingness to bring new ideas from the seminar to try out with your students.

Maxine

SESSION 7

MAKING MEANING FOR OPERATIONS

Expanding Ideas About Division in the Context of Fractions

Mathematical Themes

- Problems involving multiplication and division by positive rational numbers require contexts that allow for the objects to be broken into parts.

- Diagram solutions for problems involving division of fractions can reveal the relationships among the operations; that is, a division of fractions problem can be solved by calling on addition, subtraction, or multiplication.

DVD for Session 7	Individuals and pairs	10 minutes
	Whole group	25 minutes
Chapter 7 case discussion	Small groups	35 minutes
	Whole group	30 minutes
Break		15 minutes
Math activity: Operating with positive rational numbers, part 1	Small groups	40 minutes
	Whole group	20 minutes
Homework and exit cards	Whole group	5 minutes

Background Preparation

Read

- the casebook, chapter 7
- the detailed agenda for Session 7
- "Maxine's Journal" for Session 7

Work through

- the focus questions for Session 7
- the math activity: Operating with positive rational numbers, part 1

Preview

- the DVD, Session 7

Materials

Duplicate

- "Focus Questions: Chapter 7"
- "Math Activity: Operating with Positive Rational Numbers, Part 1"
- "Eighth Homework"

Obtain

- graph paper
- interlocking cubes
- index cards

How Can We Interpret $\frac{3}{4} \times \frac{1}{2}$?

The facilitator note for Session 2 examined situations that are modeled by multiplication and division with whole numbers. What changes when the problem includes numbers less than 1? In the facilitator note for Session 8, this idea will be extended to include multiplication with rational numbers greater than 1.

Consider these situations:

a. I run a 3-mile route when I exercise. I did this 5 times this week. How many miles did I run?

b. I run a route that is $\frac{3}{4}$ of a mile. This week I ran 5 times. How many miles did I run?

c. I run a route that is $\frac{3}{4}$ of a mile. Today I was interrupted and ran only $\frac{1}{2}$ of the route. How many miles did I run?

These arithmetic statements match the situations:

a. $3 \times 5 = 15$ miles

b. $\frac{3}{4} \times 5 = \frac{15}{4}$ miles

c. $\frac{3}{4} \times \frac{1}{2} = \frac{3}{8}$ mile

In each case, the first factor establishes the length of a single run. The second factor indicates how many times or what portion of the run takes place. The product reports the total number of miles run. Assuming the first factor is positive (as it must be in these contexts), when the second factor is greater than 1, the total number of miles is greater than the length of a single run. When the second factor is less than 1, the total number of miles is less than the length of a single run.

How Are the Two Types of Division Seen in Problems with Fractions?

A consequence of the relationship between multiplication and division is that a given multiplication situation produces two different division statements, depending on which of the two factors is missing. Consider a situation involving whole numbers:

I run a 3-mile route when I exercise. I did this 5 times this week. How many miles did I run?

There are two related division situations:

a. This week I ran 15 miles. I run a 3-mile route when I exercise. How many times did I run?

b. I ran 15 miles this week. I ran the same route 5 different times. How long is my route?

In situation (a), the quotient 5 is the number of runs; in situation (b), the quotient 3 is the length of one run.

Session 7 Detailed Agenda

> What changes when the numbers are not whole? Consider, again, this multiplication context:
>
> I run a $\frac{3}{4}$-mile route. Today I was interrupted and ran only $\frac{1}{2}$ of the route. How far did I run?
>
> The corresponding division problems are these:
>
> c. I ran $\frac{3}{8}$ of a mile today. My usual route is $\frac{3}{4}$ of a mile. How much of the route did I run?
>
> d. I ran $\frac{3}{8}$ of a mile today. I ran only $\frac{1}{2}$ my usual route. How long is my usual route?
>
> In situation (c), the quotient $\frac{1}{2}$ indicates the fraction of my route that I ran today. In situation (d), the quotient $\frac{3}{4}$ indicates the length of a single run.
>
> The mathematics of the situations involving $\frac{3}{4}$ and $\frac{1}{2}$ is not different from that of the situations involving the whole numbers 3 and 5. However, the language that is used to describe the situation may shift from "number of" to "portion of," "part of," or "fraction of" when the numbers are less than 1.
>
> In the facilitator note for Session 8, this idea will be extended to include multiplication with rational numbers greater than 1.

Session 7

Detailed Agenda

Viewing the DVD: Dividing by a Fraction (35 minutes)

Individuals and pairs (10 minutes)

Whole group (25 mninutes)

Creating a story problem (10 minutes)

Before showing the DVD segment, ask participants to write a story situation for $4 \div \frac{3}{5}$. Give them 3 or 4 minutes to think and work by themselves, then ask them to share their story with someone.

Solicit two or three story situations for the whole group to examine. Ask, "What did you have to consider to write such a problem?" See "Maxine's Journal," lines 9–43, for an example of this discussion.

Viewing and analyzing the DVD (25 minutes)

In this video clip, an interviewer is talking with an eighth grader, Rachel, as she works to create a story problem for the arithmetic expression $4 \div \frac{3}{5}$. Rachel reasons out the solution to be $6\frac{2}{5}$. She is able to create two reasonable contexts, one in which the domain is discrete (her story allows only whole-number answers) and one in which it is continuous (her second context allows answers of any positive number). However, Rachel does not see that her answer is in error.

Recommend that participants take notes about Rachel's thinking as they watch the DVD. After the segment is over, first ask questions to establish the two different contexts that Rachel created. Then ask more general questions such as these:

- What ideas are solid for Rachel?

- Explain why her answer seems reasonable to her.

- What is she missing?

- What questions might you ask, or what math tasks might you pose, to help this student continue to work on these ideas?

Case discussion: Fractions and division (65 minutes)

Small groups (35 minutes)

Whole group (30 minutes)

In the two cases in chapter 7, students are working on problems that involve division of fractions. They solve these with a variety of methods; some use addition, some subtraction, some multiplication; and some students rely on diagrams or models that help them act out the problem situations. As participants work to understand the student approaches, they will have to consider what images the students formed that led them to their particular views of the solution.

The second case, "Stretching Elastic," presents a situation of division (or multiplication) that can feel different from the repeated subtraction (or repeated addition) model. You might suggest that participants think about a similar problem with whole numbers to become familiar with the problem context before discussing the focus questions. For additional information on the elastic problem, see "Maxine's Journal," lines 165 to 201 and 440 to 512.

Small-group case discussion (35 minutes)

Organize the participants into small groups and distribute "Focus Questions: Session 7." Question 1, based on Sarita's case 28, invites participants to analyze the justifications students offer for their methods of solving the problem about serving $\frac{3}{4}$ pint of ice cream per person when they have 6 pints of ice cream. To help participants follow the logic of the thinking and highlight connections between the various operations and division, ask questions like these: "Given the expression and justification offered in each case, how do you think the student actually solved the story problem? In what ways does this expression match the action in the story situation?"

Some of the student solutions illustrate confusion. Ask, "What is right in the thinking here? In what ways do you see correct and incorrect thinking intertwined? What questions might you ask a student to sort this out?" You may also need to remind participants that their thinking does not need to agree with Sarita's.

Focus question 2 is based on Selena's case 29, the problem about stretching elastic. This problem leads participants into an examination of division of fractions. They will need to sort out the difference between making groups of size $5\frac{1}{2}$ and making $5\frac{1}{2}$ groups. Focus their conversation on the diagrams that the student groups create.

Whole-group case discussion
(30 minutes)

To prepare for whole-group discussion of Sarita's case 28, small groups need to have established the reasonableness of the four solutions Sarita has collected in the first box. Then focus the whole-group discussion on justifications she has placed in the second box. Ask, "What is right in the student thinking? What ideas appear to be missing?" Once those justifications have been analyzed, turn to the questions the teacher poses near the end of the case by asking, "What characterizes a given problem as division by a fraction?"

If participants have discussed the "Stretching Elastic" case in small groups, include that case in the whole-group discussion. Ask how this situation is different from the ice-cream situation in case 28. Then ask if the students approached the problem differently because of that difference.

Break
(15 minutes)

Math activity: Operating with positive rational numbers, part 1
(60 minutes)

Small groups (40 minutes)

Whole group (20 minutes)

This math activity begins work that continues in Session 8. Participants find sums, differences, products, and quotients of pairs of numbers; first with whole numbers, then fractions less than 1, then mixed numbers expressed as fractions and as decimals. They examine how their thinking changes or remains the same as the kinds of numbers operated on change. In their investigation, participants are asked to develop story contexts, visual representations, and also to complete computational procedures. For Session 7, participants work with whole numbers and fractions less than 1.

Small-group math work
(40 minutes)

Distribute the handout "Math Activity: Operating with Positive Rational Numbers, Part 1." Ask participants to follow the directions carefully, focusing on creating story contexts and visual representations before they do any calculations. If participants create new story contexts or representations for the fractions less than 1, remind them to see if these new ideas will apply when the numbers are whole numbers such as 3 and 5.

Let the participants know that as they approach the second set of values, $r = \frac{3}{4}$ and $s = \frac{1}{2}$, they should begin by working to modify what they tried for the whole numbers. Alert them to the fact they will be continuing this kind of work in the next session with additional number pairs, so they should keep their work on this activity available for next session.

Whole-group math discussion (20 minutes)

In the whole-group discussion, focus on these issues:

- How did participants modify the whole-number contexts and diagrams to accommodate the fractions in the second part of the activity?

- What was the same and what was different in the computational procedures they used for whole numbers and for fractions less than 1?

- Did their thinking about what the operations meant change as they moved from whole numbers to fractions less than 1?

Remind the group that they will be coming back to this kind of thinking at the next session and suggest that they bring their notes from this discussion.

Homework and exit cards (5 minutes)

Whole group

Distribute the "Eighth Homework" handout. If you have not previously assigned any of chapter 8 for your group to read, let them know this chapter is different from a set of cases. Chapter 8, "Highlights of Related Research," makes connections between the thinking of the students in the cases and the findings of mathematics education researchers.

Suggest that while reading chapter 8, they turn back to the cases that are referenced to reacquaint themselves with the details. Remind them to respond to the questions on the assignment sheet, which will be the basis of the discussion of chapter 8 at the next session.

As the session ends, distribute index cards and pose these exit-card questions:

1. What ideas about division of fractions are clear to you? What are you still thinking about?

2. What else do you want to tell the facilitators about your experience?

Before the next session...

In preparation for the next session, read what participants wrote about the math idea they are working on for themselves. For more information, see the section in "Maxine's Journal" on responding to the seventh homework. Make copies of both the papers and your response for your files before returning the work.

DVD Summary

Session 7: Dividing by a Fraction

Eighth-grade student Rachel interviewed by Deborah Schifter (4 minutes 20 seconds)

Rachel is asked to create a word problem for which $4 \div \frac{3}{5}$ would lead to the solution. Rachel offers this: "If Sally wanted to buy something that cost 60 cents and she had 4 dollars, how much of this thing could she buy?" In response to the interviewer's question about why she was using 60 cents, Rachel states that she changed the $\frac{3}{5}$ to a decimal.

Rachel solves the problem by determining that two things would cost $1.20; four would cost $2.40; another one would be $3.00, and then one more would make $3.60. Rachel states that Sally could buy six things for $3.60; so she would have 40 cents left. Since 40 cents is $\frac{2}{5}$, Rachel concludes that the answer to the problem would be 6.4 or $6\frac{2}{5}$.

Next the interviewer points out that the answer to her problem requires a whole-number answer. She asks Rachel to make up another story—one that does not require a whole-number answer. Rachel proposes this: "Sally wanted to grow 4 inches, and she grows $\frac{3}{5}$ of an inch each year. How long would it take her?"

The interviewer asks what the answer would be, and Rachel says, "6 and $\frac{2}{5}$ of a year."

The interviewer asks Rachel if she can think of a way to check her answer. The girl indicates that she would multiply 6.4×0.6 or $6\frac{2}{5} \times \frac{3}{5}$, and if the answer to that is 4, "I would know I am right."

Session 7 Detailed Agenda

SESSION 7

MAKING MEANING FOR OPERATIONS

Focus Questions: Chapter 7

1. In case 28, Sarita lists a variety of equations and explanations her students used to solve the ice-cream problem (see the boxed examples). Examine each of the statements. Which ones seem right, and why? Which ones seem wrong, and why? Your conclusions need not be the same as Sarita's.

2. In Selena's case 29, the students are working on a problem that involves the division of 33 by $5\frac{1}{2}$. Does this situation seem like a division problem to you? Why or why not? What ideas about division (or multiplication) were highlighted for you as you read the case? How are the ideas the same and how are they different from ideas involved with division (or multiplication) of whole numbers?

3. Discuss the ideas posed in the introduction to this chapter.

SESSION 7

MAKING MEANING FOR OPERATIONS

Math Activity: Operating with Positive Rational Numbers, Part 1

In this activity you will work with the four expressions $(r + s)$, $(r - s)$, $(r \times s)$, and $(r \div s)$. Do not do any calculations until you reach step 4.

1. Let $r = 5$ and $s = 3$. Create a story context and a visual representation for each of the four expressions.

2. Let $r = \frac{3}{4}$ and $s = \frac{1}{2}$. Do the same story contexts and visual representations still apply? If not, create a second set of story contexts and visual representations for these values of r and s. Do your new story contexts and visual representations apply for $r = 5$ and $s = 3$? Why or why not?

3. How does your thinking about the meaning of each expression change or remain the same for each operation? For example, does $r + s$ or $r \times s$ take on a different meaning for you, depending on whether the numbers you are operating with are whole numbers or fractions less than 1? Consider each operation separately. (*Note*: You will consider fractions greater than 1 when you continue with this activity during Session 8.)

4. Perform each of the calculations. What is the same about the procedures you used to perform each of these calculations? What is different?

Session 7 Detailed Agenda

SESSION 7

MAKING MEANING FOR OPERATIONS

Eighth Homework

Reading assignment: Casebook chapter 8

In the casebook, read chapter 8, "Highlights of Related Research."

Writing assignment: Casebook chapter 8

After reading chapter 8, respond to the following in writing.

1. What did you learn from the research article that wasn't in the cases?

2. Identify two points in the essay that particularly interested you. Explain what made them interesting.

3. What connections did you see between your classroom and the ideas in the essay?

Bring this writing to the next session to support the discussion of this chapter.

Session 7
Expanding ideas about division in the context of fractions

Maxine's Journal

April 23

As we are approaching the end of the seminar, I can see how the ideas we have been working on for the last few months are applied, even as we dig deeper into division of fractions. We began this session by viewing a DVD of an eighth grader who made up story problems for $4 \div \frac{3}{5}$. We then turned to two print cases that involved division of fractions. Finally, we began an activity which will continue into the next session, considering all four of the basic operations as they apply to whole numbers and to fractions.

Discussing the DVD: Fractions and division

Before showing the DVD, I asked participants to come up with their own story problems for $4 \div \frac{3}{5}$. They worked alone for 2 minutes and then turned to a partner. Within 5 minutes we were sharing the problems.

Elspeth offered, "Ann runs 4 miles. She stops every $\frac{3}{5}$ mile to rest. How many times does she stop?"

Maalika said, "The answer to that problem is 6, not $6\frac{2}{3}$."

Gaye added, "It doesn't make sense for her to make $\frac{2}{3}$ of a stop."

I acknowledged that Elspeth's problem requires a whole-number answer, and that $\frac{2}{3}$ isn't meaningful in this context. I asked, "What about a remainder of $\frac{2}{5}$? Does that have any meaning in this problem?"

Elspeth answered, "Yes. After Ann's sixth stop, she still has $\frac{2}{5}$ of a mile to run."

Marina suggested a second problem. "We were inspired by the gas-tank problem. *You have 4 gallons of gas. If it takes $\frac{3}{5}$ of a tank to mow my lawn, how many times can I mow my lawn?*"

Spencer said, "The answer to that question is $1\frac{2}{3}$. If it takes $\frac{3}{5}$ of a tank to mow the lawn, then if you start with a full tank, you can't even mow twice."

Marina looked confused and turned to Dofi, her partner, saying, "What did we do?"

Dofi said, "No, our problem was different. It takes $\frac{3}{5}$ of a *gallon* to mow the lawn, not $\frac{3}{5}$ of a tank."

Spencer said, "OK, the answer to Dofi's problem is $6\frac{2}{3}$. You can mow it 6 whole times, and then you can mow $\frac{2}{3}$ of the lawn. That makes sense."

Celeste said, "Or you can change Marina's problem by saying, *You have 4 gallons and that fills $\frac{3}{5}$ of the tank. How big is the tank?* The answer to that question is $6\frac{2}{3}$ gallons."

Elspeth laughed and said, "Oh, we're back to that problem again! I thought about that lawn mower in bed every night since the last session, and I still can't figure it out. What makes that division?"

I didn't want to spend any time on that issue at this moment, and so I said, "We'll see if we can get back to your question later today or in the last session. For now, let's set it aside and think about the other two problems. We've already made the point that one situation requires a whole-number answer. The other is continuous, and the answer can take on fractional values."

With that, I turned on the DVD in which an eighth grader, Rachel, is asked to come up with a word problem for $4 \div \frac{3}{5}$. Her first problem involves an item that costs $.60; if she has $4, how many of those items can she buy? When asked to come up with a problem that could have a fractional answer, Rachel says that she wants to grow another 4 inches. If she grows $\frac{3}{5}$ of an inch each year, how long will it take her to reach her goal?

There were several comments about Rachel's work, starting with her choice of problems.

Gaye said, "That's amazing, that she immediately recognized that 60 cents is $\frac{3}{5}$ of a dollar and she could use that in a problem."

Beatrice added, "She knows contexts that involve division, and she could easily think through the distinction between discrete and continuous quantities."

An-Chi said, "I was interested that she made these up as division problems, but she solved them by subtracting. So she knows how division and subtraction are related."

Karran said, "She also knows how division and multiplication are related. When asked how she would check her answer, she said she'd multiply her answer by $\frac{3}{5}$ and make sure it comes out to 4."

Cathleen said, "Too bad she got the wrong answer."

An-Chi said, "Yeah. She made the same mistake we all made when we did Wanda's cakes. She got a remainder of $\frac{2}{5}$, but that's not $\frac{2}{5}$ of a year. In her problem, if she grows $\frac{3}{5}$ of an inch each year, it would take her $6\frac{2}{3}$ years."

Cathleen said, "So why didn't the interviewer tell her she got the wrong answer?"

Joseph said, "It would have been really interesting to see how Rachel worked it through."

I said, "All we have is what's on tape. But let's think about what we would do if Rachel were in front of us. What would you do?"

Cathleen said, "I'd ask her to do $4 \div \frac{3}{5}$ using the algorithm."

Celeste countered, "Actually, I would ask her to follow through with what she said. She said she would check her answer by multiplying, so I'd ask her to do that: $6\frac{2}{5} \times \frac{3}{5}$. She'd soon discover it doesn't come out to 4. Maybe after that, I'd ask her to use the invert-and-multiply algorithm."

Marina added, "I think I'd ask her to draw a diagram. I've found the diagrams so helpful in thinking about all this."

I asked, "So what is it that Rachel needs to understand in order to see that her answer should be $6\frac{2}{3}$ instead of $6\frac{2}{5}$?"

Joseph said, "I think I'd ask her how much she will have grown after 6 years, and how much she still needs to grow to reach her goal of 4 inches. That would help her see that $\frac{2}{5}$ stands for $\frac{2}{5}$ of an inch. From there, I'd ask her how long it would take her to grow $\frac{2}{5}$ of an inch. Maybe she'll see that it's $\frac{2}{3}$ of a year."

I nodded and then suggested we move to the print cases.

Case discussion: Fractions and division

Before getting into small groups, we read the focus questions for chapter 7 together. I specifically asked if participants understood question 2: How are the ideas in Selena's case 29, "Stretching Elastic," the same as or different from division of whole numbers? I explained that I wanted them to sort out the ideas that have to do with division, whether or not they were dealing with fractions, and the ideas that have to do specifically with fractions.

Amber responded, "I know exactly what this means because I had it happen to me today!" She had been working with a special ed student who had come to her with a problem his classroom teacher had assigned, involving division of fractions. As she questioned him, she realized he didn't understand division of whole numbers. So they went back and did the same problem situations with whole numbers. She said she planned to work on that with him for another day before returning to fractions.

The teachers then got into small groups, but I wanted to move quickly to the whole-group discussion because I heard some very interesting conversation. To start out, Karran posed the following questions: "There's something I'm curious about. In Sarita's case, she said, 'In my mind the students' equations were, though not necessarily wrong, not quite correct either!' I want to know what others think of that. What's the difference between being *wrong* and *not correct?*"

Marina volunteered, "I can think of lots of examples in other subjects, but not in math." She went on to explain that when her students use double negatives or the word *ain't*, she knows what they're saying, but it's not "correct." Then Marina added, almost to herself, "I can think of examples in language, but not in math. Why is that?"

Odette interjected, "I think Sarita was thinking about something else. It happens all the time that a teacher is expecting something particular and the students go off and do whatever they do. I think Sarita just means that the students didn't do what she expected, or what she had wanted them to do. But what the students did in Sarita's first list was correct. It's like the children we read about a few weeks ago in Georgia's case [case 11, "How Do Kids Think About Division?]. Georgia gave them all these division problems, and they solved them by adding, subtracting, and multiplying. They weren't *wrong.*"

Dofi said, "But I don't think they were incorrect, either. Georgia's students solved the problem. Sarita's students wrote out number sentences that allow them to solve the problem."

I said, "So let's consider the work that Sarita's students have done. We know that Sarita wasn't sure what to do. But if this had happened in your class, and you got these equations on the board, what would you want your students to learn from this?"

Karran said, "It's interesting that they have four equations, one for each operation. The thing is, three of them involve 6 and $\frac{3}{4}$, the numbers given in the problem, but the division equation involves 24 and 3. Is there something to make of that?"

Joseph said, "It looks like Sarita ended the lesson with all the equations still on the board, including the incorrect ones. I would want to make sure there was enough discussion to eliminate the four incorrect equations. For example, from what she wrote, it seems that some students challenged $8 \div \frac{1}{4} = 6$. We don't know what the challenge was, but it seems like Sarita should push on what $6 \div \frac{1}{4}$ means. Maybe from there they'll get to $6 \div \frac{3}{4} = 8$."

Odette said, "If they finally arrive at $6 \div \frac{3}{4}$, they'll probably eliminate all the incorrect ones, since they're all division. It seemed the students knew there was a division of fractions problem in there, but they couldn't figure out which one it was."

Karran said, "Once they come up with $6 \div \frac{3}{4} = 8$, I'd want students to talk about how that equation relates to the other correct ones. At least, I'd want them to see how it related to the multiplication, addition, and subtraction equations."

Before the discussion of Sarita's case ended, Gaye and Iris wanted to explain what they were thinking about. As they were working on the diagram, they realized they had two different ways of thinking about $\frac{3}{4}$: We can understand $\frac{3}{4}$ as "this much stuff," or as "three of these little clumps." They were using the problem to talk about what it means to understand $\frac{3}{4}$ as representing a quantity of ice cream in and of itself, and also as three times the quantity $\frac{1}{4}$, which makes up the same amount of stuff. Idris has been working on this idea for weeks—what it means for a fraction to represent a quantity, that is, an "amount of stuff." These issues came up for her when we were talking about $\frac{3}{8}$ of a pizza back in Session 4.

In response, I drew a number line on the board.

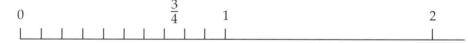

I said, "We've been working with story problems because they give us lots of insight about fractions and the operations. But remember, we have also been placing fractions on a number line. When you look at the number line, $\frac{3}{4}$ has a position, just like 0, 1, or 2. That is, $\frac{3}{4}$ is a number, just like 0, 1, or 2."

When we moved on to Selena's case, Nadra protested, "I just don't get it! I don't get what's going on in the problem with the elastic."

First there was laughter, then Labeeba said, "Neither do I," and Camisha echoed her.

"Is the difficulty about fractions or about division?" Amber asked. They all said they weren't sure, so Joseph suggested they change the terms of the problem to whole numbers. They agreed that the elastic stretches three times its original length and that, when fully stretched, it is 12 meters long.

Nadra laughed and said, "Well, I guess my difficulty isn't about fractions. I still don't get it. The cases in this chapter are about division, but this doesn't seem like division to me."

Nadra wasn't alone. Most of the participants in the seminar were confused by this problem. I think they were saying they didn't like this idea that something would be just one thing, and then be bigger all at once. They didn't want to call it multiplication or division; they didn't know what to call it, didn't know what it was, didn't have a name for it. They were picturing something that grew instantaneously, instead of through repeated addition, and that was distressing them.

Then Karran took the initiative, went to the board, and marked off a length.

———

"Look, this is the length of the original elastic. We don't really know how long it is yet, but this is what we're going to use." Then she extended the line segment by the length of the original.

———|———

"Now my line is twice as long. I can take my elastic and stretch it out to here and it's stretched twice its original length." Next she marked off a line segment that was three times the original.

———|———|———

"See, I can stretch the elastic from here to here, this entire length. We said that it stretches out to 12 meters. So can't you look at this picture and see? It's 12 meters divided into 3 parts, and that tells you the original length was 4 meters."

Labeeba said, "Oh, yeah. I get it."

Nadra made a face. "I don't know, I have to think about that some more."

An-Chi said, "So what if it's about fractions instead?"

Not everyone was ready to take that on, so I suggested they get into pairs. Those who were still thinking about Karran's whole-number demonstration got together, as did those who were ready to think about fractions again. After a while, I told participants to take a break when they felt that they had gone as far as they could for now.

Math activity: Operating with rational numbers

The next activity was designed to help participants consolidate the ideas we have been working on about the meaning of operations on whole numbers and fractions, as well as to push on whatever ideas they are still trying to sort out. First, they were asked to write word problems for $5 + 3$, $5 - 3$, 5×3 and $5 \div 3$. Then they were to write word problems for $\frac{3}{4} + \frac{1}{2}$, $\frac{3}{4} - \frac{1}{2}$, $\frac{3}{4} \times \frac{1}{2}$, and $\frac{3}{4} \div \frac{1}{2}$. I said to them, "As you work, I want you to think about two things: (1) What ideas about the operations get highlighted? (2) How do the word problems you wrote for whole numbers need to change in order to work for fractions?"

As I sat down to listen to Marina, Labeeba, Joseph, and Carol, they had completed their problems for operations with 3 and 5:

- Ryan brought 5 cakes to the party and Sue brought 3. How many cakes did they bring?

- Ryan baked 5 cakes and Sue put frosting 3 of them. How many unfrosted cakes are left?

- Ryan baked 5 cakes a day for 3 consecutive days. How many cakes did he bake?

- Ryan has 5 cakes that he wants to distribute equally to 3 friends. How much does each get?

Now they were rewriting the problems for $\frac{3}{4}$ and $\frac{1}{2}$. Labeeba read, "After the party, Ryan has $\frac{3}{4}$ of a chocolate cake left over and Sue has $\frac{1}{2}$ of a carrot cake. How much cake do they have altogether?"

Carol said, "So if we add, we get $1\frac{1}{4}$ cakes. Does that make sense? There isn't a whole cake of anything."

Joseph laughed, "This is like Jorge's pizza problem. If we think about one cake as a unit of measure, then it doesn't matter if it's chocolate or carrot. I guess what's important here is that the cakes need to be the same size in order for this to make sense."

Marina said, "That's interesting. When we talked about 3 and 5, it wasn't so important that the cakes should be the same size. You can have small cakes or big cakes; it would still be a total of 8 cakes."

Then they moved on to subtraction. Carol said, "Ryan has $\frac{3}{4}$ of a cake and he gives Sue $\frac{1}{2}$. How much does he have left?"

Marina said, "How much did Ryan give to Sue? Did he give $\frac{1}{2}$ of what he had, or did he give her $\frac{1}{2}$ of a cake?"

Joseph said, "Right. For this problem, it's not that he shared it equally with her. That would be multiplication. If he gave her $\frac{1}{2}$ a cake, then he would have $\frac{1}{4}$ of a cake left."

I had placed together some of those participants who had been trying to sort out the gas tank problem in Session 6, and this activity brought them back to similar questions. Elspeth, Karran, Spencer, and Gaye had come up with a story context for 5 ÷ 3 and were now translating it to $\frac{3}{4} \div \frac{1}{2}$. Elspeth explained to me that for 5 ÷ 3, they wrote several problems. She said, "We made up problems for the dealing version of division so that we can see what happens with fractions."

- I have 5 candy bars to share equally among 3 people. How much does each person get?

- I used 5 cups of flour to make 3 batches of cookies. How much flour is used for 1 batch of cookies?

- I walk 5 miles in 3 hours. If I walk at the same rate, how far do I go in 1 hour?

Now the group was trying out these problems with the numbers $\frac{3}{4}$ and $\frac{1}{2}$. Spencer said, "I have $\frac{3}{4}$ of a candy bar to share equally among $\frac{1}{2}$ people. That doesn't make sense."

Karran said, "It doesn't make sense because we can't have half of a person. But what if we change the question to something that allows fractions? Earlier, Maxine suggested we think about portions instead of people. *I have 5 candy bars to share among 3 portions. I have $\frac{3}{4}$ of a candy bar to share among $\frac{1}{2}$ portion.* That doesn't sound right, either. You don't share something among half a portion."

Gaye said, "Maybe, *I have 5 candy bars for 3 portions. I have $\frac{3}{4}$ of a candy bar for $\frac{1}{2}$ of a portion.* How does that sound?"

Karran built from Gaye's suggestion: "*I have 5 candy bars and that's enough for 3 portions. I have $\frac{3}{4}$ of a candy bar and that's enough for $\frac{1}{2}$ portion.* Does that work?"

Spencer had been listening quietly to his groupmates and now spoke up. "Let me look at this problem. *I have $\frac{3}{4}$ of a candy bar and that's enough for $\frac{1}{2}$ portion; how much is 1 portion?* If I had been given that problem cold, I would have called it multiplication with a missing factor: $\frac{1}{2}x = \frac{3}{4}$. But since we've derived it from a problem for 5 ÷ 3, I start to see it as division."

Karran said, "Let's look at the others. They seem to go pretty easily with fractional amounts."

By the end of the small-group discussion, they had three problems for $\frac{3}{4} \div \frac{1}{2}$.

- I have $\frac{3}{4}$ of a candy bar and that's enough for $\frac{1}{2}$ of a portion. How much is a portion?

- I used $\frac{3}{4}$ cup of flour to make $\frac{1}{2}$ batch of cookies. How much flour is used for 1 batch of cookies?

- I walk $\frac{3}{4}$ mile in $\frac{1}{2}$ hour. How far do I go in 1 hour?

I had just a few minutes at the end of the session to bring the whole group together to discuss some of the issues that arose in this activity. Odette began the discussion: "It was pretty interesting just to make up the four problems for 5 and 3. We were using the same numbers, but the meanings changed with each problem."

When I asked her to explain, Odette continued, "We started out saying that we'd make all of our problems about pizza. So, we have 5 pizzas and 3 pizzas. The worked for the first two: There are 5 sausage pizzas and 3 mushroom pizzas. How many pizzas are there? How many more sausage pizza are there than mushroom pizzas? That takes care of addition and subtraction. But we couldn't think of anything where you multiply 5 pizzas by 3 pizzas. We ended up saying we bought 5 pizzas; each cost $3. How much did the 5 pizzas cost? We needed to change what the 3 stood for in order to make a multiplication problem."

I asked, "What is it about addition and subtraction that makes it so you could keep it focused on counting pizzas, which you couldn't do for multiplication and division?"

Beatrice said, "Addition and subtraction require that the unit stays the same for all three numbers. You add pizzas to pizzas and the answer is a number of pizzas. You subtract pizza from pizza and the answer is a number of pizzas. It can be any unit, but it has to stay the same. But with multiplication, the unit changes."

Joseph brought our attention to fractions. "We noticed something interesting when we wrote the addition problem for $\frac{3}{4}$ and $\frac{1}{2}$. Our whole-number problem was to add 5 cakes and 3 cakes. They could be different kinds of cakes, different sizes of cakes; it doesn't matter. But when we added $\frac{3}{4}$ of a cake to $\frac{1}{2}$ of a cake, it seemed important that those cakes be the same size. It doesn't make any sense to add $\frac{3}{4}$ of a large cake to $\frac{1}{2}$ of a small cake."

Celeste said, "Oh, I've never thought about that before, but you're right. When you're counting discrete objects, it sometimes doesn't matter what size they are. But if you've got a situation where you're joining parts of units, those units have to be the same size."

An-Chi said, "When we were working with fractions, we had to be much more careful about the units. For example, we could say, James has 5 marbles and gives away 3. But if we say, James has $\frac{3}{4}$ of a cookie and gives away $\frac{1}{2}$, does he give away $\frac{1}{2}$ of a cookie, or does he give away $\frac{1}{2}$ of what he has?"

Dofi said, "We could easily make up problems for 3 and 5, and then it was a stretch to make those contexts work for $\frac{3}{4}$ and $\frac{1}{2}$. But once we had a context for $\frac{3}{4}$ and $\frac{1}{2}$, the story usually worked pretty well if we changed it back to 3 and 5."

These ideas were all very interesting. I told the group that in the next session, we would have some more time to work on something similar.

Homework and exit cards

I pointed out that for homework, the reading assignment is not a set of cases. Instead, the final chapter of the casebook is an essay about research related to the ideas we have been working on. "Some people find it takes time to absorb all the ideas in these final chapters. I suggest that you start reading early in the week or over the weekend." I also pointed out that the writing assignment is to address a set of questions about the essay.

I posted the exit-card questions.

1. What ideas about division of fractions are clear to you? What are you still thinking about?

2. What else do you want to tell the facilitators about your experience?

From their exit cards, I got a better sense of who is still struggling with the ideas and who feels pretty solid. Everybody sounds pretty hopeful.

CAMISHA: Not much is completely clear. I feel like I "get it" in class at times, but it is very fleeting. This is more so when it is a fraction divided by a fraction. I understand what to do when it is a whole number divided by a fraction.

CAROL: The pictures make the ideas clearer to me: groups of ___, or ___ groups. It is still not "natural" for me and I really need to think about it. But I am getting there.

SPENCER: Today's math activity really clicked with me. I know, it's about time.

CATHLEEN: I am still thinking about the connection between multiplying and dividing fractions and *how* you explain that to students.

DOFI: I'm still thinking about the division of fractions. Pictures are a helpful tool for me that I need to continue to use to understand more.

IRIS: I think I am clear on the process of dividing fractions, but still get stuck on writing story problems to use with them.

ANDREA: Fractions are complicated. I realized that I know more than I think I do about them.

LABEEBA: I am still thinking about how to show it—how to write a story for it. At the crux, I am not really sure why dividing makes the number bigger. I think I get the multiplying piece with fractions and why they get smaller. I'll keep thinking about it.

AMBER: The ideas about division of fractions that are clear to me are that you end up with an answer greater than the numbers you started with. This is different from division of whole numbers. The reason the answer is more is because you are doing the first fraction more times. Does that make sense?

When I read these exit cards, I realize I need to check on the generalizations Labeeba and Amber are writing about, and that other participants might be thinking. They seem to be saying that when you multiply by fractions, the product is a lesser number; when you divide by fractions, the quotient is a greater number. Are they also thinking about fractions like $\frac{3}{2}$ or $\frac{21}{5}$? Their generalization holds for numbers between 0 and 1, but it doesn't hold if you consider fractions greater than 1. We'll have a chance to pay attention to that in the next (and final) session.

Responding to the seventh homework

April 26

The mathematical issues that participants raised in their homework assignment were varied. They were also quite varied in terms of the depth of their thinking about them. I include two sets of responses here to illustrate.

Nadra

> I thought about a couple of ideas to write about for this assignment, but I decided to pick one. I originally thought of multiplication as just repeated addition. I have since changed my mind. I now view it as more than just repeated addition. What makes sense to me now is I think of it as groups of sets, not just repeated addition. It does make sense to me that three groups of five are not the same as five groups of three. I know a lot of teachers including myself have taught multiplication as repeated addition, even if they show the groups of sets. One thing that I am still struggling with is how can I get the students to see it differently if the total number comes out the same for both ways. They may feel that repeated addition is easier for them than groups and sets, so why bother if the result is the same in the end?

Once Nadra stated that there are other ways to think about multiplication than repeated addition, she didn't have much else to say. In my response, I wanted to show her that there was more to think about.

> Dear Nadra,
>
> You are right—it *is* important to realize that multiplication is more than repeated addition. It is good that you now feel comfortable with another way to represent that operation: as a set of equal groups. You now hold an image of the quantity, and you can think about contexts that call for multiplication. By recognizing that you can add up the total quantity group by group, you can see how repeated addition relates to a set of equal groups.
>
> In the seminar, we have worked with some other representations of multiplication—for example, an array. An array is a rectangular arrangement of objects with equal rows and equal columns. You can think about how an array is related to the other representations we have mentioned: If you add up the number in each row (or in each column), you have repeated addition. And you can think of each row (or each column) as a group.

Even if we can see how one representation maps onto another, we frequently find that some representations highlight particular ideas. In the array we can see, for example, how 3 groups of 5 is equal to 5 groups of 3.

In this picture, if we think of each row as a group, we have 3 groups of 5. But if we look at each column as a group, we have 5 groups of 3. In this way, the array demonstrates an important property of multiplication.

These three images of multiplication are all restricted to whole numbers. In the seminar, we have worked on developing images that allow us to think about multiplication of fractions, as well. For this, we have mainly been using the area of a rectangle (though we have also worked with some number line representations). That is, the area is equal to the product of the lengths of the sides.

In order to develop flexibility and have a rich understanding of the operation, we want our students to be familiar with a variety of representations. For that reason, we try to give them problems that call on different representations. But ultimately, we want them to work with multiplication in efficient ways.

Maxine

On the other hand, Gaye wrote about the two representations in Selena's case 29, "Stretching Elastic," from the chapter she had just read for homework. Wondering whether both are correct, she further considered the implications for her sense of what the field of mathematics is about.

Gaye

After reading chapter 7, Selena's case stood out for me. Her class worked on this problem:

> A piece of elastic can be stretched to $5\frac{1}{2}$ times its original length. When fully stretched, it is 33 meters long. What was the elastic's original length?

Originally, I saw what Marcus was seeing: 33 meters divided into groups of $5\frac{1}{2}$. I wasn't even thinking about the original length of the elastic. To me, this makes sense. I guess I see fractions as dividing into equal parts, groups, but I could also see Sonia's model. She drew the 33 and divided it into $5\frac{1}{2}$ groups. It wasn't until I reread the case that this model made more sense to me than the other. However, it seems to me that in order to draw Sonia's model, you have to already have an understanding that you've got groups of size 6.

I keep going back and forth between the two models, trying to see which one is "right." I feel like I could justify each model (the way they were divided), but it means I have to ignore the question about the original length of the elastic.

These two models really have me thinking: Is mathematics subjective? In a sense, this class is beginning to make me feel that way. Is my way of interpreting a problem ever incorrect, especially if I can justify my reasoning? I guess my last comment kind of goes along with Sarita's case 28, "Who Says That's Not the Right Equation?" She asks about whether her students are "wrong" or "not correct"—or are they actually correct, even if they gave her answers she didn't expect? There are many questions going through my mind, and I just want there to be a concrete answer. I am so used to a *yes* or *no*, it is hard to see the in-between. Don't get me wrong; I enjoy seeing children explore math and justify why they are correct. My fear is that when the time comes for them to be correct, will they be? And will people who haven't been exposed the way I have begin to question my math ability and knowledge?

In my response, I wanted to address both the specifics of the representations of the elastic problem and her questions about the nature of mathematics.

Dear Gaye,

I found your paper very interesting, and I'll try to address your questions.

First, there are many different ways the problem can be represented. For example, it can be represented with an equation. Either of the following is perfectly appropriate.

$$33 \div 5\tfrac{1}{2} = x \qquad 5\tfrac{1}{2} x = 33$$

The two equations are equivalent; that is, the solution for one equation is the same as the solution for the other: $x = 6$. And 6 is the answer to the problem.

We can solve the problem with a diagram. We have an elastic that is stretched to $5\tfrac{1}{2}$ times its original length. We can think of it this way:

That shows the elastic distributed over $5\tfrac{1}{2}$ sections, where each section is the original length. But as you and Selena's students point out, it doesn't actually help us figure out the original length. What is the length of each of those sections so the total length is 33 meters?

On the other hand, having recognized that we've got a division problem, we might think about how many sections of $5\frac{1}{2}$ meters we can get from 33 meters. That gives us a slightly different picture:

In this diagram, we start marking off lengths of $5\frac{1}{2}$ until we get to 33. We've marked off 6 lengths, and so the answer is 6.

We can use this diagram because of our knowledge of division. We know that we will get the same answer no matter which interpretation of division we use. However, this diagram might be less satisfying because it doesn't match the context of the problem. It shows 6 lengths of $5\frac{1}{2}$ instead of $5\frac{1}{2}$ lengths of 6.

But as I start looking at this diagram some more, I might see in it an interpretation that fits the problem. I can say, if the original length of the elastic is 1 meter, then when it's stretched out, it looks like this:

If the original length of the elastic is 2 meters, then when it's stretched out, it looks like this:

The diagram marks off each meter of the original length stretched out $5\frac{1}{2}$ times. So, you see, there is a way to interpret the diagram to match the context of the problem. Continuing to add these $5\frac{1}{2}$ meter lengths until we get to the full length, we find that it takes 6 of these stretched-out meters to reach the full 33 meters. So the original elastic must have been 6 meters long.

So you ask, does that make mathematics subjective, that we can look at the diagrams in different ways to make them match the problem? The thing is, the answer to the problem is still 6 meters, no matter which representation we consider. That is not subjective.

You also ask if any way of interpreting a problem is ever incorrect. The answer is yes. For example, one of Sarita's students wrote "$\frac{3}{4} \div 8 = 6$" as an equation to match the ice-cream problem. This equation is simply wrong. The student offered a justification, "$\frac{3}{4}$ pint is the serving; there are 6 pints of ice cream, so 8 servings," but it is still wrong. In a division equation, it matters which number is the divisor, which is the dividend, and which is the quotient. The correct division equation with these numbers that matches the problem is $6 \div \frac{3}{4} = 8$.

On the other hand, $8 \times \frac{3}{4} = 6$ is also a correct representation of the problem. The students' justification—8 servings of $\frac{3}{4}$ of a pint each gives you 6 whole pints—matches the problem and matches the meaning of multiplication.

It might be that you are discovering mathematics to be more open than you previously believed it was. There may be several correct representations to a problem, and several routes to a solution. The key is that the *reasoning* in support of that diagram or solution method must be solid. That is where mathematical rigor lies.

Maxine

SESSION 8

MAKING MEANING FOR OPERATIONS

Wrapping Up

Mathematical Themes

- The same basic principles that govern operations with whole numbers are called upon to operate with fractions or mixed numbers, but the interpretation of each operation may need to be expanded.

Research essay discussion	Small groups Whole groups	35 minutes 30 minutes
Math activity: Operating with positive rational numbers, part 2	Small groups Whole group	40 minutes 25 minutes
Break		15 minutes
Reviewing early portfolio examples of student work	Individual	20 minutes
Final homework and closing	Whole group	15 minutes

Background Preparation

Read

- the casebook, chapter 8
- the detailed agenda for Session 8
- "Maxine's Journal" for Session 8

Work through

- the math activity: Operating with positive rational numbers, part 2

Materials

Duplicate

- "Math Activity: Operating with Positive Rational Numbers, Part 2"
- "Ninth Homework"
- "Evaluation Form"

Obtain

- graph paper
- interlocking cubes
- participants' first homework assignments

Contexts for Multiplication and Division

The cases and math activities in Sessions 5–8 illustrate a variety of contexts that involve multiplication and division of positive rational numbers. In this facilitator note, we identify four categories of contexts.

Portions of portions: Erin has $\frac{3}{4}$ of a yard of fabric and she needs $\frac{1}{2}$ of that to make a place mat. How many yards does she need? (Erin needs $\frac{3}{8}$ yard of fabric.)

Shrinking or stretching: My scarf was $\frac{3}{4}$ yard long. After I washed it, it was $\frac{1}{2}$ that length. How long is my scarf now? (It's now $\frac{3}{8}$ yard long.)

Area of a rectangle: The length of a rectangle is $\frac{3}{4}$ inch. Its width is $\frac{1}{2}$ inch. What is the area of the rectangle? (The area is $\frac{3}{8}$ square inch.)

Rate and time: I am walking at a rate of $\frac{3}{4}$ mile per hour, and I walk at this rate for $\frac{1}{2}$ hour. How far do I go? (I go $\frac{3}{8}$ mile.)

Each of these contexts has two associated division problems. One is solved by $\frac{3}{8} \div \frac{3}{4}$. (For example, I have traveled $\frac{3}{8}$ mile, walking at a rate of $\frac{3}{4}$ mile per hour. How long have I been walking?) The other is solved by $\frac{3}{8} \div \frac{1}{2}$. (I have walked $\frac{3}{8}$ mile in $\frac{1}{2}$ hour. At what speed have I been walking?)

The same four contexts can be used with mixed numbers.

Portions of portions: Erin has $3\frac{1}{2}$ yards of fabric, but she needs $1\frac{3}{4}$ as much as that amount to make a dress. How many yards does she need?

Shrinking or stretching: I have a scarf that was $3\frac{1}{2}$ feet long. Then it got stretched out to $1\frac{3}{4}$ times that length. How long is the scarf now?

Area of a rectangle: The length of a rectangle is $3\frac{1}{2}$ inches. Its width is $1\frac{3}{4}$ inches. What is the area of the rectangle?

Rate and time: I am walking at a rate of $3\frac{1}{2}$ miles per hour, and I walk for $1\frac{3}{4}$ hour. How far do I go?

Each of these contexts has two associated division problems, one solved by $6\frac{1}{8} \div 3\frac{1}{2}$; the other solved by $6\frac{1}{8} \div 1\frac{3}{4}$.

SESSION 8

Detailed Agenda

Research essay discussion (65 minutes)

Small groups (35 minutes)

Whole group (30 minutes)

Small-group discussion (35 minutes)

Suggest that participants begin by sharing within their small group the points they wrote about for homework in response to the chapter 8 essay, "Highlights of Related Research." Suggest that they first discuss points related to section 1, then section 2, and so on.

Once they have commented on each section of the essay, ask them to turn to their writing about the connections between their own classroom and the ideas in the essay. Remind participants to be sure that each person in their group has an opportunity to share.

Whole-group discussion (30 minutes)

Begin the whole-group discussion by asking participants to think over the conversation at their table and to share something someone said that they found interesting. Then turn the conversation to the connections they noted between their own classrooms and what they read in the essay.

Math activity: Operating with positive rational numbers, part 2 (65 minutes)

Small groups (40 minutes)

Whole group (25 minutes)

This math activity continues the work begun in Session 7, as participants continue to find sums, differences, products, and quotients of pairs of numbers. In Session 7, the pairs were two whole numbers and two fractions less than 1. In this session, participants will work with two pairs of mixed numbers, one pair expressed as fractions and one as decimals. They examine how their thinking changes or remains the same as the kinds of numbers being operated on change. In their investigation, participants are again asked to develop story contexts, visual representations, and also to complete computational procedures.

Small-group math work (40 minutes)

Distribute "Math Activity: Operating with Positive Rational Numbers, Part 2." Remind the participants that they began this work in the last session and that the whole-group discussion will refer to all four pairs of numbers. As they begin this session's work, they should review the contexts and representations they used with whole numbers in Session 7. Participants should begin by working to modify what they tried for the whole numbers as they approach the new number pairs with mixed numbers ($r = 3\frac{1}{2}$, $s = 1\frac{2}{3}$) and decimals ($r = 4.2$, $s = 0.3$).

Take note of which problems provoke different diagrams or create confusion so those can be brought up in the whole-group discussion. In particular, if the group did not work in depth with the mixed numbers in Sarita's case 26 (Session 6), the diagram solutions for parts (c) and (d) may need discussion. You might ask some participants to put their solutions on posters which can be displayed during whole-group time.

Whole-group math discussion (25 minutes)

Begin the whole-group discussion by clarifying any questions that surfaced during the small-group work. While it will be useful for the group to see some examples of diagram solutions for $\frac{3}{4} \div \frac{1}{2}$, $3\frac{1}{2} \times 1\frac{2}{3}$, and $3\frac{1}{2} \div 1\frac{2}{3}$, do not commit the entire whole-group time to a discussion of solutions. It is important to set aside time to ask questions that encourage participants to talk about how their concepts of the operations changed as they worked with different kinds of numbers.

Points that are likely to come up in this conversation include these:

- In addition, we combine things that are alike. This works for whole numbers (add hundreds to hundreds, tens to tens, and ones to ones), fractions (make them all the same denominator and then combine them), and decimals (add hundredths to hundredths, tenths to tenths, and so on). In fact, this same principle is also true when using algebraic notation (add x's to x's, x-squareds to x-squareds, constants to constants).

- In multiplication, the conception of this operation as repeated addition needs to change to accommodate non-whole numbers. However, once we arrive at an image of multiplication that suits fractions and decimals, that conception does also work for whole numbers. (For instance, how you think of $\frac{2}{3}$ of $\frac{4}{5}$, or $3\frac{1}{2}$ of 4, also works for 3 of 5.)

- When operating with numbers expressed as fractions and decimals, many people find it easier to conceive of division as "how many portions of $\frac{1}{3}$ or $2\frac{1}{3}$ are there in $3\frac{1}{2}$?" than as placing a quantity into $\frac{1}{3}$ of a group or into $2\frac{1}{3}$ groups. The latter might be thought of as having some quantity as equal to $\frac{1}{3}$ portion or $2\frac{1}{3}$ portions; how much is one portion?

- Changing from thinking about *how many?* to thinking about *how much?* accommodates fractions and decimal numbers.

Break (15 minutes)

Reviewing early portfolio examples of student work (20 minutes)

Individual

Let the group know that they will have the opportunity to examine how their ideas may have changed over the seminar. For homework, they will review and comment upon their portfolio assignments. In this activity, they will begin that process by reflecting on the assignment they completed for Session 1.

In that assignment, participants collected and analyzed examples of their students' work. Return this set of student work and analysis to each participant and ask them to read over what they had written. In that analysis, they had responded to this set of questions for each piece of student work:

- What does the student understand?

- What is the student missing?

- What is your learning goal for the student?

Ask them to write about how their ideas have changed. After 10 minutes, open the group to a discussion by asking, "What did you notice as you did this?" or "How has your thinking changed?"

Final homework and closing (15 minutes)

Whole group

Use the final 15 minutes to provide a close to the seminar experience. First distribute "Ninth Homework" sheet and explain the final reflections assignment, which participants are to do as homework. This assignment has two purposes. One is to encourage participants to examine how their own thinking has changed over the course of the seminar. The other purpose is to provide you, the facilitator, with information about what your participants have learned. Let participants know that it will be helpful if they can indicate specific parts of their work that helps them to see the changes they are writing about.

Announce the date by which you want the assignment completed and explain the process for returning it to you. If you are using a seminar evaluation form, distribute that form and make clear how participants will return it and by what date. Providing a stamped self-addressed envelope for the final reflection and the seminar evaluation form may be helpful.

SESSION 8

MAKING MEANING FOR OPERATIONS

Math Activity: Operating with Positive Rational Numbers, Part 2

This assignment builds on work started in Session 7. Review the work you started on the value pairs (a) and (b) in that session, and then continue by working on pairs (c) and (d).

Consider $(r + s)$, $(r - s)$, $(r \times s)$, and $(r \div s)$ for the following pairs of values:

(a) $r = 5, s = 3$

(b) $r = \frac{3}{4}, s = \frac{1}{2}$

(c) $r = 3\frac{1}{2}, s = 1\frac{2}{3}$

(d) $r = 4.2, s = 0.3$

1. Create a story context and a visual representation for each expression.

2. How does your thinking about the meaning of each expression change or remain the same for each case; that is, for example, does $r + s$ or $r \times s$ take on a different meaning for you when the numbers you are operating with are whole numbers, fractions less than 1, or fractions greater than 1? Consider each operation separately.

3. Perform each of the calculations. What is the same about the procedures you used to perform each of these calculations? What is different?

Consider each operation separately; that is, answer these questions first for addition for all values given for r and s, then for subtraction, and so forth.

SESSION 8

MAKING MEANING FOR OPERATIONS

Ninth Homework

Writing assignment: Portfolio review and final reflections

Throughout the *Making Meaning for Operations* seminar, you have been compiling a portfolio that contains your reflective writing, examples of your students' thinking, and your analyses of that thinking, as well as facilitator's responses to your writings. Look through the material you have collected to see how your ideas about *learning*, about *mathematics*, or about *teaching* have changed.

1. Locate two examples from your portfolio for each of these three aspects of the seminar and write about each example.

2. Likely there are issues, mathematical and pedagogical, that came up for you during the seminar and that still puzzle you. Pick an issue that is still "alive" for you. Explain what it is and describe your current thinking about it.

SESSION 8

MAKING MEANING FOR OPERATIONS

Evaluation Form

Please respond to the following questions and send your responses to your facilitator.

1. What worked for you about the way the seminar was conducted? Be specific.

2. What didn't work for you?

3. What changes would you suggest if this seminar were to be offered again?

4. What else would you like to tell seminar facilitators about this experience?

Session 8
Wrapping up

Maxine's Journal

May 10

We had our last seminar meeting several days ago. The session itself went very well, and the teachers had powerful things to say about what they had learned from the seminar. We spent the first hour talking about the "Highlights of Related Research" essay, and the second hour on the math activity. In the last hour, participants spent time beginning their portfolio reviews, and then we got together to mark our closing.

Research essay discussion

For homework, the group had read the essay on research related to the themes of the seminar, *Making Meaning for Operations*. When I asked what they thought about it, Maalika said, "It was hard."

Idris joined in, laughing, "Yeah. When I began reading, I was underlining the parts that were hard for me. Pretty soon I realized that I was underlining so much of the chapter, it was a joke."

Then Maalika added, "It wasn't the way it was written, or anything like that. But the ideas were hard to grasp."

I explained to participants that they would get into small groups to discuss the essay. I said, "For homework, you've written about points that particularly interested you. I suggest that you go through the essay, section by section, discussing those points. Then I'd like you to share your thoughts about how the content of the essay connects to your teaching."

Once we got organized, participants dug into the text. After a few minutes, I noticed that Karran's group recognized that the chart I had distributed in the first session, "Classification of Word Problems," was relevant. They had taken out a copy of that chart and were figuring out how to classify the problem about Electra's rocks, as well as the other problems in those paragraphs.

When I got to Gaye, Amber, and Dofi, they were discussing section 4, "Making Meaning for Multiplication and Division." Dofi said, "It was hard. I had to keep going back to the words *partitive* and *quotitive* to figure out which is which."

I asked if the others in the group had experienced particular trouble with those words, and they nodded. I asked, "If you don't worry about which is which, do you know what the author is talking about when she uses those words?"

At that, Amber and Gaye started to talk at the same time, realized what they were doing, laughed, and then sat back. Gaye said, "Sure, it's all about grouping and dealing; they're the same as our two ways to think about division."

I recalled to this group that they had found this to be an important idea when we started talking about it in Session 2. Many of the teachers had then decided they needed to make sure both of those actions were represented among the problems they brought to their students. "So if you have the idea, does it matter if you have the words *partitive* and *quotitive* attached to it?"

At which Amber complained, "If those words aren't important, then why do they use them?"

Gaye answered Amber's question. "Those are the words the researchers made up. We used different words; we talked about *grouping* and *dealing*. Well, they use *partitive* and *quotitive* so they have a way to talk about it."

Dofi added, "Right. And you're certainly not going to test your students on which situations are partitive and which are quotitive. The children will just solve the problems and use their own language. So will we."

Then Gaye said, "As long as we're not having conversations with researchers, we don't need to remember all those words. We don't need to pay so much attention to the labels as long as we are thinking about the ideas behind them."

When I came to Beatrice, Spencer, Camisha, and Elspeth, they were discussing section 5, "Encountering Fractions in Sharing Situations." Elspeth was saying, "I still find it amazing that, to answer $5 \div 39$, you just say $\frac{5}{39}$. That feels to me like saying, 'The answer to 5 divided by 39 is 5 divided by 39.' I don't know, that seems so weird."

Spencer said, "I guess the trick is to start seeing $\frac{5}{39}$ as a number. It has a place on the number line; it's not just an operation."

In another group, sitting with casebooks open to MaryAnn's "Sharing Brownies" case in chapter 5, the teachers were talking about Jackson. "Before I took this course, if I had a student like Jackson, I would have taken one look at his paper and said, 'Forget it.' But it's really interesting to see that he was thinking really hard. He was making those fractions make sense, even though he sometimes got confused."

When we came back together as a whole group, I wondered what people were now feeling about this essay. Camisha spoke up. "I think this was hard to read, but I know I'm going to reread it. After some time goes by, I'm going to want to refer to it again. I think there are some important ideas here that will help me with my teaching."

Odette said, "I think the same thing."

Maalika added, "Before, I said the ideas are hard to grasp. They are, but talking about them in groups this way helped."

Cathleen said, "Actually, in my homework, I said that I didn't think the essay offered anything new. It just seemed like it was repeating everything we did in the seminar. But discussing these ideas in small groups, I realize there's more to it."

Spencer said, "Actually, even if it was everything we did in the seminar, I found it helpful to have it all written out in one essay. Throughout the spring, it seemed like each session we took on a new topic. Reading the essay helped me to see how connected the ideas are."

I really appreciated the tone of this discussion. Those teachers who talked about how hard the essay was weren't whining; nor were they putting themselves down. They were simply saying that they found the material difficult, and some of them, like Camisha, said they were going to continue working on it. And those who first didn't see new content in the essay now could talk about how it added a new dimension to their thinking.

Karran continued in this vein: "I found it really interesting to see the same issues written about in such a different way." I asked her what she meant, and she went on. "All the cases earlier in the book are written from the classroom point of view—teachers describing their students. In this essay, they're writing about the same issues, but from a different perspective. Like, in the essay, they say, 'Children arrive at school with an intuitive understanding of mathematics. They are able to model and solve word problems without ever being taught how, using a variety of strategies.' And then they list all these researchers who say that. But that's what we were reading about all along in the seminar. The cases show children who have their own ways to model and solve word problems without ever being taught how."

Marina added, "I think it feels good to have all the ideas we've been talking about put down in this way. The researchers came to the same conclusions we did."

"Yeah," Carol agreed, "But I guess what's so hard in this essay is that it's so dense."

"We need more think-time," Andrea said.

Camisha spoke again: "That's why I said I'd need to reread it later. I need more time for the ideas to sink in. We talked about all those cases, and there were lots of ideas to think about. If I read the essay next September, I'll be able to get more out of it. And if I read it again a year from now, I'll get still more."

Math activity: Operating with positive rational numbers

I explained that today's math activity is a continuation of the one from the last session. "In the last class, you made up story problems for the four operations, first using the numbers 5 and 3, then using the numbers $\frac{3}{4}$ and $\frac{1}{2}$. Today I'd like you to review the work you did in the last class and then make up another two sets of story problems: one set with mixed numbers, $3\frac{1}{2}$ and $1\frac{2}{3}$, and the other set with decimals, 4.2 and 0.3."

I changed the groups from the last session to cross-fertilize some of the ideas. For the first few minutes, participants got out the problems their groups had created and made decisions about how to proceed with the next set of numbers.

When I got to Joseph's group, he was describing some of the changes they had needed to make in the problems when they changed from whole numbers to fractions. He said, "For the multiplication problem, we wrote, *Ryan baked* 5 *cakes a day for* 3 *consecutive days. How many cakes did he bake?* Then when we went to fractions, we had to think about how that context needs to change since it doesn't make sense to bake a portion of a cake. So then we thought about mowing a lawn. *If Ryan can mow* $\frac{3}{4}$ *of a lawn in a day, how much does he mow if he works for* $\frac{1}{2}$ *day?*"

Spencer said, "OK. I see how that works. Now let's see if we can use that problem for mixed numbers. *If Ryan can mow* $3\frac{1}{2}$ *lawns in a day, how much can he get done in* $1\frac{2}{3}$ *days?*"

Joseph, who has been paying attention to what happens with the unit, said, "That will work if all the lawns are the same size. It doesn't make sense if you have some large lawns and some small ones. When we're multiplying $\frac{3}{4} \times \frac{1}{2}$, we didn't have to think about it because the context didn't have more than one lawn."

An-Chi then did the calculations in her head. "OK, so in 1 day, he does $3\frac{1}{2}$ lawns. In $\frac{2}{3}$ of a day, he does another 2 lawns and $\frac{2}{3}$ of $\frac{1}{2}$. So $3\frac{1}{2} + 2 + \frac{1}{3}$ is $5\frac{5}{6}$. Is that what you get when you apply the regular multiplication algorithm?" Then she quickly wrote out $\frac{7}{2} \times \frac{5}{3} = 3\frac{5}{6} = 5\frac{5}{6}$. "Yep," she said, "it checks out."

Karran showed the problems her earlier group had created for division:

- I have $\frac{3}{4}$ of a candy bar and that's enough for $\frac{1}{2}$ of a portion. How much is a portion?

- I used $\frac{3}{4}$ cup of flour to make $\frac{1}{2}$ batch of cookies. How much flour is used for 1 batch of cookies?

- I walk $\frac{3}{4}$ mile in $\frac{1}{2}$ hour. How far do I go in 1 hour?

Now the group checked to see if all those problems still work for the mixed numbers.

- I have $3\frac{1}{2}$ candy bars and that's enough for $1\frac{2}{3}$ portions. How much is a portion?

- I used $3\frac{1}{2}$ cups of flour to make $1\frac{2}{3}$ batches of cookies. How much flour is used for one batch of cookies?

- I walk $3\frac{1}{2}$ miles in $1\frac{2}{3}$ hours. How far do I go in 1 hour?

Dofi said, "The problems seem to make sense, but it's a lot harder to see what's going on with mixed numbers. Let's draw some diagrams."

Karran took the lead on this. "OK, so we've got $3\frac{1}{2}$ candy bars. They look like this. Now that amount represents $1\frac{2}{3}$ portions, and we have to figure out how much one portion is."

The group looked up at me, stumped. I said, "What if we were to write $1\frac{2}{3}$ as $\frac{5}{3}$. Would that help at all?"

At first everyone said, "No, that doesn't help," and laughed. But then Beatrice said, "Wait a minute. If that stands for $\frac{5}{3}$, then we can draw in what $\frac{1}{3}$ is. We take $\frac{1}{5}$ of that amount and that will tell us what $\frac{1}{3}$ of a portion is." Beatrice filled in the picture. She first divided two whole candy bars into halves. She said, "This makes 5 halves of a candy bar, so I'll start by shading in one half."

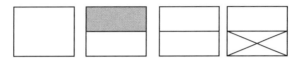

Beatrice continued, "Now we have one whole candy bar left, so I'll shade in $\frac{1}{5}$ of that. So now I've shaded in $\frac{1}{5}$ of the total amount of candy bar we started with. And that stands for $\frac{1}{3}$ of a portion."

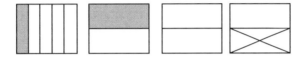

She concluded, "If that's $\frac{1}{3}$ of a portion, I need to multiply that by 3 to get one portion. So that gives me $1\frac{1}{2} + \frac{3}{5}$, which is equal to $1\frac{5}{10} + \frac{6}{10} = 2\frac{1}{10}$."

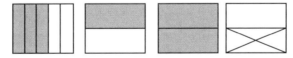

In the meantime, Cathleen had applied the algorithm: $\frac{7}{2} \div \frac{5}{3} = \frac{7}{2} \times \frac{3}{5} = \frac{21}{10} = 2\frac{1}{10}$. She said, "Yep, you got the right answer. But that seemed like a whole lot of work, when you can just apply the algorithm."

Dofi said, "But look at what she did. She first took the amount of candy bars that we start with and divided that by 5; then she took the answer to that and multiplied that by 3. I can see the steps of the algorithm in what Beatrice did."

Cathleen replied, "Still, it's easier to do the algorithm."

Apparently Karran had thought about this a lot since the last session and could explain the algorithm now in terms of the context. She said to Cathleen, "Yes, the algorithm is easier. But once I've done this picture, it gives me a new sense of what is going on with the algorithm. Like, let's say I have $\frac{a}{b} \div \frac{c}{d}$. I can think of $\frac{a}{b}$ as the amount of something I have, and $\frac{c}{d}$ is the number of, or amount of, a portion that represents. So, if I divide $\frac{a}{b}$ by c, and get $\frac{a}{bc}$, that tells me the amount of stuff that represents $\frac{1}{d}$ portions. And if I multiply that by d, I get $\frac{ad}{bc}$, and that's the size of one portion. The diagram helps me see why $\frac{a}{b} \div \frac{c}{d} = \frac{a}{b} \times \frac{d}{c}$. When I just want to divide fractions, I'm going to use the algorithm and not draw pictures, but having drawn the pictures, I have more confidence in that algorithm."

Then Dofi said, "Karran, I know you wanted to make up all those problems to see the *dealing* kind of division. Let's make up a problem with the other kind of division to see what that looks like."

The group quickly followed through on Dofi's suggestion: *We have $3\frac{1}{2}$ candy bars and a portion is $1\frac{2}{3}$. How many portions do we have?*

They drew a picture of $3\frac{1}{2}$ candy bars.

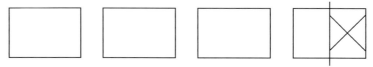

And then they marked off portions of $1\frac{2}{3}$.

Dofi said, "OK. You can see the 2 portions. And then what's left? It's $\frac{1}{2} - \frac{1}{3}$, and that's $\frac{1}{6}$."

Karran said, "But remember, you have to pay attention to what it's $\frac{1}{6}$ of. It's $\frac{1}{6}$ of a candy bar. So how much of a portion is that?"

Beatrice said, "Right. A portion is $\frac{5}{3}$ of a candy bar; that's $\frac{10}{6}$. So $\frac{1}{6}$ of a candy bar is $\frac{1}{10}$ of a portion."

Cathleen asked, "So, can we do the same thing with *a*, *b*, *c*, and *d*? How does this explain the algorithm?"

Beatrice, who had felt solid with her understanding of Wanda's cakes, offered an explanation. "You have $\frac{a}{b}$ candy bars and each portion is $\frac{c}{d}$ bars. What we figured out with Wanda's cakes is that means that each bar has $\frac{d}{c}$ portions."

Dofi said, "Wait a minute. I need to think about this here." She drew a few pictures to satisfy herself of Beatrice's claim.

1 portion is $\frac{2}{3}$ of a bar.   1 portion is $\frac{5}{6}$ of a bar.   1 portion is $\frac{5}{4}$ bars.
1 bar is $\frac{3}{2}$ portions.   1 bar is $\frac{6}{5}$ portions.   1 bar is $\frac{4}{5}$ of a portion.

Once Dofi was satisfied, Beatrice finished her argument. "So, if you have a certain amount of stuff, like the number of candy bars, that's $\frac{a}{b}$, and you know the size of a portion, that's $\frac{c}{d}$, you can figure out the number of portions you have by dividing the number of candy bars by the size of a portion—$\frac{a}{b} \div \frac{c}{d}$—or you can multiply the number of candy bars by the number of portions you get from one candy bar."

I've explained the work of the groups that spent most of their time working on division. Other groups spent quite a bit of time thinking about contexts for decimals. At one point, Nadra said, "*Sean was getting $4.20 an hour and then got a raise of 0.3 of a cent.*"

An-Chi pointed out that it needs to be 0.3 of a dollar, which is 30 cents. She said, "So then the problem is, *Sean was getting $4.20 an hour and then got a raise of $.30 an hour.*"

Odette commented, "Contexts that work for decimals are money, miles, or any metric measurement."

Because groups were working on such different aspects of the content, and because in Session 7 we'd had a chance to discuss many of the issues that come up when you move from whole numbers to fractions, I let the small groups run long. There was just one point that I wanted to clarify for the whole group. After I brought them together, I said, "One thing I frequently hear is that students develop the idea that 'multiplication makes things bigger' and 'division makes things smaller.' Then, when they encounter multiplication and division of fractions, they see that these generalizations no longer hold, and they conclude that mathematics makes no sense. Over the last few sessions, we've had a chance to take a close look at multiplication and division of fractions, and I'd like you to comment on that generalization. What happens to the size of the numbers when you multiply and divide?"

Spencer spoke first. "I frequently hear my students say, 'Multiplication makes things bigger,' but my response to them is, 'What about multiplying by 1? What about multiplying by 0?' Then they say that those are exceptions. When this comes up again, I'll help my students think about fractions as exceptions, like 0 and 1."

I nodded and said, "Yes, you can think about the exceptions. But can you think about what happens with multiplication and division to make it make sense?"

Amber spoke up, "Yes, I've been thinking about that. If you want to know how many times 2 goes into 8, the answer is going to be less than 8. But if you want to know how many times $\frac{1}{2}$ goes into 8, the answer is going to be more than 8."

Gaye said, "Oh, right! I see it. You've got more little pieces, and so the answer is going to be more than what you start with."

I asked, "What if the size of your portion is $\frac{3}{2}$? It's a fraction. Is the answer going to be greater than or less than the dividend?"

Maalika said, "Even though it's a fraction, it's more than 1. So you'll have fewer portions. Your answer will be less than the number you started with."

I asked, "And what about multiplying by $\frac{3}{2}$? What happens to the product?"

Elspeth skipped my smaller steps to summarize the larger idea: "If you multiply a number by a factor between 0 and 1, the product will be less than the original number. If you multiply a number by a factor greater than 1, then the product will be greater. And it's the opposite with division. If you divide by a number between 0 and 1, then the quotient will be greater than the number you started with. If you divide by a number greater than 1, then the quotient will be less than the number you started with."

Because of what Amber had written on her exit-card in Session 7, I knew that she had been thinking about these questions, but I hadn't been sure what her conclusions were. But now I saw her nodding. I asked if she wanted to paraphrase Elspeth's conclusions, which she did.

Although many of the small groups had worked on a different set of ideas in the session, I felt satisfied that the last piece of mathematics we did as a whole group involved the statement of an idea that everyone seemed to understand.

Beginning the portfolio reviews

I was about to ask participants to begin their portfolio reviews when Gaye said, "I'm sorry. We can continue in a minute, but already for 2 hours I've wanted to tell this story and I'm about to burst. We can think of it as related to our portfolio discussion because it's about one of our activities.

"After our last session, I gave Wanda's cake problem to my fourth graders—the one about 4 cakes with servings equal to $\frac{3}{5}$ of a cake. We've done a little bit of fractions work in my class, but we hadn't done anything like this. Nobody knew anything like 'invert and multiply.' So all the children solved the problem by drawing pictures or using manipulatives. They figured out there would be 6 whole servings, but they confronted the same issue we had—some thought the extra should be $\frac{2}{3}$ and some thought it should be $\frac{2}{5}$. And so I told them I had just worked on this problem with a group of teachers and we had been confused about it, too, because the problem seemed to have two different answers. The children were excited to learn that a group of teachers had come up with the same question. So I asked them, could it be both $\frac{2}{5}$ and $\frac{2}{3}$? That was their journal assignment.

"We worked on that problem for the next couple of days. But I want to tell you what happened today. We're doing parent conferences right now, and today I was talking to these two parents—in two different conferences—and they each asked if I would show them how to do that problem. They said that their children were working on it at home, and they thought the children understood it, but they (the parents) didn't, and they wanted to. And so, in each conference, I got out the child's math journal and we went through it together, the parent and I. And we read how the child explained that you could look at the answer as being $\frac{2}{3}$ and you could look at it as being $\frac{2}{5}$." Gaye paused and laughed. "OK, you can start the other activity now."

"Hold on," Elspeth said. "In a second, but I just want to say that there's a lot of really neat stuff in your story. What a good way to answer the parents' questions. They were asking you about math—they weren't asking about the child—but you took them back to their children's work. You were showing the parents that they could learn math from their children."

Andrea chuckled. "Yeah, isn't that what we learned in this seminar, that we could learn math from children? Weren't we learning math from all those children in the cases? I remember back in the first chapter of *Building a System of Tens*, there's a case called, 'Learning Math While Teaching,' and this teacher is saying that her second grader showed her a completely new way to subtract. I've started learning from my kindergartners! Remember when the idea—that we would learn math from our students—seemed so strange to us?"

I considered keeping everyone in whole group since they seemed to want to all be together. But just then there was a lull in the conversation and it occurred to me that Gaye's story was going to be a hard act to follow. I decided the participants needed a few minutes of individual time and then the intimacy of the small group to start talking about themselves; we would come back together, later, for one last time.

I think I was right. Once they got settled, participants looked over their first portfolio assignment and took some notes; then they got into small groups to share. Most of them talked about either a shift in the way they listened to their own students' ideas or an insight into the power of those ideas.

Final homework and closing

When we came back together as a whole group, participants continued to share their stories. We all recognized that we had come far together.

Among the things that were said, I find myself thinking a lot about Elspeth's remark: "For years I've been asking my students to explain their thinking, to say how they solved a problem. I always asked questions. But now I think about my students as reasoning beings, and the kinds of questions I ask are different."

The others nodded; they seemed to understand what she was saying. I'm still thinking about it. I guess you can ask students to explain their reasoning. and what they say gives you important information about what they understand. But it's still another thing to assume that whatever the child says issues from some form of logic. And so, to Elspeth, the idea that her first graders are "reasoning beings" is novel.

I explained to the group that this was the first step in their final assignment. They would read over their entire portfolio and locate two examples that illustrate changes in their ideas about mathematics, learning, or teaching. This is what they would write about. I distributed the homework assignment that included my e-mail address; they were to send me their portfolio reflections within the next two weeks.

I told them they would also hear from me one last time. I would be reading their eighth homework assignment and would send them a response.

In closing, I thanked the participants for being so open; their ideas and their learning had taught me an incredible amount. I explained that, between sessions, I thought about them a lot and I expected to continue thinking about them for a long time to come.

After that, everyone milled around, continuing to talk. There was lots of hugging, and soon the room was empty.

Responding to the eighth homework

May 8

Participants' writing about the research essay was quite varied. Some of it was very thoughtful, some perfunctory. Some people said they found it difficult; some said there wasn't much new in the essay. I do feel reassured that the discussions that took place about the essay were very thoughtful and covered lots of content. Those who said in the homework that there wasn't much new in it came to see, through the group discussion, that they had missed a lot in their first reading.

Since this was the last time I would write to each of the participants, my responses weren't confined to what they had written. I used this as an opportunity to address any issues that had registered for me that might be left hanging for the individual. I also commented on each person's participation in the seminar as a whole.

Amber's writing this time was quite thoughtful. I decided to include it in my journal because she posed some important questions about teaching and learning, and I needed to put some thought into my response.

Amber

I found section 5, "Encountering Fractions in Sharing Situations," particularly interesting. This article relates the research accounts of young children connecting sharing to fractions and having a firmer grasp of whole numbers than fractions. This section was about the great brownie problem in which 4 children shared 7 brownies. The research indicates that children may share an equal number of pieces, but the pieces themselves may not be the same size. I find this very interesting because that is what happened in my after-school remediation class. The third-grade child who solved the problem gave three children two whole brownies and the fourth child one whole brownie cut into two pieces. She was very proud of herself for solving the problem and not at all concerned that the fourth child got half as much as the other three. In the research of how children learn, her solution is documented as a common answer to the problem, which was new knowledge for me.

This makes me curious about the possibility of predictable stages of math understanding, even as we know there are predictable stages of literacy development. In language acquisition, we know there is an integral relationship between listening, speaking, reading, spelling, and writing. These skills develop simultaneously. It seems to me that mathematical ideas also develop simultaneously and in relation to each other. This leads to fundamental competence in thinking about math and the ability to handle more complicated math skills with a depth of understanding.

The research article summarized many of the exercises we have worked on in class. It made me wonder about the role of explicit instruction. For much of my career, as well as my experience as the mother of two sons with learning disabilities, direct instruction has been a critical component of learning. Where is the place for this in the questioning manner and the exploration I have seen modeled in class for the past few months? Is there a right or wrong method of teaching and learning? Is there a place for balance in both questioning and direct instruction? Is there a point at which I can have any level of confidence that I know what I'm doing as a teacher?

This class and this research article confirm that rote memorization and algorithms can actually limit a student's understanding of math. A child can come to believe that an understanding of math is both unlikely and unrealistic. He may lose his sense of curiosity and wonder about a fascinating world of intricate relationships and order. Memorizing a formula may help in the short term, yet restrict flexible thinking of how the operations relate to one another.

When I read this paper, I felt that Amber was writing out questions she had been pondering since the beginning of the seminar. Early on, the tension she felt around these questions was sometimes expressed as agitation. By now, she could formulate them calmly, not as a threat to her practice, but as something to be considered. I was happy to have the opportunity to consider them with her.

Dear Amber,

I am pleased that you found the essay so interesting and that, at least in parts of it, you found connections to experiences with your own students. Isn't it fascinating when one of our students solves a problem in a way that we at first think is idiosyncratic, only later to learn that it is, in fact, quite common? This led you to pose a very interesting question: Are there predictable stages in learning mathematics?

For years, it seemed that an underlying assumption guided the mathematics curriculum: you needed to establish building blocks before you could get to the next stage. For example, you first master your addition facts and then go to place value, then two-digit addition without carrying; then two-digit addition with carrying; then three-digit addition, and so on. Many curricula are now designed with the assumption that learning mathematics isn't so linear. For example, researchers now understand that students can develop an understanding of place value while working on multidigit computation. Just as you specify different skills in literacy that develop simultaneously and in relation to each other, we might identify some of the skills in mathematics that also develop in relation to each other: creating representations for story problems; learning what the operations are; learning addition, subtraction, multiplication, and division facts; developing computation procedures. These are just some examples.

On the other hand, some researchers are working to specify predictable stages within particular mathematical domains: for example, addition and subtraction of whole numbers, whole-number place value, measuring length. This work is still in process, but researchers are trying to figure out how teachers can use such trajectories to guide their practice. Teachers pose questions to try to locate individual students on the trajectory and then give them tasks to help them move forward.

This brings us to another interesting question you posed: Is there a balance between questioning and direct instruction? The simple answer to your question is yes. But it's complicated to figure out just what that balance is.

In the context of the MMO seminar, we can identify what might be considered direct instruction on my part. Assigning this essay for you to read is an example. The essay lays out a body of research very explicitly. Handing out the chart "Classification of Word Problems" is another example. There were other times when it may not have looked like direct instruction, but I was very explicit about a particular idea I wanted everyone to understand: for example, making sure everyone could represent addition and subtraction on a number line; distinguishing between different ways of thinking about whole-number division.

However, when we offer direct instruction, we must be careful about our assumptions. Just because we explained something, that doesn't mean it was understood. If we rely on direct instruction, we frequently need to follow it up with questions, to see how our instruction was received.

In your paper, you name another important consideration. That is, we want our students to maintain the expectation that they should and can understand math; and we want them to be curious and have a sense of "wonder about a fascinating world of intricate relationships and order." That must be another goal as we work to figure out that balance between questioning and direct instruction. I expect that in order to maintain a sense of curiosity, students would need to have a sense of their own ability to investigate a mathematical question.

Finally, you bring up the role of memorization and algorithms. We know that at a certain point, we do want students to know their math facts. For example, when fourth graders are working on a complicated fractions problem, we don't want them bogged down by having to think about the sum 8 + 6. By that point (actually, quite a bit earlier), they should automatically know that 8 + 6 = 14, leaving that mental space to figure out the ideas that make fractions complicated. But as you point out, exclusive focus on rote memorization may lead children to believe that understanding math is unlikely and unrealistic. This, too, is part of the balance. In the early grades, math facts and calculation procedures are objects of study in themselves. When do we expect them to become automatic so that they can be used as tools in support of learning new content?

I haven't answered your questions. Mainly, I am trying to communicate that the questions you've posed are important and complex. I am sure that as you continue to incorporate these principles into your practice, an excellent teacher will become even stronger.

I appreciate the hard work and thoughtfulness you have brought to the seminar.

Maxine

Final reflections

May 23

It has been two and a half weeks since the last session of the seminar, and I've been reading participants' portfolio reviews and final reflections. Now it's time for me to write about my own reflections of the seminar.

In each of the sessions I felt satisfied that, as a group, we addressed the goals I had in mind as I began the lesson. Of course, each individual engaged with the ideas from his or her own perspective. Some participants finished with a solid understanding of most of the mathematics content; others will need more time. But as I read their portfolio reviews, I saw all of the main points highlighted in one set of writing or another. It is interesting, perhaps to be expected, that the primary-grade teachers tended to highlight issues from early in the seminar; upper-grade teachers from later sessions. First-, second-, and third-grade teachers wrote about whole-number operations and the implications of these new ideas to their teaching. Iris wrote:

> In the past, I would have checked that students could add and subtract. But now I am more interested in the strategies that students are using and whether or not they match the context of the word problem. For example, if the problem is posed as a missing addend problem, do they solve it that way?

Camisha wrote:

> I now see how important it is to expose children to many kinds of story problems. The story problems that involve subtraction are not always separating situations. They can also be situations that involve comparing numbers or missing addends. I have learned how important it is to expose my students to various contexts. This will help them deepen their understanding of the operation involved.

Odette wrote:

> One area where my ideas of mathematics changed was when we did the addition and subtraction problems where the context of the problems changed. The idea that subtraction problems could be solved with addition was completely new to me. Or that a division problem can be solved using multiplication, addition, or subtraction. These assignments really made clear to me how important the context of a story problem is. If you do not understand the context of the problem, you will not know how to solve it correctly. It is not simply about the numbers and "key words."

Higher-grade teachers tended to write about fractions. Spencer wrote:

> In one of my class assignments, I gave my students a word problem with fractions and asked them to prove their solution with a diagram. At first they did not know what I meant. After some discussion, they solved the problem and drew a picture supporting their answer. Later, the class explained that the picture made it easier for them to see what was happening. I realized I needed to present more problems with drawings and models to support their understanding, and I need them to create drawings and models so that I can see what they are doing. Simply applying traditional algorithms doesn't offer the opportunity for students to see the relationships between numbers and operations. It is by understanding these relationships that students build a strong foundation that they can rely on in the future.

At one point as I was reading the portfolios, I started to wonder about the wisdom of including such a wide span of grades, K–9, in one seminar. Should I have put the primary teachers together to concentrate on whole-number operations and the upper-grade teachers together to concentrate on fractions? But as I kept reading, I felt more and more strongly the power of having the teachers work together on content that arises from kindergarten through middle school. First, all of our work on fractions depended on establishing meaning for the operations with whole numbers. Maalika wrote:

> In the past, I viewed operations as separate and distinct entities that each accomplish a unique task. However, these operations are far more interchangeable than I realized.

Marina wrote:

> I do hope to continue to wrestle with the meanings of operations and to finally understand why we invert and multiply!

Several people wrote about how, when confronted with a fractions problem they didn't immediately know how to solve, they could change the numbers to think through the operations implied by the context. Karran wrote:

> I realized how helpful it is, as a learner, to change the numbers in a word problem so that they are friendlier. I found myself changing the fractions to whole numbers in order to better visualize why division was being used.

On the other hand, teachers of lower grades wrote about how their own study of fractions gave them insight into the experiences of their students working with whole numbers. Iris wrote:

> The idea that came clear to me during this class was how complex the ideas of addition and subtraction can be to my first graders. I always need to remember that they are dealing with brand new ideas. They will need things explained and taught in a number of different ways, and it still may not be completely clear to them. I learned this

the most when we were doing problems in class that involved multiplying and dividing fractions. A lot of these activities brought me out of my comfort zone, and I was able to experience what my first graders may be experiencing when dealing with whole numbers.

Over and over again, I read about the importance of being put in the position of the learner, and how this throws new light on the experience of teaching. Gaye wrote:

> Jorge's pizza and the kids in Mary's class just about put me over the edge. However, they also put me in the shoes of a student again. It was very humbling to leave a class feeling as though I understood that because Jorge's whole was the same (one pizza), I could add those fractions. And then I go home and add the boys and girls in Mary's class together. Agghh! Being in the role of a learner is, I think, the most valuable lesson I took away from this seminar. Being asked questions to further my thinking, being encouraged, and then being taken back to the foundations of my understanding were all so helpful.

As I read participants' reflections, I also reviewed my overall goals, which I had identified before the first session. Back then, I wrote, "I want teachers to come to see that mathematics is about *ideas*, that *they* have mathematical ideas, and so do the children they teach. I want them to learn how to analyze their students' thinking, to follow the reasoning of the students' thought process, to identify the conceptual issues the students are working through. And I want teachers to learn how to help students build on their own and, importantly, their classmates' mathematical ideas."

Several of the teachers, especially those who had already taken a DMI course, had already encountered mathematics as a realm of ideas. But this notion was new to many of the teachers at the beginning of the seminar. For example, Labeeba wrote:

> What I have come to realize about my learning of mathematics is that I had never really learned how to do math! Sure, I learned the steps of how to find the right answers (and I was good at that), but I never learned the "why" behind the steps. I thought memorizing the steps and being able to do them in the right order without making any computational errors was "doing" math. Now I do not feel that way. This was especially true when it came to fractions. Our fraction work was very challenging for me, but it helped me to understand how fractions work.

Throughout the seminar, there were two participants I had been concerned about: Nadra and Cathleen. Especially at the beginning of the seminar, both of them seemed to be somewhat prickly, almost hostile. I interpreted that to mean that the seminar threatened them in some way, and so I tried to remain supportive. In their final writing assignments, both indicated a shift in their thinking. Nadra wrote about some changes in her practice.

> I was taught that there is only one right answer and one way to get there. Now I am teaching my students that there may be one right answer, but there are many ways to get there. Some ways might be quicker or more efficient, but they all head toward the same place.

It seems that Cathleen, a middle school teacher, hasn't yet made significant changes in her practice. However, she is beginning to ask questions about a different way of engaging with mathematics and implications for teaching. Now the edge of hostility has dropped and I appreciate her candor:

> I'm curious as to what kind of mathematician and learner I would be if my learning experiences had been similar to what we did in class rather than being taught algorithms. Because of the way I have been taught, I was extremely uncomfortable at times in the seminar. Math was a lot easier when I was told what to do! How uncomfortable do middle school students get when being taught this way? I would surmise that teaching math by guiding and questioning would create more independent thinkers. Does this ultimately show up on the standardized tests? Is there time to teach math this way and address the concepts you are expected to cover in middle school?

Throughout the seminar, as I thought through my interactions with Cathleen, I found myself thinking about Karran and the way she began *Building a System of Tens*, the seminar I offered last fall. Back then, Karran had been uncomfortable and resistant to engage with many of the ideas of the seminar. But by the time she began *Making Meaning for Operations*, some of those ideas were more settled for her. She entered our discussions with considerable thoughtfulness and participated in mathematics activities with enthusiasm. Perhaps Cathleen, similarly, needs more time. I wonder if she will follow through and sign up for another seminar.

That is not to say that Karran is "done." In fact, her writing reveals that she is just beginning to incorporate some changes into her practice:

> Several times in the course of these weeks and in my writings, I have questioned whether my eighth-grade students were beyond the point of being able to fill conceptual holes in their mathematical abilities and understanding. Before now I would have preached memorization of facts and formulas, and "Practice, practice, practice!" I understand now that learning by rote or memorization does not facilitate understanding and may even hinder further development of mathematical skills. Because the ability to work with fractions is a major issue for all of my students, I have paid particular attention to those lessons in this class. There are many formulas, mantras, and rules one can teach to prod students into operating with fractions accurately. After working with my students for several months, I have noticed that these formulas and rules are mixed up, misused, misunderstood, and massacred in the mind of a student with no real

concept of *why*. Genuine learning takes place when that focus isn't as much on answers as on understanding.

Although she sees the problematic outcome of her current teaching practice, Karran is unsure of how to begin to make changes. She asks:

> How can I promote this type of learning and provide the amount of time it requires to step back and let a student attempt to traverse some mathematical mountain on his own, when our pacing guide says that I should be farther down the road on the list of items of our curriculum framework? How do I motivate my students and turn them on to this kind of learning so that they begin to make mathematical connections with their prior knowledge and experience?

Whereas Cathleen and Karran have yet to begin to interact with their students in new ways, many of the participants wrote about what they learned about their students from the assignments in which they collected and analyzed work from their own classrooms.

Dofi wrote:

> I have been pleasantly surprised at the intuitive understandings of math that my first-grade students have exhibited. Normally, I would not have posed a problem like "Sharing Brownies" to my first graders. I was amazed at their reasoning and at the different levels of thinking going on. I am now looking for more problems like that.

Joseph wrote:

> One thing I've discovered is the importance of finding out what students understand about math concepts in order to move them forward. It is important to take the time to ask questions in order to see things the way they do.

An-Chi wrote:

> I'm learning that it's very important for my students to understand the reasoning and steps for solving a problem. It's not just saying "yes" or "no" or "that's incorrect," but asking how they got to that answer. When I have been doing this in the last few weeks, I notice that when my students are explaining their answers, they see where they went wrong without my having to step in. It's neat for both of us!

Elspeth wrote:

> Since I have been questioning their work and their steps in solving, they are more confident in their work and comprehend the material more quickly. At first my students were very confused when I asked them how and why they chose to solve a problem the way they did. Now they are able to tell me and even write out their steps to

show their comprehension. This is what I have wanted for so long as a teacher, but I did not know how to get to this point. I feel much success as a teacher, knowing that my students also feel the same success.

The structure of these assignments also caused teachers to reflect on how their planning can affect the outcome of a lesson. Celeste wrote:

> In more than one assignment, the importance of thinking about what I was expecting to see from my students was clear to me. Philosophically, I know that this prior planning about what to expect is best practice. However, I don't always have the time I'd like. These assignments encouraged this aspect of lesson planning, and I have noticed a difference in student understanding when I have taken the time to do so.

Marina wrote:

> One aspect of my teaching that has changed is the way I analyze students' understanding of a topic. The guiding questions—What does the student understand? What is the student missing? What is my learning goal?—help to focus my attention in better ways. I used to focus more on what the student is missing and where I want to go with him/her next. I think it is important to first clearly highlight what the student is doing well and does understand before jumping right into what the student doesn't understand.

Beatrice wrote:

> I learned that math discussion requires careful planning. Which work do I want to share, what order makes the most sense for progression of learning? The discussion allows students to have open dialogue about important math concepts. Children are asked to explain their own work, ask questions about others' work, and state someone else's strategy in their own words.

As did Karran's, Andrea's writing also brought me back to the seminar last fall. Throughout *Building a System of Tens*, Andrea was very timid, fearful of what was being asked of her, quiet in whole-group discussions. During this seminar, *Making Meaning for Operations*, I was pleased to see how her confidence has developed. I had been curious about how she would engage with our work in fractions, especially since, as a kindergarten teacher, she is not responsible for teaching that content. But she took on the challenge and learned a lot.

However, in her final reflections, even as she wrote about her work in fractions, Andrea says that the homework assignments in which she interacted with her students were what meant the most to her:

> When MMO assignments call for us to present a task to our students, ask them to perform, write about the experience, and then

converse in small groups about the event, it's utopia. That's what teaching should be. I think I'm tasting a little of this utopia during our grade-level math meetings. A few times a month, for 30 minutes, is nowhere near sufficient. However, I find it very stimulating to hear what others are doing, get their feedback, and have that experience drive my next lesson. In talking about ideas from this seminar, I have piqued the interest of my colleagues. I think I may persuade them to take advantage of the next round and build a kindergarten think tank!

I realize now that when I set down my goals, I left out something significant. I did say that I wanted the teachers to develop a stance of communal inquiry, by which I meant they should learn to pose their own questions and then find ways to think about those questions. But when I wrote that, my own vision didn't extend beyond the life of the seminar. Now, what seems to me so important is that the seminar initiated the teachers into a process of inquiry that will continue.

Their inquiry will continue as they delve into mathematics content, wonder what this student is thinking, listen for the sense in that student's ideas, and reflect on the impact of their own actions. Some of that work will happen alone, as teachers interact with their students. And some teachers, like Andrea, are learning about the power of meeting with colleagues, to discuss these questions together.

Made in the USA
Charleston, SC
25 May 2016